HANDBOOK OF EDUCATION

other recent books on similar topic

ENCYCLOPAEDIA OF EDUCATIONAL ADMINISTRATION.
in 5 Volumes
Edited by Paul Monroe

ENCYCLOPAEDIA OF HISTORY OF EDUCATION.
in 4 Volumes
Edited by Paul Monroe

ENCYCLOPAEDIA OF PHILOSOPHY OD EDUCATION
in 2 Volumes
Edited by Paul Monroe

ENCYCLOPAEDIA OF PSYCHOLOGY OF EDUCATION.
in 2 Volumes
Edited by Paul Monroe

INTERNATIONAL ENCYCLOPAEDIA OF EDUCATION
New Edition
in 12 Volumes
Edited by Paul Monroe

ENCYCLOPAEDIA OF SEX EDUCATION.
in 3 Volumes
Edited by A. Bigelow

ENCYCLOPAEDIA OF MORAL AND VALUE EDUCATION.
in 5 volumes
Edited by S. R. Sharma

INTERNATIONAL ENCYCLOPAEDIA OF HIGHER EDUCATION.
in 10 Volumes
Edited by S. R. Sharma

HANDBOOK OF EDUCATION

By

Sir Gooroo Dass Banerjee

Cosmo Publications

2003 New Delhi

HANDBOOK OF EDUCATION
© Cosmo Publications
This COSMO Print 2003
First Published by COSMO in 1984
Reprinted in 1993

ISBN 81-7020-401-1

Published by
MRS. RANI KAPOOR
for COSMO PUBLICATIONS Div. of
GENESIS PUBLISHING PVT. LTD.
24-B, Ansari Road, Darya Ganj,
New Delhi-110 002, INDIA
Ph.: 327 8779, 328 0455
Fax : 324 1200

Printed at
Mehra Offset Press

PREFACE TO THE FIRST EDITION.

The educational problem in India presents many peculiarities not to be met with in any other country. Thus, Indian students have to acquire knowledge through the medium of a difficult foreign language, and this not only overtaxes their energies, but also cramps their thoughts. Then again, while on the one hand, the circumstances of the country and the habits and sentiments of its people, make Western methods and systems in their integrity often inapplicable to them, on the other hand, the control of Education rests with those who, from their early training and their imperfect knowledge of the East, naturally consider those methods and systems equally efficacious here, and seek to enforce them accordingly. The diversity of the creeds, moreover, which our students profess, renders religious Education in public schools and colleges extremely difficult. Owing to these and other peculiarities, much remains to be said about Indian Education notwithstanding the existence of many excellent works on Education generally.

I have had some opportunities of observing the operation of our system of Education, first as a student, and then as a Lecturer on Mathematics in the Calcutta Presidency College and afterwards as a Lecturer on Mathematics and on Law in the Berhampur College, and latterly as a Fellow of the Calcutta University, and for some years as a member of its Syndicate. I have found similar opportunities also in supervising the teaching of those whom Nature has committed to my care, and in giving occasional instruction on Sundays to the students of the Entrance Class of a High School in my neighbourhood. It was when thus employed, that various suggestions for improving our system of Education occurred to me, from time to time, and these have been embodied in the following pages. Most of them are trite and are generally accepted in theory as correct, and they have been deemed fit for formal statement and inclusion in this book, only by reason of their being persistently disregarded in practice. There are some few again which afford room for doubt and discussion ; and they are submitted for the consideration of those engaged in teaching or in controlling teaching.

One main object of these suggestions is to make the work of the learner easy and interesting, by suitable explanation of complex and obscure matters, and by timely stimulation of his curiosity for knowledge. Though we may not be able to discover a royal road to learning, we should try to help the learner by removing unnecessary obstructions in the ordinary road to it.

If the presentation of my suggestions to the public leads to the adoption of any of them, or induces any one better qualified than myself to make more acceptable suggestions for educational reform, I shall consider my humble efforts amply rewarded.

NARIKELDANGA, G. D. BANERJEE.
The 6th September, 1904.

PREFACE TO THE SECOND EDITION.

The first edition being exhausted, this second edition is published. The book has been revised, and a few additions and alterations have been made, of which the remarks relating to the direct method of teaching language, the supersession of Euclid, and education on national lines, may be specially mentioned.

NARIKELDANGA, G. D. BANERJEE.
The 18th December, 1909.

CONTENTS

INTRODUCTION

CHAPTER I.

EDUCATION IN INFANCY.

Introductory Remarks.

Section I.—Physical Education.

Section II.—Intellectual Education.

Section III.—Moral Education.

Section IV.—Religious Education.

Section V.—Instruments of Education.

CHAPTER II.

EDUCATION IN BOYHOOD.

Introductory Remarks.

Section III—Moral Education.

Section IV.—Religious Education.

Section V.—Instruments of Education.

CHAPTER III.

EDUCATION IN YOUTH.

Introductory Remarks.

Section I.—Physical Education.

Section II.—Intellectual Education.

CHAPTER IV.

PROFESSIONAL AND TECHNICAL EDUCATION, AND EDUCATION ON NATIONAL LINES.

Introductory Remarks.

Section I.—Legal Education.

Section II.—Technical Education.

Section III.—Education on National Lines.

A

Few Thoughts on Education

INTRODUCTION

1. The object of the following pages is, not to present to the reader a finished systematic treatise on Education, but to place before him a few stray thoughts on the subject, having special reference to the circumstances of India. Object of the book.

2. Education is one of the most powerful agencies in moulding the character and determining the future of individuals and of nations; and the question, how to regulate education so as to secure the best results, has engaged the attention of speculative thinkers and practical administrators in all ages and countries. At the present moment in India, that question is occupying a large share of public attention. Importance of Education.

It may not, therefore, be deemed inopportune now to offer a few suggestions relating to educational reform in this country for the consideration of the public.

The different divisions of the subject.

3. The subject is large and may be viewed from many different points of view.

Education in its most comprehensive sense should aim at storing the mind of its recipient with useful knowledge, and training his powers of mind and body to healthful and harmonious action.

Considered with reference to its objects, education has to be dealt with under the different heads of Physical Education, Intellectual Education, Moral Education, and Religious Education.

Or it may be considered with reference to its historical development, in which case, the different divisions of the subject will be, Education in the Ancient World, and especially in Ancient India, Greece, and Rome, Education in the Middle Ages and the rise of Universities, and Education in Modern Times and the different Educational Theories.

Viewed again with reference to the nature of the agencies employed, the subject may be treated under the heads of Home or Private Education, Education at Public Schools and Colleges, and University Education.

Then, again, viewed with reference to the different stages of the pupil's progress, we have to consider Education during Infancy, Education during Boyhood, and Education in Youth.

Plan of this book.

4. From a practical point of view, the last-mentioned division of the subject is the one that may be most conveniently adopted. This division is not

arbitrary, but is based upon reason, as different considerations apply to the conduct of education during the above-mentioned three different periods; and it is the division according to which every father or other guardian guides himself in educating his son or ward.

The remarks I wish to make will accordingly be arranged under the three heads of—

Education in Infancy,

Education in Boyhood, and

Education in Youth.

And these will be followed by a few general observations on

Professional and Technical Education, and Education on National Lines.

CHAPTER I.

EDUCATION IN INFANCY.

INTRODUCTORY REMARKS.

5. The Indian aphorist Chānakya says, "A child should be nurtured for five years, disciplined for ten years, and treated as a friend on his attaining the sixteenth year."[1] The French philosopher, Rousseau also, in his Emile, fixes the age of five years as the limit of the first period of life with reference to education. When two such men, in two countries so different, fix the same limit, it may be fairly presumed that the limit has been properly fixed ; and I shall, under the present head, deal with education during the first five years of childhood.

Infancy to be taken to include the first five years of childhood.

6. Though the child receives very little education in the ordinary sense of the term, that is, education from teachers and books, during this period, yet it is an important period in his educational life. He is taught by Nature from her own great book. It is during this period that the child learns the use of his limbs, his senses, and his organs of speech. This is no small progress in physical education. As regards intellectual education, he learns to express

Educational progress in infancy, Nature the chief educator.

---

[1] लालयेत् पञ्चवर्षाणि दशवर्षाणि ताड़येत् ।
प्राप्ते तु षोडशे वर्षे पुत्रे मित्रवदाचरेत् ॥

simple ideas in his vernacular; he learns to remember simple things; and he learns to identify and discriminate simple things. In moral education also, he takes the first steps. He learns the distinction between good and evil in simple matters, and he learns to feel joy and sorrow, hope and fear, love and hatred. Even religious education has its foundation laid during this period, and the child learns, though vaguely, to look above for a higher Being.

But she should be aided in her work by the child's parents.

7. But though Nature is, and must be, the chief educator during this period, it is not enough to leave the child entirely to her. Nature must be aided in her work, and the duty of assisting her must devolve on the parents. And even if they do not assist Nature, they must learn not to thwart her. But how few parents are there that can properly discharge this great duty of assisting Nature, and how few are they that know where to abstain from interfering with her. Herbert Spencer[1] justly complains of our neglect to teach young men and women how to bring up children. It should be the duty of every young man and woman before entering married life, to acquire some knowledge of the mode of training children; and if they are married when too young, it should be the duty of their parents to help them in acquiring such knowledge before they begin to live together.

It might be said that the inability of parents to give proper training to their infant children may

[1] Education, Stereotyped Ed., p. 21.

be made up by the ability of experienced nurses. But training by a nurse, however able and experienced, can no more form a fit substitute for parental training, than artificial food, however nourishing, can be a fit substitute for the mother's milk. Necessity may oblige us to have recourse to the one substitute as to the other; but we should avoid being placed under such necessity. The nurse works chiefly for gain, the parent solely for love; the child's future well-being, moreover, must be of much more momentous consideration to the parent than to the nurse; and the child will be likely to respond more readily to a parent's appeal than to that of the nurse. Parental training must, therefore, be more efficacious than training by a nurse. The nurse may, and often must, assist the parents in doing their duty; but the work must be done under their supervision.

8. It might also be said that the child learns so little during the first five years of its existence, that any deficiency in its training during that period will be amply made up by proper training under able teachers in boyhood and youth. But we must carefully guard ourselves against being influenced by any such mistaken notion. It is true that during this period the amount of book learning, if anything, must be very small. It may be true also that the number of facts learned is not large. But the faculties of the child have their first exercise during this period, and receive their first bent, and if that is not

Influence of early education.

in the right direction, it may cause much future harm; for, as has been truly said,

"Just as the sapling's bent the tree's inclined.

And even if owing to the plasticity of our nature in early age, you may succeed in setting right a wrong bent, it will be at the cost of much time and energy which might otherwise be more profitably employed.

Sub-divisions of the Chapter.

9. I shall now offer some remarks with reference to each of the four different sorts of education—Physical, Intellectual, Moral, and Religious—appropriate to this piriod, and conclude the Chapter with a few words touching the Instruments that may be employed for the education of the infant.

SECTION I.—PHYSICAL EDUCATION.

Importance of Physical Education in Infancy.

10. Physical education demands special attention during infancy, because it is the first and the most important period of growth and development, and also because it is the period of utmost helplessness in resisting adverse forces.

Matters requiring consideration.

11. The matters chiefly requiring consideration under this head are, feeding, clothing, exercise, and play.

Food.

12. In infancy, food should be given at short intervals of three or four hours in suitable quantity. During this period of rapid growth, the demand for

food is great, and underfeeding should be as carefully avoided as overfeeding. The food should be nourishing but simple. Patent foods should not be given except under medical advice. Next to the mother's milk, cow's milk is the best food for an infant. But unfortunately the difficulty of obtaining pure and good milk in large cities is gradually increasing. If any educated gentlemen, who have studied the subject, will open well-conducted dairy farms near our large cities, for the supply of pure good milk, they will not only find it a profitable business for themselves, but will confer a real benefit on their customers.

13. In a warm climate like ours, a child does not require much clothing. Too much clothing in this country, instead of doing any good, only increases the susceptibility to catch cold on the slightest exposure. The growing tendency to imitate the practice of cold countries in giving too much clothing to a child, should be checked, and children should be exposed to the light and, in a moderate degree, to the heat of the sun, as they used to be in former times. Clothing.

14. There should be no difference between a child's exercise and his play, during the first five years of his existence. All his exercise during this period should consist in play. In the earliest years, the child should be left free to choose his own modes of exercise or play, and to indulge in exercise or play as long as he chooses, care being taken only Exercise-Play.

to prevent his hurting himself or others. As the child grows, his exercise or play may be slightly regulated so as to make it helpful in training all his powers harmoniously. Thus if a child exercises his arms too much to the neglect of his legs, he should have inducement offered to exercise the neglected limbs. So, again, if a child exercises his sense of hearing too much by repeating or listening to nursery rhymes, and neglects to cultivate his sense of vision by observing and discriminating varieties of colour and form, he should be induced to exercise the neglected sense, by having beautifully coloured flowers and leaves and pictures of various things placed before him.

Though a child's exercise or play may be regulated by *inducing* him to take to certain forms of it, it must not be interfered with by *constraining* him to have his exercise or play only in certain ways; for in that case it will lose the character of play, cease to be attended with pleasure, and may prove injurious to healthy and vigorous growth.

The plays of children have been considered by great educators to be of deep significance. Froebel in his Education of Man[1] says, "Play is the highest phase of child development."

By proper direction, and without using any compulsion, we can make a child's play serve much useful purpose in training him.

---

[1] § 30. Hailmann's Translation, p. 54.

SECTION II.—INTELLECTUAL EDUCATION.

15. Intellectual education in infancy is conducted mainly by Nature; but we can help her materially in many ways.

Intellectual Education in infancy conducted by Nature.

After the child has learnt to speak, he shows a great desire to know the name and nature of everything that he sees; and by judiciously placing before him useful and amusing things of varying degrees of simplicity, and telling him their names and pointing out to him their simple qualities, we may gradually help the child in *increasing his knowledge of words and things.*

May be helped by simple things being placed before the child.

16. To *exercise his memory,* the same things should be presented to him after suitable intervals, a second time, and oftener if need be.

Exercise of memory.

17. To *call into play the faculty of comparison,* things of varying degrees of similarity should be placed before the child, and he should be shown their prominent points of resemblance and difference, and gradually led to find them out for himself.

Exercise of discrimination.

It must not be thought that this would be too much for little children. They often find out resemblances between unlike things, notably in calling a new thing by the name of an old one which, in their view, it resembles most. A child of about three years, who had seen many black kids, but no black cat before, was heard to call the first black cat it saw a kid.

Discrimination of differences is perhaps a more difficult process than the identification of resemblances; but still the two are connected processes.

Number.

18. The next step should be the awakening of the idea of *number* by the exhibition of similar things. The child should be taught the names of the *first ten* numbers, the names being illustrated by the presentation of the corresponding numbers of similar things; and the numeration table should be gradually extended to *one hundred*, but no further.

As the memory is very active during this period, it may be usefully employed in getting up the Multiplication Table up to Ten times Ten, the table being illustrated by the exhibition of beads or *cowries*.

Space.

19. From number or repetition in *time* we may pass on to *space*; and infant Arithmetic may be followed by infant Geometry, by the notions of *up* and *down*, *before* and *behind*, *right* and *left*, of *straight line* and *curve*, of simple figures, such as *square* and *circle*, and of simple solids, such as *cube* and *sphere*, being gradually called forth by suitable illustrations.

Names of the letters of the Alphabet.

20. The names of the *letters of the Alphabet* in the child's vernacular may next be taught, and the child asked to commit them to memory. As these names in most of the Indian vernaculars are only the articulate sounds of the letters, and are

arranged in systematic groups, the letters of each group being connected together by reason of their being pronounced by the aid of the same part of the vocal organ, the learning of the names may be made a little more interesting than the mere mechanical memorising of an unconnected series of names. The teacher may pronounce the groups of gutturals, palatals, cerebrals or front palatals, dentals, and labials, from the throat, the palate, the front palate, the teeth, and the lips; and the infant pupil, whose power of imitation is strong, will be found ready to imitate him with pleasure.

21. I have made many suggestions above, which might seem to embody a course of study too long and difficult for an infant under five years. I shall now make a few general remarks regarding them to explain my meaning and object.

Acquisition of knowledge Exercise of the mental powers.

The modes recommended above, aim at *making the child acquire knowledge, and exercise his mental powers*, which are the two objects of all intellectual education. As the progress in the attainment of the former can be more easily observed and more definitely measured than that in the attainment of the latter, the acquisition of knowledge has often been erroneously regarded as a more important object of education than the cultivation of the mental powers. But the importance of the latter is unquestionably much greater than that of the former. If the mental faculties are well trained, acquisition of knowledge becomes easy. We must therefore take care that *the training of the intellect does not suffer in any way from our endeavour to store it with information.* This caution, which is always necessary, is indispensible in education during infancy. For it is the period of first growth and development, and any undue strain arising from overcrowding of information will impede mental growth materially.

Training of the senses of seeing and hearing.

22. The training of the intellect *must begin with the training of the senses.* For what we call differences in intelligence, are, in the opinion of some psychologists, often the results of differences in acuteness of the senses of seeing and hearing. Thus, a child with keener eyes and ears than another, will not only perceive things presented before him more quickly, but will also understand things explained to him more easily, owing to his greater facility in marking the gestures and movements and the words and intonations of the teacher when giving the explanation. As the senses of seeing and hearing are the two principal gateways of knowledge, and are exercised from the first dawn of intelligence, it can never be too early to begin to train them. Little children should therefore be accustomed to find out points of similarity in objects generally dissimilar, and points of dissimilarity in those generally similar.

Education should be attended with pleasure.

23. There is one thing, however, which must never be lost sight of. The education of the infant (as indeed that of the boy and of the youth) should,

whether it consists in the imparting of knowledge, or in the training of the faculties, be so conducted as to be *attended with pleasure.* Some are of opinion that it is play alone that is pleasant, and that a serious business like education must involve effort, and therefore also pain, at least in the commencement. But this view is not correct. For play often involves much effort, and yet it is pleasant. And why? Because play, so long as it does not degenerate into task, is voluntarily indulged in. It is not the employment of effort, but the use of constraint, that constitutes the source of pain. That this is so may be seen clearly by introducing compulsion into play, which will then cease to be play attended with pleasure, and will become task attended with pain. As Manu has well said:—"All that depends on another is pain, all that depends on one's self is pleasure. Know this to be a short definition of pleasure and pain."[1]

How to make education, which must involve the guidance of the pupil by the preceptor, matter of voluntary exertion by the former, free from constraint by the latter, is one of the chief problems for the educationist. One of the proposed solutions of this problem is that furnished by the Kindergarten system. It has its merits, but it has also is defects

---

[1] सर्व्वं परवशं दुःखं सर्व्वमात्मवशं सुखं ।
एतद्विद्यात् समासेन लक्षणं सुखदुःखयोः । IV, 160.

consisting in its tendency to degenerate into a mere mechanical plan involving much needless constraint. The real solution of the problem is not very difficult as regards education in infancy; for that is practically left to the free exertions of the child under the safe guidance of Nature, what little help man renders being only by way of giving amusement to the child and not of imposing any task on him. The difficulty increases as we proceed to education in boyhood; and I shall have to revert to this matter when I come to that part of the subject. For the present, it will be enough to say, that every one who wishes to help an infant in learning sooner or faster, should remember that the mode of rendering such help is *to excite the infant's curiosity*, which is generally keen, *by presenting things in an interesting form* so as to induce him to put forth his voluntary effort in exercising his powers to gain knowledge about them. If this is not borne in mind, our most anxious and loving care will fail to help the child. Notwithstanding the pliancy and docility of childhood, the infant learner is more intolerant of constraint and discipline than the grown-up boy. If you give him information or put him any question when he is not in a mood to hear or answer, he tries to evade you by introducing some other topic; and if you do not take the hint, but persist in proceeding, he then puts on a morose reserve, impervious to your earnest appeals to excite interest. Every one who has any experience of the ways of little children knows this well.

24. One of the best modes of stimulating a child to exercise his faculties and to increase his knowledge, is *to return simple but suggestive answers to his questions*, which are often sensible, but which we often in our carelessness consider silly. We must never tease an infant with questions; and while imparting knowledge, we must carefully avoid making him feel ashamed of his ignorance. Infants, especially those of keen intelligence and sensibility, are found extremely loth to admit their inferiority in anything. You will repel instead of attracting them, if you treat them otherwise than as your equals.

Education by answering and suggesting questions.

The suggestions made above as to the course to be followed will, I fear, be considered too general and indefinite in many places. But it is not easy to give more detailed and definite directions; and the trainer of infant minds will always have to supplement and modify, as occasion requires, any rules that may be laid down for his guidance.

SECTION III.—MORAL EDUCATION.

25. It is never too early to begin moral education, that is, education, not by insipid admonitory lecturing, but by earnest loving effort to make the child good. *We should endeavour to place before the child for imitation all that is good, and should avoid placing before him anything that is bad.* And this is all the more necessary in the case of an intelligent than in that of a dull child. As has been well said,

Moral education should begin early.

> "Vice quickly springs unless we goodness sow;
> The rankest weeds in richest gardens grow."

2

Nor must we rely too much upon the supposed innocence of childhood. Mendacious and thievish propensities are often found in little children, and can be reconciled with innocence, as Herbert Spencer remarks,[1] only on the ground of the child not knowing fully their evil nature, but indulging in those propensities according to the dictates of the selfish instinct which is strong in him, and which has not had time to be restrained and regulated by training.

It is of the greatest importance *that good habits are formed as early as possible*; for if habits of lying and stealing are once formed, it will cost no small effort to overcome them.

Granting then that early moral education is necessary, the question is, How is it to be given? I would answer it by the suggestions contained in the following paragraphs.

By the repetition of simple precepts.

26. In the *first* place, an infant should be taught *to repeat simple moral precepts* in *simple* but *melodious* language. With grown up men of mature minds, thought, word, and action are in the natural order of sequence; but in the case of infants whose minds are every moment receiving accession of new words followed by new ideas, word, thought, and action often come in the order in which they are just stated. And even in the case of grown up men, as has been well said, though they may suppose that their thoughts regulate their words, the reverse is often

[1] Education, Stereotyped Ed., p. 135.

true, and words oft repeated come to govern their thoughts and guide their actions. It is of importance, therefore, to teach an infant to say good things, so that their frequent reiteration may lead to good thoughts and eventually to good actions.

But these moral precepts must be simple, and couched in simple and melodious words, taken so far as possible from the infant's vocabulary. Thus an infant may be taught to repeat—'Hurt no one,' 'Take not another's things,' 'Tell the truth,' 'It is good to give food to the poor,' and other similar precepts.

By illustration of their meaning.

27. In the *second* place, the texts taught should, as far as possible, be *illustrated by examples*, so that the child may gradually realize in thought the meaning which the words of the text are intended to convey.

By reducing precepts to practice.

28. In the *third* place, the child should be *taught to act, as the precepts require*, so that he may learn to reduce to action the thoughts which a text awakens. And this is really the most important part of moral education, that is, to be trained *to reduce precepts to practice*. It requires constant care. Every moral slip committed by a child should be noticed, though gently, and sought to be corrected, not with any severity of manner, but with the most loving earnestness.

Evil environments to be avoided.

29. Not only should we *do* what has been indicated above, but we should also *avoid doing* certain

things which often prove morally injurious to the infant.

We must avoid placing him under the care of an ill-natured nurse, or in the company of ill-natured children. For the faculty of imitation being strong in infancy, the child may. through the mere exercise of that faculty, learn evil ways.

Emulation to be encouraged cautiously. False fear not to be excited.

30. Then again, though the feeling of emulation, which is keen in the infant, may be rightly enlisted in the cause of improvement, we must avoid exciting this feeling, as some nurses and even parents often do, to an unhealthy excess, by telling the child that he alone is good and all the other children in the neighbourhood are bad.

We should also avoid securing obedience by working upon the fear of the child and frightening him with stories of ghosts and demons.

Teaching by example more necessary than teaching by precept.

31. And *lastly* we must remember that our precepts and teaching will all prove fruitless, *unless we by our acts and conduct shew that we ourselves scrupulously follow them.*

Though not able to express in clear language what he observes, an infant is generally a shrewd observer of things. Not only the words you speak to him, but the mode in which you behave towards him and towards others in his presence, produce an impression on him ; and you should not be surprised if you find, that he follows your practice rather than your precept, when they differ, it being easier for him to imitate the former than to act up to the latter.

The affirmative rules suggested above, that is, those in which I have recommended certain things to be done in giving moral education, are, partly from the nature of the case, and partly, I regret to say, from my own inability to make them more clear, somewhat vague and indefinite. Every one who has experience of the ways of little children, will see that it is not easy to lay down anything but general, and therefore necessarily vague directions for training them. The case of each child has to be dealt with specially, according to his powers and susceptibilities.

The negative directions, that is, those recommending what we should avoid doing, are more definite, and should be carefully followed.

SECTION IV.—RELIGIOUS EDUCATION.

Religious education in infancy difficult but not to be omitted.

32. The religious education of an infant is a difficult matter, the difficulty arising from the fact that the mental powers in infancy are not sufficiently developed to form a conception of the Supreme Being. I once observed a child of about three years, during a heavy shower of rain, looking at the spouts through which water was flowing from the roof, and saying 'That is a God, that is another God;' and on inquiring I learnt that a few days before, in answer to his question, 'whence

came rain ?' the child had been told that it was God who sent rain to the earth.

This incapacity of the infant mind is not to be wondered at, when we remember that the most gifted intellects in their full maturity have but imperfectly comprehended the Divine Being, whom, as the *Mahimna Stotra* (Hymn of Glory) says "Even the Vedas do but feebly apprehend, and describe only by his negative attributes."[1] The only wonder is, that things should have been so ordained as to make the "Great First Cause least understood."

That is no reason, however, why religious education should not commence in infancy. If we are to help the growth of the infant's physical frame by giving him proper food and exercise, if we are to aid the development of his intellectual faculties by presenting and explaining new things to him, and if we are to endeavour to awaken his moral sentiments by suitable precepts and examples, should we do nothing to assist the unfolding of his spiritual nature, the noblest part of man, and that which ought to dominate all his other powers? Nor must we suppose that the infant is wholly unfit for religious education. His earnest inquiries about the cause of things, and his plaintive cries for help in hours of pain and fear, often proceed from an unconscious yearning to know that which would gratify his curiosity, and to have that which would allay his pain

---

[1] अतद्व्यावृत्त्या यं चकितमभिधत्ते श्रुतिरपि ।

and fear. Fond parents, watch those precious moments when your child is in this inquiring or plaintive mood, and give him that which will in the end satisfy his thirst for knowledge, and remove all pain and fear. If you seek the true happiness of your dear child, try every means early to awaken in his mind some notion, imperfect as it must be, of Him who is the Supreme Good. Teach him the name of God, the priceless gift which Dhruva in the *Purana*[1] obtained from his mother when he was only five years old, and which gave him bliss beyond measure for endless ages.

The child may fall into strange mistakes in realizing the idea of God, as in the instance referred to above. When this happens, we should correct the mistake and offer further explanation. This is the direction which Locke gives in his 'Thoughts on Education'[2] when he urges that "there ought very early to be imprinted on the mind a true notion of God."

Let it not be thought that when the infant's conception of God must be imperfect and incorrect, it is not right to endeavour to awaken it in his mind, and that his religious education should be postponed until his mind becomes fit for it. Our first notions, even of things within our power of comprehension, are often incomplete and inaccurate, at whatever age

---

[1] Srimadbhagavata Sk. IV, Ch. VIII,

[2] Paragraph 136.

we begin to study them. And it would be unreasonable to expect that our conception of the Incomprehensible Being will be at once complete and correct, if only we begin to study Him in mature years.

Idea of God. 33. The infant should be told that God is the Creator and Supreme Ruler of the universe; that He is almighty; that He knows and sees everything and is present everywhere, though we cannot see Him; that He is just and merciful; and that we should revere and adore Him. But we should be content with telling him a few things like these, and should not attempt to teach him any dogma or doctrine.

It might be urged that the teaching of even the few things indicated above, would puzzle and bewilder the child; for he may say, if God is everywhere, why should we go to a temple or a mosque or a chapel to worship him; or if God is almighty and omnipresent, how can the image which his parents worship be that God. But it is the raising, and the removal so far as possible, of these apparent difficulties, that would itself be a reason for early religious education. To remove the first mentioned difficulty, the child should be told that as God is everywhere, he is in the temple, mosque or chapel where we sit to worship Him, and we select a particular place because it is suitable and convenient. And his second difficulty may be met by telling him that an image is worshipped only as a symbol of God.

SECTION V. – INSTRUMENTS OF EDUCATION.

34. This part of the subject may be disposed of in a few words.

Instruments of education in infancy.

I shall consider the instruments of education under two heads, *first*, Personal Agency, including principally the teachers employed, and, *second*, Impersonal Agency, including books and other appliances used.

Infant to be taught by parents or relatives, not by school teachers.

35. *I. Personal Agency.*—The education of an infant should be *exclusively home education*, and the teachers employed should be the parents, any other near relatives of whom the child is fond, and the nurse if any. This is necessary, not only for the comfort of the infant, which requires that he should remain only with those in whose company he is happy, but also for the success of the education to be given, which requires that the teacher should be one who loves the pupil and is loved by him.

No books to be taught.

36. *II.*—*Impersonal Agency.*—Books *for reading* should be wholly discarded; but picture books and cards printed with pictures should be largely resorted to, and so also interesting and instructive toys. Some of the Kindergarten appliances, such as coloured balls, and variously shaped cards and models, might be used, but not according to the ordinary elaborate rules, which make the method mechanical and not rational. *Each child must be individually taught*, and a very great deal will depend upon the teacher, who will have to modify and supplement, as occasion may require, all rules laid down for his guidance.

The infant should have the use of a slate and pencil, not for *writing*, which it would be too early to begin, but for *scribbling* freely, which is necessary *to train his hand*. The child lisps before he can speak, and so he must scribble before he can write. He may be asked to draw straight lines and crooked lines and circles and the like, but he should not be troubled with too many directions.

Nursery Rhymes and Tales.

37. I shall here add a few words with reference to one class of books which may be read to the infant, though they may not be read by him, I mean books of Nursery Rhymes and those of Nursery Tales. The former are resorted to much more than the latter, because rhymes interest little children long before tales can be appreciated. These Nursery Rhymes and Tales form a literature by themselves, and are to be found in every language, preserved partly in writing and partly by oral tradition. They are endeared by the associations that cluster round the nursery; they are hoary with antiquity; and they are full of interest for the antiquarian and scholar as containing valuable traces of the manners and customs of by-gone ages. I like them and have respect for them. I would have them preserved as interesting records of human thought and sentiment in the past. But because they deserve a place in the library, that is no reason why they should be used in the Nursery, if they are out of date, any more than because flint spades are fit to be preserved in the museum, that can be a reason for using them in the

field. Though they are entitled to be preserved, it does not follow that they must continue to be used for the purposes for which they were composed, notwithstanding that they have fallen out of date, and might be displaced by others more suitable for instruction and entertainment. I speak only with reference to the nursery literature of my country, leaving it to the people of other countries to speak of their own.

Their revision.

38. The suggestion I would make with all earnestness is, that competent writers should revise the Nursery Rhymes and Nursery Tales in Bengalee, retaining what is both interesting and instructive, substituting for the rest what is more interesting and more instructive, making them few and short, and arranging them in some order. The nursery rhymes might be arranged under the following heads, namely, those relating to :—

(i) Concrete household objects familiar to the child, such as his articles of food, clothing, and furniture.

(ii) Other familiar cencrete objects of the mineral kingdom, such as ordinary metals, earth, water, air, fire, the heavenly bodies.

(iii) Other familiar concrete objects of the vegetable kingdom, such as ordinary flowers, fruits, trees and plants.

(iv) Familiar concrete objects of the animal kingdom, such as ordinary animals.

(v) Days of the week, months of the year, the four cardinal points of the compass, and the first ten numerals.

(vi) The fundamental moral truths.

The nursery tales might be arranged in order of simplicity, omitting all that involves anything that is unnatural or shocking to tender sentiments.

Conclusion. Avoid meddling too much.

39. I have indicated many directions above, and I shall conclude this Chapter with one general direction, which is of greater importance than all others, in the education of the infant, namely, that errors of omission are better than those of commission, and that we should carefully *avoid meddling too much with the voluntary efforts of the child to exercise his powers and gain knowledge.*

CHAPTER II.

EDUCATION IN BOYHOOD.

INTRODUCTORY REMARKS.

40. The second educational period in the life of man I have termed Boyhood. According to Chánakya,[1] it extends from the beginning of the sixth to the end of the fifteenth year, and is the only period of compulsory discipline. Rousseau in his Emile makes the second period extend to the end of the twelfth year; but he would leave the child free to follow his own inclinations during the second as well as the first period, and he strongly condemns all attempts at compulsory training during this period as mischievous and cruel. Dr. Chamberlain in his work on "The Child as a Study in the Evolution of Man" has an interesting Chapter (Chapter IV) on the periods of childhood, in which he quotes the following lines from "Tussur's Five Hundred Points of Good Husbandry" published in 1557 :—

Period of boyhood.

> "The first seven years bring up as a child ;
> The next to learning for waxing too wild ;
> The next to keep under Sir Hobbard de Hoy ;
> The next a man and no longer a boy."

He then cites Dr. Sanford who in readjusting the Seven Ages[2] of Shakespeare, makes the second extend

---

[1] Quoted in note 1, p. 5.

[2] As You Like It, Act II, Scene VII.

from three to fifteen years. The Indian Universities Commission unanimously recommend the completion of the fifteenth year as the minimum age-limit for entering the University and commencing collegiate education. I do not intend to enter into any detailed discussion as to what should be the proper limit of the second educational period. I think the limit fixed by the Indian aphorist Chánakya long ago, and recommended by the Indian Universities Commission so late as 1902, may conveniently be adopted in this country. It is true, the period of ten years from five to fifteen, is a little too long, and involves much change in growth, and it might have been subdivided into two periods of four and six years. But as the remarks I am going to make are of a general nature, this subdivision will not be necessary, except for certain purposes which will be noticed as I proceed.

Sub-divisions of the Chapter.

41. As in the preceding Chapter, I shall offer my remarks under the heads of Physical, Intellectual, Moral and Religious Education, and conclude with a few observations on the Instruments of Education in Boyhood.

SECTION I.—PHYSICAL EDUCATION.

Matters requiring consideration.

42. As in infancy so in boyhood, the matters requiring consideration under the head of physical education are, food, clothing, and exercise and play.

43. As boyhood is a period of growth, the food of a boy should be wholesome in quality and sufficient in quantity. But on the other hand, it should be simple and moderate, excessively rich food and overfeeding being carefully avoided. **Food.**

I do not wish to inculcate severe asceticism, or to condemn altogether the pleasures of the palate. That would be wrong, seeing that Nature has endowed us with a delicate sense of taste which is, on the whole reliable,[1] has furnished for us in her vegetable kingdom so many articles of food which are delicious and at the same time wholesome, and has so regulated the process of digestion that what we eat with relish is digested more easily than what is taken with repugnance. But what I earnestly wish is, that a boy should be told as early as he is able to understand it, that *we take food not for gratifying the palate but for satisfying our hunger, and supplying the wants of our physical system* which gets exhausted by work and requires food to renew its vigour, and that, in the beneficent economy of Nature, the performance of this necessary function of eating is attended with exquisite pleasure experienced in the palate. A boy should also be told early, that while food in suitable quantity is necessary, *excessive eating is positively harmful.* As Manu[2] says, "Excessive eating is prejudicial to health, to longevity, and to attainment of heaven;

---

[1] See Diet and Digestion by Sir W. Roberts, p. 156.

[2] II, 57.

it is vicious and detested by people; therefore let him avoid it."

Though, not being a medical man, I must speak with some diffidence, I would venture to say that meat and stimulating drinks, including tea and coffee, should be avoided by boys in this country.[1] If it is true that extreme abstinence as well as excessive indulgence in the matter of food should both be avoided, it is equally true that natural inclination will be a sufficient safeguard against the former kind of excess, while the only corrective of the latter is early discipline. The boy who is early trained in ascetic self-denial, will be none the worse for fighting the battle of life, but will, on the contrary, be a great deal better prepared for it than the child nursed in the lap of luxury. Nor need we apprehend that this implies any appreciable diminution of the boy's happiness, if the training in self-denial is given gradually, and the boy is made to practise it, not *under coercion*, but *voluntarily* by following the precept and imitating the example of the trainer.

Clothing.

44. In regard to clothing we should bear in mind that too much of it is not necessary in this climate. The dress of a boy should be neat and clean, but simple and not gaudy; and even in the choice of

[1] See Diet and Food by Dr. Haig. There is some difference of expert opinion on the general question, but scarcely any so far as this country is concerned.

his holiday apparel he should be asked to follow Polonius's advice to his son—

"Costly thy habit as thy purse can buy,
But not expressed in fancy : rich not gaudy.
For the apparel oft proclaims the man."

Before a boy becomes a man, it is well that he should be taught that economy is a virtue and extravagance a vice, and that following fancy and fashion is foppishness and folly.

Exercise and Play.

45. A boy should have plenty of healthful exercise and play. They are necessary for his healthy physical growth, and they may be utilized to help his mental development. During the earlier years, that is, up to the ninth year, they should occupy the greater part of the boy's time, only a small portion of it being devoted to work strictly so called, that is, to intellectual, moral and religious education ; and the time for exercise and play should be gradually reduced as the extent of that work increases.

There are two things to be kept in view in regard to a boy's exercise and play. *First*, they should be healthful and free from risk ; and, *secondly*, they should be utilized to help intellectual, moral, and even spiritual development.

Play to be healthful and free from risk.

A boy's play and his exercise are not necessarily healthful. He may, under the excitement of the moment, be playing or taking exercise in the heat of the sun, and if he continues so doing long, he may in the end have a bad headache. So, again, there are several sorts of play and exercise which are attended with risk, and these should be carefully avoided.

Sir Steuart Bayley, Lieutenant-Governor of Bengal, in addressing an audience at a Prize Distribution ceremony at which gymnastic performances by students were exhibited, strongly deprecated risky exercises, and pointed out that exercises should be resorted to for gaining health and strength, and not for becoming acrobats.

Play to be regulated so as to help mental development.

Plays of boys may be so regulated as to help the development, not only of their bodies, but also of their minds. Thus, in walking or running, a boy may be made to describe different figures; in playing with small coloured balls, he may be taught the numerals and portions of the Multiplication Table; in playing with pieces of card, he may learn to make solids of different shapes; and so on. But care should be taken not to make play, which should be free and spontaneous, degenerate into rigid routine, as the Kindergarten method sometimes degenerates when followed unintelligently and mechanically.

SECTION II.—INTELLECTUAL EDUCATION.

Questions to be considered under the head of intellectual education.

46. Intellectual education in its comprehensive sense, as conducted by Nature aided by man, begins with the dawn of intelligence, and goes on in a more or less marked manner all through life. But the

sense in which I use it now is a restricted one, it being taken to mean intellectual education professedly given and consciously received as such. When it is used in this sense, the questions requiring consideration are :—

(1) When should it begin ?
(2) What subjects should it embrace ?
(3) How should they be taught and learnt ?

Time when it should begin.

47. Some great educators[1] would put off intellectual education till the twelfth year. The practice of civilised countries is to begin much earlier. In this country, intellectual education formally begins in the fifth year. By putting off education for some time, we may make the earlier years of boyhood more pleasant, and a boy beginning later, and therefore with better developed powers, may, to some extent, make up for lost time. But remembering that the struggle for existence is daily increasing, and remembering that life is short but art is long, I do not think it would be for the real good of the boy to postpone the formal beginning of his intellectual education later than the fifth or the sixth year. Nor need we apprehend that this will interfere with his early happiness. Education, to be successful, must be so conducted as to be attended with pleasure, whether we begin it early or late; and during the first four years of boyhood, that is, up to the end of the ninth year, it should never be too exacting.

[1] See Rousseau's Emile, Books II and III.

i.—COURSE FOR THE SIXTH YEAR.

Earliest subjects of study and mode of teaching them—Language and Arithmetic.

48. The earliest subjects of intellectual education should be Language (the boy's Vernacular), and Arithmetic. A boy during his first five years must have made fair progress in Language, and some progress in Arithmetic; for he must have learnt to speak his vernacular, and to count and add small numbers and subtract one small number from another. One main point of difference between that and the education in Language and Arithmetic which I am now speaking of, consists in this, that the latter involves the teaching of reading and writing, and teaching with the help of books. This is no small matter of difference. The teaching of reading and writing marks an important period in the education of a child; and books, notwithstanding the disfavour shown to them by some teachers, are, and must always be, necessary appliances in education. It is through books that one learns to commit to memory lessons which may not be retained in recollection from oral teaching, unless it is often repeated; it is through books that one learns to think over lessons orally taught; and it is through books that one can have access to the thoughts of master minds in distant ages and countries. A boy should therefore be told to approach books with love and reverence.

I shall now offer a few remarks on education in each of the above two subjects; and then consider what other subjects should be gradually included in a boy's course of study.

49. The learning of language with the help of books, which must be preceded by the necessary preliminary learning of *reading* with its concomitant *writing*, is different from the learning of language in infancy, the latter being in what may be called the *synthetic* method, words and sentences being learnt as the equivalents of things and thoughts, while the former is in what may be styled the *analytic* method, the elementary sounds or letters composing words being learnt first, words composed of them next, and then sentences composed of those words. The earlier steps of this process, however interesting to the philologist, must be somewhat tedious to the child. Language.

50. To make these steps agreeable to the child, in other words, to convert his *work* of learning the alphabet into a sort of *play*, Locke[1] recommends the use of dice with letters pasted on their faces; others use pictorial alphabets or charts, each letter having the picture of an animal or a fruit the name of which begins with that letter, printed by its side. Rousseau,[2] considers all these to be useless effort, and he would substitute for these devices, a desire to learn, which may be created in a child if he is made to feel the inconvenience of not knowing to read, by being unable to respond to invitations to pleasure parties conveyed in short notes addressed to him. I Reading.

---

[1] Education § 150.

[2] Emile (abridged translation in the International Education Series) p. 82.

think we may employ the devices usually resorted to, and at the same time endeavour to create in the child a desire to learn; only, we must here, as in other similar matters, be careful not to attach any disproportionate importance to either of the two modes of creating interest, nor to make unduly elaborate efforts to overcome a boy's reluctance to learn to read; for happily for us, the reluctance after all is not very great, and boys take pleasure in learning anything that is new, even if it be the alphabet, provided the teacher deals with them pleasantly.

Writing.

51. As writing impresses on the mind the forms of the letters of the alphabet, and is helpful in enabling the boy to learn reading, besides being useful in various other ways, *the teaching of writing should proceed hand in hand with that of reading.* The best mode of teaching writing is, as Locke[1] recommends, to write the letters in large size in red ink on a sheet of paper, and to make the learner trace his pen with black ink over them in the proper direction a large number of times, so that his hand may be trained in moving in the required manner. The difficulty which a boy feels in writing a letter after seeing you write it, arises from his having to perform two mental operations at once, namely, the operation of working his memory to remember what you did, and that of working his will to make his hand do what he recollects you to have done. In tracing the letters placed before him, he has not to

[1] Education § 160.

work his memory, the direction which his hand is to take being visible to his eyes; and all that he has to do is to work his will in moving his hand.

A slate may be used for the same purpose.

Teaching of the alphabet and alphabetical primer of the Sanskritic vernacular languages.

52. I may here add a few detailed remarks on the teaching of the alphabet and alphabetical primer in the Indian vernaculars derived from or allied to the Sanskrit, they being the most important among the vernacular languages of India.

Leaving out of consideration certain minor points on which opinions differ, these alphabets, though differing in form, are the same as regards the names and sounds of letters. The letters are fifty in number, whereof fourteen are vowels and thirty-six consonants, to which should be added three more which are signs rather than letters, namely, the nasal signs *Anuswara* and *Chandravindu* which being added to a letter indicate that it is to have a nasal sound, and the aspirate sign or *Visarga* which added to a letter indicates that it is to have an aspirated sound. The *names* of the letters being their *sounds* with the vowel (a) added in the case of the consonants, a boy learns the sounds of the letters almost as soon as their names are repeated before him. We should be satisfied with this at first, and should reserve for a future lesson the explanation and understanding of the beautiful and scientific *arrangement* of the alphabet in the Sanskrit and its allied languages. (See para. 80).

The learner should be asked to observe and point out the similarities and differences in the forms of the letters, and to note that while some few of them are composed of straight lines only, and a few others of curve lines alone, the majority are composed of straight and curve lines joined together. And he should then be taught the different forms which the vowels take when joined to consonants. Next he should be exercised in forming words composed of one, two, or three consonants, with vowels joined to them. And here a special precaution, which is often lost sight of, should be carefully observed. The words which the boy should be exercised in forming, and which should find a place at this stage in the Alphabetical Primer, *must be only those that are already known to him. and all new words must be carefully excluded.* To form and read out words composed of their elementary sounds represented by corresponding letters, is sufficiently new and difficult work for the beginner, and we should not add to the novelty and difficulty of his work, by requiring him to make words unknown to him. To be taught to make with their component letters words already known to him, is to the boy a source of pleasure, somewhat similar to that of recognizing an old friend in a new guise; but this element of pleasure will be wanting if you attempt to teach him all at once to make new words with their component letters.

Nor should we take a boy through long columns of unconnected words, in the belief that we thereby give him sufficient exercise. Instead of having one monotonous form of exercise, it is better to vary its form so as to make it *interesting* ; and we can make it so by making the boy *learn to read short and simple sentences composed of words already known to him.*

The learner should next be taught the sounds and forms of *consonantal compounds*, of which there are a great many in the Sankritic languages ; and he should be exercised in reading words, and short sentences composed of words, containing these compounds. Here it would not be easy to avoid introducing new words ; but they should be as few and simple as possible. We should be satisfied at first with teaching only the ordinary consonantal compounds, and should not trouble the beginner with all possible compounds and with unusual words to illustrate them.

An alphabetical primer in any of the Sanskritic Indian vernaculars, written in accordance with the foregoing suggestions, need not contain more than *thirty* pages; nor need it consist of two parts, and detain the learner more than *six months* in getting through it. I shall have to say a few words more about elementary books in Section V of this Chapter, when dealing with text-books. Simultaneously with reading the alphabetical primer, a boy should be taught to write

53. Along with his Alphabetical Primer a boy should be taught his Arithmetical Primer, the two studies being taken up at two different times of the day. He should be taught to *read* and *write* first the Arithmetical Primer.

first ten numbers, and then the next ten, and so on, up to one hundred. The fact of the scale of notation being the *decimal* scale should be brought to the learner's notice, or rather, should be barely hinted at, so that he may carefully observe it for himself. But the explanation of the reason for the origin of the fact, simple and interesting as it is, should be postponed for a later stage of his progress. The learner should then be taught to *read, write, and commit to memory* the Multiplication Table up to 10 times 10. To make his knowledge, as far as possible, *intelligent* instead of leaving it to be merely *mechanical,* the correctness of each result in this table should be *shown to him by a concrete example.*

The table of the quadruples called the *Karania* or *Karakia* table in Bengali, showing what multiple of four with how much over, each number up to 100 is, may also conveniently be committed to memory. But the other tables such as *Gandakia Burkia, Punkia, &c.,* with which Bengali Arithmetical Primers are filled, should be left out as useless incumbrances on the memory. The arithmetical primer thus abridged, will consist of not more than *six* pages, and may either be kept separate, or incorporated with alphabetical primer.

Subhankari mechanical system need not be taught.

I know it is the opinion of some educationists that the tables I would exclude, are helpful in the application of the method of mental arithmetic known as *Subhankari,* which is useful for the ready solution of many ordinary arithmetical problems, and that they should therefore be committed to memory. With all respect for Subhankar, the inventor of the method, I must say that it is unnecessary and burdensome, not only for boys who are intended to receive liberal education, but also for those who may not advance beyond the standard of primary education; and my reasons are two. In the *first* place, the method is a mechanical one for the solution of problems which may, intelligently and no less readily, be solved by the ordinary methods of Compound Multiplication and Practice; and the little saving of time which it may apparently secure, is more than counterbalanced by the cost of time and trouble which the preliminary preparation, in committing the tables to memory must entail,—time and trouble with the expenditure of which a boy can easily learn the ordinary methods. And in the *second* place, the method is of use only so long as rupees, annas, and *gandas* are the units of money; maunds, seers, powas, and chittaks, the units of weight; and bighas, kathas, and chittaks, the units of area; and if you change the units of weight to hundredweights, quarters, and pounds, or the units of area to square feet, square yards, and acres, the method becomes inapplicable and useless.

54. Along with Language and Arithmetic, a boy should be taught in his sixth year, Drawing, that is the drawing of *lines* and simple *figures*.

55. He should also be taught Object Lessons, that is lessons on familiar objects, by having the objects *placed before him*, and by being made to

Object Lessons.

observe their simple qualities, such as their shape, size, colour, sound, taste, and smell.

ii.—COURSE FOR THE SEVENTH YEAR.

Book of Reading Lessons.

56. The learning of the Alphabetical Primer of 30 pages or so, and of the Arithmetical Primer of 6 pages, ought not to take an ordinary boy more than one year. In his seventh year, a boy should begin a book of simple Reading Lessons and an Elementary Arithmetic.

The book of reading lessons should be *interesting* as well as *instructive,* that is, calculated to impart pleasure as well as knowledge, as regards both its language and subject.

Its languag should be simple and pleasant.

57. For the language to be interesting, it must be *simple* and *pleasant,* that is, easy to read and understand and agreeable to hear; hard, inexact, and unnecessary words should be avoided; and the lessons should be *partly in prose and partly in poetry.* And for the language to be instructive, it must *contain new words* to increase the boy's vocabulary. But to prevent this from interfering too much with simplicity, care must be taken not to introduce too many new words at once, but to *graduate* successive lessons and even successive sentences in the same lesson, so that *not more than a small fraction,* say *about one tenth, of the words in it should be new words.* When a book observes no such rule, as is the case with many otherwise good reading books, I have found

little boys who have to read such books, look despondent and helpless on seeing that the lesson they are reading in their own vernacular is utterly unintelligible to them.

It will no doubt cost an author some time and labour to write a reading book, observing the foregoing rule; but if we want to make reading pleasant and not irksome to the beginner, we should not grudge that the preparation of his book of reading lessons entails such cost.

In regard to the subject-matter of a boy's first book of Reading Lessons, the principle points to be borne in mind are the following:— Its subject matter should satisfy certain conditions.

I. The book should treat of matters *some* of which are *already known* to the boy, and the *rest* are *new matters* such that the boy's attention, in due course of things, should be soon called to them.

II. The matters, if they relate to the physical world, should be such as are, or can be made, *known in their reality* to the boy; and scenes and events of foreign countries which have no counterparts in his own, should be avoided.

III. Matters relating to the moral world or the physical world which are likely to be *beyond his comprehension* should be *excluded*.

A striking illustration of the futility of our attempt to make a child understand matters before his mind becomes fit to comprehend them, is furnished by the story told by Rousseau,[1] of the little boy and the incident about Alexander and Philip. The incident was this, that Alexander, having been informed by a letter from Parmenion that Philip, his most esteemed physician, had been bribed by Darius to poison him, at the same moment that he gave Parmenion's letter to Philip to read, drank the beverage which the physician had presented to him. The tutor of the boy had related the incident to him, and commented on the intrepidity of Alexander which it proved, believing that the pupil fully appreciated the lesson. But when questioned as to what the courage of the hero consisted in, the boy could only say that it was in the fact of his having swallowed at a single draught a disagreeable potion without hesitation or disgust.

IV. The reading lessons for a little boy should not only be *instructive*, but should also be *interesting* and even *amusing*. They may be grotesque, but they should never be absurd.

With all respect for ancient wisdom and approved authority, I would *exclude* from the child's first book of reading all lessons which make animals speak and involve other similar *fiction*. Not that fables like Æsop's are not useful reading, but they should not be placed in the hands of a boy until he is able to discriminate between fact and fiction. It is true, a little boy no more believes that the animals in his

---

[1] Emile F. 77 (Translation in the International Education series).

fables did actually speak than a grown up man does; but the mischief is this, that not being able adequately to appreciate the real purpose of introducing the fiction, he may be led to think that it is allowable to tell tales; and the result may be to weaken his regard for truth at a time when every effort should be directed towards strengthening it.

V. Even at this early stage, each lesson, whatever its subject may be, should be presented in a manner such that it may have as much of *literary grace* imparted to it as is consistent with simplicity of language and directness of statement. Some eminent scientists seem to think that the facts of the material world, stated in a matter of fact style, are all that knowledge should consist of. Such knowledge might feed the intellect, but it would starve the emotional side of the mind, which plays an important part in life, and the culture of which is necessary in all true education.

Method of teaching Reading Lessons—Reading.

58. Boys should be taught to read their lessons with *correctness* and *ease*. For this purpose, the words composing a sentence should be read first, slowly and separately, care being taken to avoid the naming of the letters making up a word, except mentally and inaudibly, and then the sentence should be read out as a whole. This will cost the boy some trouble at first, and his reading will for a time be halting; but his difficulties will soon be overcome. On the other hand, if instead of making him read out the words, the teacher helps him too readily, and

reads out each sentence for him, and then asks him to read it, it will be often found that the boy reads more by *reproducing from memory* (which is strong at his age) what he *heard* his teacher read, than by *observing the words himself.*

Nothing but constant practice will enable a boy to read out whole sentences without going through a conscious effort of pronouncing separately every letter and syllable in it. He should, therefore, be *exercised in reading his lessons aloud* as often as he can find time.

Explanation. 59. After a boy has read out a sentence, he should be asked to *explain* it; and for that purpose, he should first *give the meanings of the words*, unknown words being explained, and then he should *state the meaning of the sentence as a whole.*

After an entire paragraph is read and explained, the boy should be asked *to give its substance in his own words*, and he should be required to do the same thing after the whole lesson is finished. This should never be neglected, as it is not only the best test for judging whether the boy has understood the lesson, but is also the best way of making him think out for himself what the lesson teaches. He will require to be helped a good deal at first, and it will be found that though able to repeat portions of the lesson, he is unable to give its substance as a whole. The peculiarity of growing minds, as indeed even of grown-up minds when untrained, is to see the parts separately and distinctly, without being able easily to take a comprehensive view of the whole.

Classification of words, number and case of nouns, person and tense of verbs.

60. After a boy has made some progress in his first book of Reading Lessons, he should be taught that words belong to different *classes* or Parts of Speech, and he should be told *to mark the differences in the termination* of the same word, if a *noun*, indicating differences in *number* and *case*, and if a *verb*, indicating differences in *person* and *tense*; but too much of detail in grammatical instruction should be avoided.

Arithmetic to be learnt intelligently and not mechanically.

61. Along with his first book of Reading Lessons, a boy should be taught Arithmetic. The teaching of Arithmetic is not very easy; but whatever the difficulty attending the teaching may be, it should be taught *rationally* and not *mechanically*. It is the first scientific subject that a boy learns, and it is desirable that he should learn it intelligently.

Teaching of Notation and Numeration.

62. I shall assume that the pupil has already learned to count up to 100 or a little upwards, and has learnt also the Addition, Subtraction, and Multiplication Tables. The first thing to be taught after that, is Notation and Numeration. To teach this, I think we may proceed somewhat in the following manner (as has been more fully stated in my Elements of Arithmetic.)

The boy should be asked how to express numbers by *signs* or *symbols*. Perhaps he will not be able to

4

give any answer to the question put in such general terms. To lead him on, he may be told that *one* may be conveniently represented by a single *stroke*, and then asked how to represent the succeeding numbers *two, three,* &c. Probably the boy will say, or if he does not, he may be easily led to say,—'by repetition of the *stroke*.' Then he should be shown the difficulty of representing large numbers in that way, and asked to consider what device to adopt to avoid this difficulty. The analogous case of writing different words which are so *many* in number, by combinations and permutations of the letters of the Alphabet which are so *few* in number, should be pointedly placed before him. He will then understand when told (if he cannot say so himself) that the plan to be followed must be, to have *a few distinct symbols* for *some of the numbers* and to adopt certain *rules* for expressing *other numbers* by *combinations* of those symbols.

The stroke method, which is the basis of the Roman system of notation, may be then explained, and illustrated by the marks on the dial of a clock or a watch; and the pupil may be told that the number *ten* which forms the turning point in our nomenclature of numbers, would naturally be represented by X, that is, one stroke crossing another, its half, *five*, by the upper half of the cross or V, and other numbers by the *addition* or *subtraction* of the stroke for *one*, according as it comes *after* or *before* a symbol of higher value, *six* being thus represented by VI, and *four* by IV.

The common system of Notation should then be explained as consisting in the adoption of,—

(1) the *nine digits* and *0* to represent the first *nine* numbers and *nought*, and

(2) the rule that *the value of every digit should increase tenfold at each step of removal towards the left.*

The teacher should next point out that this system must have been *suggested* by the ordinary method of *naming* numbers, which proceeds by *periods of ten*; and he should then ask the question, how that method of naming came to be adopted; and in answer explain the commonly accepted *theory*, that the method, in all probability, owes its origin to the fact of the ten fingers having formed the readiest counters in the infancy of Arithmetic, and numbers above ten being counted with the help of the fingers of successive assistants of the first computer.

If the explanation is given slowly and step by step in the course of several lessons, it will be quite intelligible and very interesting to boys of seven or eight years, as I have found. But we must not carry the numeration table higher than one hundred at first.

The first four operations of Arithmetic.

The *rules* for the four fundamental operations, Addition, Subtraction, Multiplication, and Division, should then be gradually taught, and *the reasons for the rules* explained, by amplifying the operations after analysing the numbers involved in them into their component units, tens, hundreds, etc. The only rule, the explanation of the reason for which will give some trouble, is, the rule about increasing by ten a figure in the minuend if it is less than the corresponding figure in the subtrahend, and adding one to the next figure in the subtrahend to keep the difference unchanged. But a few repeated efforts to explain the matter will generally be found sufficient.

Drawing and Object Lessons.

63. Drawing and Object Lessons should from part of the course for the seventh year, the syllabuses in those subjects being made a little fuller than those for the sixth year.

iii.—STUDIES FOR THE EIGHTH YEAR.

A second Reading Book and the compound operations in Arithmetic.

64. The seventh year will generally be taken up in learning the first Reading Book and the four fundamental operations of Arithmetic with abstract numbers. In the eighth year, a second Reading Book in prose and poetry, containing lessons slightly more difficult than the first, and the fundamental operations of Arithmetic with ordinary concrete numbers (not involving any fraction) should be taught.

Additional subjects.

65. The question then arises, whether any additional subjects, and if any, what sŭbjects, should be taken up in the eighth year.

English

Though I am opposed to undue multiplication of subjects which is calculated to distract attention, yet considering the importance of the knowledge of

English to the Indian student, I would recommend that an English Alphabetical Primer should be read by all Indian students in their eighth year.

I know there are some high authorities who are against this view, and who are of opinion that no student should begin to learn a foreign language until he has properly mastered his vernacular; and they cite in support of this view, instances of the successful progress of boys who learn English after passing one of the lower scholarship examinations in the vernacular. With all respect for their opinion, I would venture to adhere to my own. The boy who begins reading English after having made some progress in his vernacular, is no doubt better able to understand English idioms and English ideas than one who begins reading it earlier; but so far as the learning of an alphabetical primer, properly prepared, is concerned, that is, a primer which aims only at teaching how to read and write simple English words and short English sentences, dealing with familiar and not foreign things and thoughts, I do not think that the boy who begins reading English later is in a better position; while, on the contrary, the boy who begins earlier has the advantage of having a keener memory and more plastic vocal organs when he commences, and of having a longer training in its study before he closes. And as for the instances cited, they do not prove much, because they are only cases of boys of more than average merit, as is shown by the fact of those boys having passed a previous examination; and their success may be due more to their superior parts than to the fact of their commencing to read English later.

But though recommending the reading of English early, I must not be understood as encouraging its study to the neglect of the boy's vernacular. And I must insist upon English alphabetical primers and early reading books being prepared in the manner indicated above, *so as to avoid reference to unfamiliar things and thoughts.* We should always bear in mind that the difficulty of learning the spelling and pronunciation of words, and the structure and meaning of sentences, in a foreign language, is enough to occupy the attention of the beginner; and we ought not to add to it the difficulty of understanding foreign things and thoughts all at once. I shall revert to this point later when speaking of text books.

Teaching of English Alphabetical Primer.

One easy mode of teaching an Indian boy an English alphabetical primer is to begin by teaching him the sounds of the English letters or rather their equivalents in his vernacular, and by making him pronounce English words by combining the vernacular equivalents of its constituent letters, as is sought to be done in Peary Charan Sarkar's First Book of Reading. But this method is obviously defective, English letters not having their exact equivalents in sound in any Indian vernacular; and it is not after all the simplest mode, as every one knows, because a little boy finds it much easier to pronounce correctly a word after it is once uttered in his hearing, than to do so by combining the vernacular equivalents of its letters. In the former mode, the boy has only *to imitate*, while in the latter, he has *to reason*; and his power of imitation is much stronger than his power of reasoning.

The English alphabetical primer should, like the vernacular alphabetical primer of which I have spoken already, *avoid giving long lists of hard words* in the spelling lessons, and *sentences involving abstract ideas* in the reading lessons. The simple sentence "To be" occurring in the very first reading lesson in many primers is perhaps more difficult to explain to a boy of eight years, than the sentence "To be or not to be that is the question" to the student of Shakespeare.

Explanation.

In explaining a sentence, the teacher should not adopt what may be called the synthetic method, namely, that of giving the meaning of the sentence as a whole; but he should follow the analytic method of *giving the meanings of the component words, placing before the pupil*, whenever possible, *the things signified by the words*, and of *leaving it to the pupil to make out the sense of the whole from the meanings of its constituent parts*, giving him such help as may be necessary. To assist the pupil in this, the teacher should call his attention to the main points of difference in the structure of sentences in English and Bengali, such as the *position* of the *preposition*, which in English comes before the word it governs, but which in Bengali comes after, the governed word taking the possessive case-ending. It is in this way that the power of making out the meaning of a sentence with the help of a dictionary, can be gradually developed, and the habit of self-reliance formed and encouraged.

Direct method should be supplemented by the method of translation and re-translation.

Here I ought to say a few words about the applicability of what is called the 'direct' method of learning a language to the case of an Indian boy learning English. The direct method of teaching a foreign language aims at associating in the learner's mind words and sentences of the foreign language *directly* with the things and thoughts they signify, instead of going through the indirect process of first translating them into words and sentences in the learner's vernaculars, and then through these latter, referring to the things and thoughts signified. That is the method in which an infant learns his mother tongue, and it is doubtless a very efficacious method under favourable circumstances. But the efficacy of the method depends upon the force and frequency of the associations between the linguistic signs and the things signified; so that unless the learner is so circumstanced that the language to be learned is his sole or at least his chief means of communication with others, the force and frequency of those associations will not be such as will make the method efficacious. Now an Indian boy begins to learn English when ordinary things and thoughts have already become well associated in his mind with their expressions in his vernacular, and his surroundings are Indian and not English except for a short time during school hours. Hence the direct method cannot be of full advantage to him, nor can the case of an English boy learning French be said to be similar to that of a Bengali boy learning English, when in vocabulary and structure, Bengali differs from English much more than English does from French. In teaching English to an Indian boy, therefore, the direct method, though it may be resorted to with advantage so far as circumstances are favourable, should not be exclusively employed, but should be supplemented by the method of translation and re-translation.

Writing.

In teaching writing, the teacher should exercise the pupil in finding out similarities between small and capital letters, and between the forms of the letters as used in manuscript and in printing, with a view to develop the faculty of observation, and to arouse intelligent curiosity. The similarity is sometimes not at first sight quite apparent, as in the case of the letter Q. But in old books (I am referring to one printed in 1816) Q sometimes appears as Q, between which form and that used in manuscript (𝒬), the similarity is obvious. In teaching writing in English, the teacher should in the first place give certain general directions, such as, using ruled paper, dividing the ruled spaces properly, making the oblique lines of the letters parallel, &c.; and he should then correct the defects in each individual letter, the very first time he notices them, so as to prevent the pupil's contracting the bad habit of persevering in his error.

Drawing and Object Lessons.

66. Drawing and Object Lessons should continue to form part of the course, the syllabuses being amplified.

IV.—STUDIES FOR THE NINTH, TENTH, AND ELEVENTH YEARS.

Sanskrit Primer.

67. In the ninth year, that is, after the boy has made some progress in his English alphabetical primer, he should, if he is a Hindu, and is intended to have a liberal education, be made to begin the reading of Sanskrit. A knowledge of Sanskrit is necessary for a Hindu to enable him to perform his religious ceremonies intelligently; and it is also helpful in facilitating the study of his vernacular which is based upon Sanskrit. The Sanskrit alphabet being in most cases the same as that of the boy's vernacular, with only some difference in the forms of the letters, will be readily learnt. The Sanskrit vocabulary also is not very different from that of the boy's vernacular. The real difficulty in learning Sanskrit consists in mastering the grammatical forms, that is, the declension of nouns and adjectives, and the conjugation of verbs. Before commencing to read Sanskrit Grammar, the boy should learn a little of the grammar of his vernacular; he should know the simple rules of phonetic combination or *Sandhi*, and something about the cases of nouns and the moods and tenses of verbs. He should then begin to commit to memory the ordinary forms of declension of nouns and adjectives, and conjugation of

verbs, as given in the paradigms in some elementary grammar such as Iswar Chandra Vidyasagar's Upakramanika. And to make his work pleasant, he should read simple and melodious verses such as those of the Ramayana in Vidyasagar's compilation entitled Rijupatha, Part II. I may here add that simple Sanskrit poetry is more pleasant for the beginner to read and much easier for him to learn than Sanskrit prose; and we need not be anxious to select prose pieces for him. I know I have introduced Sanskrit a little too early. My main reason for doing so is to enable the boy to have some knowledge of Sanskrit before his *Upanayana* or initiation into religious study, which in the case of the Brahmins takes place generally between the ninth and the eleventh year. To be taught the daily prayers which are in Sanskrit, when the neophyte has no knowledge of that language, is most undesirable.

68. The ninth year will be occupied in reading the subjects indicated above. In the tenth year, an additional subject should be taken up, namely, Geography. And the subjects of study will thus be— Geographical Primer.

(1) A Vernacular Reading Book.
(2) A Vernacular Grammar.
(3) A Sanskrit Reading Book.
(4) A Sanskrit Grammar.
(5) An English Reading Book.
(6) Arithmetic.
(7) Geographical Primer.

I have already made my remarks on the mode of teaching most of these subjects; and I shall here add only a few words regarding the way in which Geography should be taught. The text-book in Geography for the beginner should be in the boy's *vernacular*, and should be as *simple and short* as possible. It should contain something about the shape and size of the earth, its main divisions, and the definitions of the principal Geographical terms, and should explain, so far as a beginner can understand, how it is known that the earth is round; but it should not enter into any elaborate explanation or statement of all the proofs of the rotundity of the earth, such as that derived from the roundness of its shadow, nor into any account of its motions, or its distances from the sun and the moon. We must not attempt to teach the beginner too much. To do so would be to confound him. I was once asked by a relation of mine to advise him as to whether his son, a boy of ten or eleven years, should go on reading for the Minor Scholarship Examination, or should be admitted into a High School; and before answering him, I wanted to see the boy. The boy was then preparing his lesson in Geography. I asked him how large the earth was and how far the sun was from the earth, and he answered me correctly. I then asked him how far he was from the earth; and the boy, though fairly intelligent, began scratching his fore-head; showing that the high-pressure stuffing of his mind with geographical knowledge was displacing his common sense.

Perhaps the best mode of teaching Geography would be to begin at the nearest point, the learner's home, and then to take him gradually to distant places with the help of a globe or a chart, *too much of detail being carefully avoided.*

History of India.

In the eleventh year, the subjects mentioned above should be studied more fully, and only one new subject taken up, namely, History of India.

Languages—Parsing, Translation and Dictation.

69. In teaching the three languages, namely, the vernacular, English, and Sanskrit, the teacher should exercise the pupil in *Parsing*, *Translation* and *Dictation.*

Arithmetic—Working out examples—statement of the process.

In Arithmetic, the boy should in the eleventh year learn Vulgar and Decimal Fractions, and should be exercised not only in working out examples but also in *stating correctly the steps of the process.* He should understand that the statement of the steps of any arithmetical or other mathematical *process* should consist of *complete intelligible sentences in logical order*, the only difference between such statement and any piece of ordinary prose consisting in the use of signs and symbols in lieu of words.

Geography-Map-drawing.

In learning Geography the student should be practised in *drawing rough maps.*

History of India to be first taught in the boy's vernacular.

The new subject, History of India, should be taught in the boy's *vernacular.* The text-book should be *simple and short*, but written in an elegant style so that it may take the place of a Prose Reader. It should not aim at teaching too much, and it should, after giving a general idea of what history is, begin at the nearer end, that is the present time, and take the student by rapid marches backwards from the British to the Mahomedan and from the Mahomedan to the Hindu period. The suggestion of having the first historical text-book written in the reverse instead of the direct chronological order, I make with some hesitation, as I have not seen the plan tried, and it is in one sense opposed to the natural order of narration; but it has for the beginner the advantage of taking him from things that are nearer and more known to matters more remote and less known; and this mode of presentation will not involve much difficulty, as the book is intended to be *a historical reader*, giving a general view of the present and the past, and not *a catalogue of events* crowding upon one another. After the historical reader is gone through, the boy may read a poem like the Bharatagatha by Akshaya kumar Chowdhuri, which gives the substance of Indian history shortly in beautiful verse.

V.— STUDIES FROM THE TWELFTH TO THE FIFTEENTH YEAR.

English Grammar and Geometry.

70. In the twelfth year, to the subjects mentioned above, two new subjects should be added, namely, English Grammar in systematic form, and Geometry. In the old subjects also, there should be some change in the method of teaching and in the text books.

Whether English should be read only as a second language or should also form the medium for teaching other subjects.

71. Here the question arises whether English should continue to be read only as a second language, or should form also the medium through which the other subjects are to be taught. There are reasons in favour of both alternatives. Those in favour of the former are, that a subject is better understood and more easily learnt if taught in the learner's vernacular, than it would be if it is taught in a foreign language; and that it would be subjecting an Indian student to unnecessary hardship to make him learn his subjects of study through the medium of the English language, when there are suitable text-books up to the standard of the University Entrance or Matriculation Examination available in most, if not all, Indian vernaculars; and these are certainly cogent reasons. In support of the other view, it may be urged that the reading of all subjects in English is helpful to the learning of English, which Indian students must thoroughly know; that it is helpful also to the study of the higher branches of the different subjects which must be read in English; and that owing to the multiplicity of Indian Vernaculars, neither the University nor the Government Education Department can conveniently conduct public examinations through the medium of the vernaculars. The first two of these reasons are not of much real force, as English, if properly taught, may be thoroughly learnt as a second language, and as the advantage to which the second reason refers may be equally secured by having the English technical terms of the different

subjects parenthetically noted beside their vernacular equivalents in the text-books; but the third reason is no doubt a strong one, and it will take some time before it can be sufficiently met. It may, however, be hoped that with the progress of the vernaculars, text-books of superior merit will come into existence, and the number of vernaculars under each local Government reduced practically to not more than two, that is, Bengali and Urdu for Bengal; Hindi and Urdu for the United Provinces and the Punjab; Mahratti and Gujrati for Bombay; and Telugu and Tamil for Madras; and the different subjects of study may then be conveniently read by the Indian student in his vernacular. But till then, in most cases he will, from his twelfth year, have to read them in English.

Further remarks on teaching.

72. The above proposition being premised, I shall now offer a few additional remarks as to how the different subjects should be taught to a boy from the twelfth to the fifteenth year.

The object of the teacher in intellectual education is, not to make the pupil gain knowledge and improve his powers without labour, for that is impossible, but *to lighten his labour and lead him to voluntary exertion, by making his work interesting and pleasant.* And the suggestions I am going to offer are intended to help the teacher in attaining that object.

Teaching English.

73. From his twelfth year the Indian student must for some years give to English the first place among his linguistic studies, partly by reason of the

importance of the subject, and partly owing to the difficulty of learning it.

In teaching English, the teacher should bear in mind that there are two things to learn, English *language*, and English *literature*, that is, the *manner* of expressing thoughts in English, and the *matter of the thoughts* expressed by the leading writers in that language. In one sense the two are inseparably connected, every sentence in the English language expressing some thought, and every thought in English literature being expressed by a sentence in English; but the learner may direct his attention principally to the one thing or to the other. In the earlier years of his progress, the student must aim at *learning the language*; and it is only when he has acquired some knowledge of the language, and attained some maturity of understanding, that he will be able *to appreciate its literature.*

English language.

The learning of the English language consists in the student being able to read, write, and understand English words and sentences correctly.

Reading English.

To read English properly, the student must learn to *pronounce distinctly and correctly* the words composing each sentence, to *stop duly* at the pauses, and to *modulate his voice* according to the sense conveyed, avoiding, however, all mannerism and affectation. The beginner must, in pronouncing a word, pronounce its component letters; and it is only by practice that he becomes able to pronounce words and read sentences without going through the conscious process of analysing words into their components. Mr. Landon in his Principles and Practice of Teaching[1] gives detailed directions for teaching reading, which I need not reproduce, but shall only refer to. There is much that is useful in them; but, like all detailed directions in teaching, they are open to the objection that they are *more than necessary* for *general* guidance, and *less than sufficient* for *all particular* cases.

In these matters, all that is really profitable is to give a few general directions, and to leave the rest to be supplied by the good sense of the teacher as occasion requires.

Digression on the difference between a text-book on a subject and a book on Education.

It might be said that directions for teaching and learning a subject should find their proper place in text-books on that particular subject, and not in a book on education generally. I do not think that this would be a correct view. It is true that if directions as to how a subject should be taught and learnt are given in a text-book on the subject, it cannot be said that they are wholly superfluous there; but their proper place is in a book on education. A text book is no doubt intended to teach a subject; if it is an elementary one, it should deal with the subject so as to make it intelligible to a beginner of average intelligence; and if an advanced treatise, it should have in view an intelligent student, who has made some progress in the subject. A text-book

[1] Chap. VIII.

must deal with *every part of the subject*, but it is not expected to deal with *every class of students*. On the other hand, a book on education, while dealing with the mode of teaching and learning a particular subject, must keep in view *different classes of students* with varying mental peculiarities, and the different ways of presenting the subject and of giving prominence to particular portions of it, so as to make its study easy and attractive ; but it cannot be expected to deal with *every part of the subject.*

Returning from this digression, I would here relate an incident in connection with the teaching of pronunciation that occurred in my personal knowledge, and then make a general remark on it.

When we were in the third class of the Hare School, there occurred in our History lesson one day the name 'Bajazet' which, with the exception of a few students, the rest pronounced either as Bajajet or as Bazazet. Our teacher was so anxious to correct this mistake, that he spent the whole of the History hour that day over that one word, and he succeeded in helping about 25 out of 30 students to pronounce it correctly. Some may say that we wasted an hour over a trifle. I venture to think differently. A teacher should not pass over any error in his pupils, but should do his best to correct it. The task is hard and may sometimes involve conflict of duties, as in a case where a teacher in charge of a large class spends an undue portion of his time in correcting an error of a single student, when the rest of the class are free from such error. The case I noticed above was, however, different, as the error there was one which almost the whole class fell into. Moreover, the indirect moral effect of the teacher's earnest effort was immense, tending, as it did, to show that errors, however small, should be carefully avoided.

Error to be corrected at once.

The general remark I intended to make, is this, *that errors, whether of pronunciation or of any other kind, should be corrected at the earliest opportunity,* and before they have been persevered in for any length of time. An error persevered in, can be got rid of, if at all, only with difficulty. I know it may be said that a beginner cannot be expected to be perfect in his pronunciation any more than in most other matters, and that things must be left to improve gradually. This view, however, involves a misconception. It is quite true, we cannot expect perfection in anything at once, and matters must be left to improve gradually; but there is a clear difference between *imperfection,* which is a negative fault, that is, a fault of *omission,* and an error, which is a positive fault, or one of *commission.* A beginner may not be able to pronounce some hard letters just in the same way as he may not know the meanings of many words, and may not understand the reasons of many things. But it cannot be right that he should begin by interchanging the letters of a word that he may in the end pronounce it correctly, any more than it would be right that he should begin by knowing wrong meanings of difficult words and wrong reasons of difficult things, the right meanings and right reasons being learnt subsequently. Omit teaching difficult things in the beginning, but do not attempt to teach them if you cannot teach correctly.

A foreigner may be excused for missing nice points, but he must learn early to avoid broad mistakes. Distinct articulation and correct pronunciation are as necessary for those who have to listen to long arguments, as legible writing and correct spelling are for those who have to go through lengthy manuscripts.

74. I have just indicated above that writing should be legible and free from mistakes in spelling. If you cannot write a good hand, still try to write legibly, neatly, and correctly. **Writing English**

To make writing legible, one good rule to follow is to *dot* every *i*, to *cross* every *t*, and to *avoid omitting any of the slanting strokes* in letters such as *e, i, m, n, u, w.*

To write neatly, one must write with care so as to *avoid the necessity of erasures and interlineations*; and one must not squeeze a word at the end of a line, as is often done to avoid either the inconvenience or the difficulty of syllabication. It is very desirable to avoid having one part of a word in one line and another in the next, but the better way to do this is to write sparsely when nearing the end of a line.

To make writing free from orthographical mistakes, the learner should be told to *look carefully at every word when he first comes to learn it*; and he should also carefully *read the rules about spelling and syllabication* given in books.

To learn to write legibly, neatly, and correctly, the beginner must have a little patience. He must proceed slowly at first, and he should be told that when once he has acquired the habit of writing carefully, what is irksome and slow at first, will become easy and fast in the end; and *the habit once acquired will not be easily lost*. This is true not only of the habit of writing carefully, but also of every other habit, good or bad; and the student should have it impressed upon him, that this law of habit is at once our encouragement in acquiring good habits, and our warning against falling into those that are bad.

Understanding English.

75. One can be said to understand English fully, only when he can express in his vernacular what is given in English, and can also express in English what is given in his vernacular. To acquire this twofold capacity, the student must learn English analytically as well as synthetically, that is, he must not only learn the meaning of a sentence in English as a whole, but must also know the meaning and effect of every word that enters into its composition. He must know how each word enters into the construction of the sentence, and what part it contributes to its meaning as a whole. It is only when he knows all this, and not merely the meaning of a sentence as a whole, that he will be able to explain the meaning

of a new sentence from his previous knowledge of it component words, aided by a dictionary for explaining new words, and to form a sentence expressing a new thought in his vernacular. The student must *acquire the necessary stock of words and phrases*, and he must *know the rules for combining them into sentences.*

To enable the learner to acquire his stock of words and phrases, two modes may be resorted to —one being to make him commit to memory select and well classified lists of vocables, and the other being to make him go through well graduated interesting reading lessons which may or may not be committed to memory by conscious effort, but which, if the passages are well written, will, without much effort, acquire a firm hold on the memory. The former method used to be resorted to about fifty years ago in this country; but it has now fallen into disuse, and the latter is the only method now in use. I would not discontinue the former mode altogether, but would make it a supplement to the latter. To make the latter effective, there should be reading lessons in both prose and poetry, and if need be, some preponderance should be given to poetry; for poetry is more easily remembered than prose. In saying this, I know I am going against the opinion of Dr. Bain[1], who says that in poetry the form and the touches of lofty diction transport us with the piece as a whole without our troubling ourselves

[1] See Education as a Science, 4th Edition, pp. 332—33.

with the meanings of the component words. With all respect for such a high authority, I must say, as I gather from my own experience, that the very form and diction in poetry impress on our mind the meanings of the component words, more than a prose piece can do; and I would venture to think that the poet when he says,

> "What can a boy learn sooner than a song?
> What better teach a foreigner a tongue?"

has come nearer the truth than the psychologist.

The pieces whether in prose or in poetry, that are prescribed for the purpose of enabling the student to learn English, must be carefully selected. They must be *sufficiently interesting and easily intelligible* to the reader, considering the stage of mental progress he has attained; and they must be well written and free from verbosity and ambiguity, and every word in each sentence must have a clear meaning and a distinct effect. Pieces abounding in peculiar idioms or obscure allusions should at first be avoided, not because idioms and allusions are not good things to learn, but because the time for learning them does not arrive until a working knowledge of the language has been acquired. And as regards allusions, I may be permitted to add that too much of them reminds one of the couplet

> "Pride often guides the author's pen.
> Books as often are affected as men."

The profuseness of allusions is an affectation in writing; they show the erudition of the author; and unless they are well-known, they serve not to illustrate but to obscure his meaning. The wide range of English literature affords ample field for selection: only we should keep in view our main object, which is to enable the reader *to acquire knowledge of the language.* The selections may be made to serve other objects as well, such as moral training or the acquisition of useful general knowledge; but these should form secondary purposes, the primary one being never lost sight of. To illustrate my meaning, I may add that though extracts from Smiles' writings are excellent in their own way for purposes of moral teaching, they are not equally well suited to help an Indian boy in learning English, their style being somewhat verbose. Pieces whether in prose or poetry that deal with scenes and incidents of life peculiarly English, should be excluded from an Indian boy's course of reading, the subject matter of which ought to be of general interest such as a foreigner can easily appreciate.

To learn the grammatical peculiarities of words, and the rules relating to the structure of sentences, the student should *read some simple and short book on grammar.* But it should be borne in mind that the reading of grammar is only a means to an end. It is necessary only so far as it helps the student in learning the language, but is superfluous at an early stage of his progress so far as mere grammatical technicalities and niceties are concerned.

Use of text books.

76. At this point an important question arises, namely, whether an Indian boy of twelve to fifteen years who reads English more for acquiring a working knowledge of that language than for studying the masterpieces of English literature, should, for the purpose of acquiring such knowledge, read a few select pieces in prose and poetry thoroughly and critically, or should go over a wider range of reading less thoroughly and less critically. Opinion is divided upon this question, those in favour of the former alternative holding, that it is the only practical method, while the advocates of the opposite view contend that the method of learning English from text-books encourages cramming. I am in favour of the former alternative, and my reasons are shortly these: In the *first* place, considering the stage of his progress, the student cannot be expected to be able to read with profit any book in English unless he reads it carefully and critically, and an extensive reading must therefore be out of the question. And in the *second* place, thorough and critical study of a limited number of well selected pieces, will enable the student to learn more about the meaning of words and the structure of sentences, than superficial reading extending over a wider range, to say nothing of the difference in the indirect effects, of a habit of thorough and careful study and one of superficial and desultory reading. The student who acquires knowledge of a language by *carefully studying every word and every sentence* in his text-book,

will be better able *to apply practically his knowledge*, though limited in quantity, than one who has a wider range of less critical knowledge. And as has been well said, "Half the knowledge with twice the power of applying it, is better than twice the knowledge with half the power of application." [1]

There are certain pieces in prose and poetry, such as De Foe's Robinson Crusoe, Johnson's Rasselas, Gray's Elegy written in a Country Churchyard and Ode to Adversity, Goldsmith's Traveller and Deserted Village, Pope's Universal Prayer and Ode on Solitude, and Longfellow's Psalm of Life, which every boy ought to read before his fifteenth year.

77. Not only should a proper course of reading be selected, but the right mode of teaching it must be followed.

How to teach English.

One important principle to bear in mind in this connection is, that while it is often necessary and always useful *to help* the learner, it is injurious in the end *to embarrass him with help*.

We help the learner in order *to lighten his labour* and *increase his pleasure* in acquiring knowledge; but excess of help will in the end fail to secure either of these purposes. If the knowledge of any particular thing is acquired with too much help, it may be acquired soon and with slight labour, but it will not be likely to be retained long unless there is renewed effort to retain it: and the pleasure of acquiring it,

Help needed to lighten the learner's labour and increase his pleasure in his work.

[1] Quoted by Sir J. Fitch in his Lectures on Teaching, p. 252.

which depends not merely upon the consciousness of having made the acquisition, but also upon the consciousness of having made a successful effort, will be less in so far as such effort has been wanting. Much as all men may wish, and much as some great educators like Pestalozzi and Froebel have striven, to find out a royal road to learning, the truth must be admitted that labour is inseparable from work, be it the acquiring of knowledge or the doing of anything else. Too much anxiety to shirk difficulty and to seek for easy methods has been justly deprecated.[1] But we should try to direct labour so as to secure large results with small labour, as far as possible. Nor need we consider labour as our primeval curse. Within proper limits, uninfluenced by coercion, and undertaken from interest in the work to be done, all labour is attended with pleasure. *The great art of the teacher is to eliminate coercion, and to create in his pupil an interest in learning, such as will make him work willingly.*

What I have said above, perhaps somewhat vaguely in abstract terms, I shall try to make more definite by referring to concrete cases. In teaching a lesson in English, the teacher should give the pupil on the day the lesson is set, the meanings of any unusual words and the explanation of any allusions occurring in it leaving it to the pupil to find out with the help of a dictionary

[1] See Lectures on teaching by Sir J. Fitch, p. 199. Bain on Education, p. 236.

the meanings of other words, and to enter them in a note book; and he should discourage the use of ready made meaning-books, and prohibit reference to explanatory keys. This mode would cost some time and labour which at first sight may seem to be spent unnecessarily, and to be capable of being saved by reference to meaning-books; but a little reflection will show that the advantages gained more than compensate the cost of time and labour entailed. For in finding out from the dictionary the meaning of a word, the student has to read carefully the sentence in which it occurs, and to exercise his mind in ascertaining, tentatively of course, to what part of speech the word belongs, if it can belong to more than one, and which of the different meanings given in the dictionary will suit the context; and the exercise thus gone through, affords no small training to the mental powers, while it is attended with pleasure each time the boy is able to hit a meaning which fits in with the context. And in looking into the dictionary, and writing the words with their meanings in the note book, the correct spelling of the words is deeply impressed on the memory, while handwriting is improved at the same time. These are advantages which will be wholly lost by the use of meaning-books and keys. After this preliminary preparation by the pupils, the teacher should, on the day for which the lesson is prescribed, make each boy read and explain a portion of it, helping him on as he

Use of the dictionary to be encouraged. Its advantages.

proceeds, and then explain the lesson as a whole to the class collectively.

To help the student in remembering the meanings of words, the teacher should tell him to enter in his note book their roots, and to observe how different words have a common element in their meaning by reason of their being derived from a common root, while they differ in their signification by reason of the root being joined to different prefixes and suffixes; and he may be asked to consult books like Oswald's Etymological Dictionary which gives in their alphabetical order words derived from the same root. Con*tract*, ex*tract*, re*tract*, and un*tract-able*; ac*cede*, pre*cede* and re*cede*; ap*pend*, de*pend*, *pend*ant; *pecu*liar, *pecu*niary, and im*pecu*nious may be cited to him as instances. It will also be helpful to the Hindu boy to know that, *daughter* and *duhitri* (दुहितृ), *pecuniary* and *pasu* (पशु), *equestrian* (*equus*) and *aswa* (अश्व), *two* and *dwi* (द्वि), *three* and *tri* (त्रि), *I* and *aham* (अहम्), *thou* and *twam* (त्वम्), not to mention *paternal* and *pitri*, *maternal* and *matri*, *fraternal* and *bhratri*, and a host of other words, are of common origin.

To make the meanings of words interesting to boys, the teacher should give them accounts of important words such as are to be found in "The Study of Words" by Trench. It would certainly be interesting to the student to know how *candid* and *candidate*, *desiderate* and *sidereal*, *cerumen* and *sincere*, *heathen* and *heath*, come to be connected in meaning.

Use of keys to be discouraged.

I have dwelt somewhat at length upon this topic, because I feel convinced that it is in our mode of teaching English, that one of the chief defects of the present system of education lies. The ill-directed zeal of teachers to make their pupils learn a great deal in a short time, and an excusable ease loving propensity of boys to save time and trouble, have led to the lazy habit of depending upon meaning-books and keys, and getting that ready made for them which ought to be made by the pupils themselves with occasional assistance from their teachers. Not that it lessens their labour in the long run; for it leads to the over-burdening of the memory in learning by rote the contents of the keys, to the neglect of legitimate exercise of the other faculties of the mind. The result is lamentable, and should be strenuously prevented if there is to be any improvement in education. But to ensure the wished-for change, *we must avoid prescribing unsuitable text-books and long lessons.* Unless we do this, resort to meaning-books and keys will continue as being inevitable. If from a vain desire to raise the standard of education, we set for our boys tasks which they cannot perform by themselves, we cannot complain that they seek to have their work done for them by others. We should never forget *that the object of education is not merely to store the mind with useful knowledge, but to train the faculties of the mind* so that a comparatively small equipment of knowledge may be turned to really good account; and that *the standard of education is raised more by increasing the learner's power of applying his knowledge, than by increasing merely the amount of knowledge acquired.* If a boy has not read much, the deficiency is more than compensated when he has learnt intelligently and thoroughly all that he has read; for the habit of thoroughness which he is thus helped to acquire, is of incomparably greater value than most other acquisitions.

Dictation, Translation, Composition.

78. As aids to learning English, the student should have exercise in Dictation, Translation, and Composition. What most boys are found wanting in, is, not so much a knowledge of the rules for writing English correctly, as the habit of doing so readily; and that can be acquired only by constant practice.

Exercises necessary; they should be frequent but easy.

The exercises should therefore be *frequent*, and for that very reason they should be *short*. For if long, they take much of the pupil's time, and have not much chance of being carefully looked over by the teacher. Another point to bear in mind in connection with exercises is, that they should be generally easy with a few hard ones at intervals. Some teachers are in favour of hard exercises, because they think that a student who is trained for hard work is necessarily trained for work that is easy. This principle, though true generally, should be followed with some qualification in practice. For in the *first* place, if the hard work be unusual work, training in it will not be good preparation for ordinary work; in the *second* place, it is a few alone who are capable of doing hard work, the great majority being fit only for ordinary work; and in the *third* place, hard exercise generally loses a good deal of the benefit of exercise, by reason of its requiring much help and affording small scope, even to the best, to work unaided.

In regard to exercises in Dictation, I have nothing particular to say.

With regard to Translation, I would suggest that the passages selected should be such as can be easily rendered from one language into another, and should not be like those of which we find specimens in certain examination papers, and which even the best experts can translate only awkwardly into Indian vernaculars.

The exercises in Composition should consist of (1) short letters on ordinary topics, (2) short essays, narrative and descriptive, but only rarely didactic, on different subjects, and (3) the giving of the substance of previously unseen passages read out to the student. The teacher may, and it is desirable that he should, observe some order in selecting these topics, subjects, and passages, not of course capable of being foreseen by the pupils; and he may *make the exercises in composition serve other useful purposes such as moral training.* He should be careful not to select any subject or passage which is beyond the capacity of his pupils to deal with; and he should impress on them the desirability of their dealing with each subject according to their own powers, of their saying nothing which they do not thoroughly understand, and of their writing methodically and in a simple style.

The exercises should be returned to the pupils after careful correction of the errors, with the teacher's remarks.

I would recommend students to read Abbott's "How to Write Clearly," the great merit of the book being that it is short and always to the point.

In the subject of Grammar, I would recommend Lennie's Grammar for the beginner, and Sir W. Smith's or Bain's Grammar for the advanced student. But I would strongly deprecate the use of books on Composition or on the Analysis of Sentences. A few general directions should suffice for the former, and the rules of grammar ought to be enough for the latter purpose. There has been a tendency to multiply books and spin out small matters, to the no small embarrassment of the learner.

In regard to Essay writing, it will be enough for the student to know that he should *think out* what to say on the subject, and *arrange his thoughts* in some order, the logical order being preferable in didactic and descriptive essays, and the chronological, in narrative essays ; he should now and then explain his meaning by *apt illustrations* ; and he should express his thoughts in *simple and clear language.* Any more elaborate directions would lead to the repression of spontaneous exertion, and the encouragement of cramming. The above remark does not apply to works on Composition and Rhetoric which deal with the principal qualities of style, and lay down rules for attaining them. Such books may be read by the advanced student: Abott's little book just referred to comes under this description.

79. What has been said above will be applicable, more or less, to the teaching of Sanskrit; and the following are the only special remarks I have to make on this subject.

Sanskrit.

In the *first* place, Sanskrit ought to be written in Devanagari characters; and boys should be enjoined to adhere to this course, if for no other reason, for the simple purpose of having Sanskrit written in a way which is understood all over India, and indeed all over the learned world.

To be written in Devanagari characters.

In the *second* place, Sanskrit ought to be read as Sanskrit, the letters being pronounced in the manner required by the rules of Sanskrit grammar. I know there is a strong feeling entertained by some eminent Sanskrit scholars of Bengal in favour of the Bengali mode of reading Sanskrit. That mode is highly melodious and musical, and the feeling in favour of it is no doubt natural; but the mode is none the less an erroneous one, and the feeling, a mistaken patriotism. This mode of pronunciation ignores the distinction in sound between words such as *satya* (सत्य) and *satwa* (सत्व), *sakrit* (सकृत्) and *s'akrit* (शकृत्), *swagana* (स्वगण) and *s'wagana* (श्वगण); and it is not understood in any part of India except Bengal; and the feeling, if given effect to, would make

To be read in the Sanskrit and not in the Bengali mode.

the Sanskrit scholars of Bengal, an exclusive body, and stand in the way of their holding converse with the general body of Sanskrit scholars, Indian and European.

Use of keys to be discouraged.

In the *third* place, the use of keys should be discountenanced. There are running commentaries on many of the standard Sanskrit works, such as those of Mallinatha on the poems of Kalidas, which, though not all that might be wished-for, are nevertheless useful for the student. But the keys to Sanskrit courses of reading that are now generally prepared, are of a very different type. They say all that could be said, and much that should have been left unsaid for the exercise of the learner, relating to every word in a *sloka* or couplet; and not content with that, they give full translation in English of every *sloka*; and the misdirected student from his anxiety to pass his examination, goes through the drudgery of learning them by rote, when he might have spent his time more profitably and saved a good deal of it too, by committing to memory the text and a few rules of grammar. This lamentable waste of time and energy should be discouraged by every one interested in the welfare of students.

Sanskrit Grammar.

80. The last remark I have to make in connection with Sanskrit, is, that Sankrit Grammar should be taught first from an elementary text-book written either in the boy's vernacular or in English, his knowledge of Sanskrit at the stage of his progress at which he must begin his grammar, not

being sufficient to enable him to read a grammar written in that language. A few of the *sutras* or rules expressed in simple Sanskrit may however be included in the text-book. Declension and conjugation should be taught by paradigms, and should not be left to be deduced from general rules.

The alphabet of the Sanskrit and Sanskritic languages—Its beautiful and methodical arrangement.

The student may, at this stage, be asked to turn back to his alphabet for a moment, and the beauty and method in the arrangement of the letters may be pointed out to him in the manner indicated in my little book on the Devanagari Alphabet. The teacher should, by pronouncing the letters himself, and making his pupil pronounce them, shew him that the first twenty-five *consonants* are arranged in five groups of five letters, the letters of the successive groups being pronounced with the help, respectively, of the throat, the palate, the front palate, the teeth, and the lips, that is, the different parts of the roof of the mouth commencing from within and proceeding outwards; and the five letters of each group being respectively the sharp, its aspirate, the flat, its aspirate, and the nasal articulate sound pronounced with the aid of the part of the roof of the mouth corresponding to the group. He should then shew that the next four letters are *semi-vowels* pronounced respectively with the aid of the palate, the front palate, the teeth, and the lips; and that the next four letters are *sibilants* or breath letters, which, with a slight change of order [ह (*h*) coming first] are pronounced with the help of the throat, the palate, the front palate, and the teeth. And lastly, the boy should be shown that the first ten *vowels* taken in groups of two (one short and the other long), with some change of order, are the vowels pronounced with the aid, respectively, of the throat, the palate, the front palate, the teeth and the lips.

For convenience of reference I subjoin in a tabular form the substance of the above remarks.

			Gutturals.	Palatals.	Cerebrals or Front Palatals.	Dentals.	Labials.
Vowels.	Simple		अ आ	इ ई	ऋ ॠ	ऌ ॡ	उ ऊ
Vowels.	Complex			ए ऐ			ओ औ
Consonants.	Consonants Proper or formed by contact of parts of the mouth.	Sharp	क ख	च छ	ट ठ	त थ	प फ
Consonants.	Consonants Proper or formed by contact of parts of the mouth.	Flat	ग घ	ज झ	ड ढ	द ध	ब भ
Consonants.	Consonants Proper or formed by contact of parts of the mouth.	Nasal	ङ	ञ	ण	न	म
Consonants.	Semi-vowels			य	र	ल	व
Consonants.	Breath Letters		ह	श	ष	स	

The rules of phonetic combination or *sandhi* (सन्धिः) should be sought to be rationally explained so far as possible, the learner being made to understand that they are no arbitrary rules, and that phonetic combinations have resulted from conscious or unconscious effort *to avoid hiatus and obtain facility in pronunciation.* In the case of vowel combinations, this may be easily shown by stating the general rules in the following form :—

I. Similar vowels combine into their corresponding long vowels.

II. Dissimilar vowels combine in such a manner that,

(*a*) अ (a) or आ (á) + इ (i) or ई (í) = dipthong ए (ai).
„ „ + उ (u) or ऊ (ú) = „ ओ (au).
„ „ + ऋ (r) or ॠ (r) = अर् (ar).
„ „ + ऌ (l) or ॡ (l) = अल् (al).
„ „ + ए (ai) or ऐ (ái) = ऐ (ái).
„ „ + ओ (au) or औ (áu) = औ (áu).

(*b*) इ (i) or ई (í), ऋ (r) or ॠ (r), ऌ (l) or ॡ (l), उ (u) or ऊ (ú),

following any dissimilar vowel, change into their corresponding semi-vowels

य् (y), र् (r), ल् (l), व् (w),

to which the vowel following is added.

(*c*) ए (ai), ऐ (ái), ओ (au), औ (áu)

followed by any vowel, resolve into their component simple vowels of which the second changes into its corresponding semi-vowel य (y) or व (w) to which the vowel following is added.

These rules clearly shew that the object of the combination is to prevent hiatus and facilitate utter ance.

The rules of consonantal combination are somewhat more complex, and their detailed explanation may be deferred, the teacher taking care, however, to refer to the simpler instances to illustrate the principle stated above.

Another point which sometimes puzzles the beginner, should be explained to him, namely, that in Sanskrit, as in certain other languages, words have gender, which is sometimes different from that of the objects signified by them; thus देवता (god) is feminine, कलत्र (wife) is neuter.

Vernacular languages.

81. In regard to the teaching of Indian vernaculars derived from or closely allied to Sanskrit, two important questions arise for consideration :—

(1) How far should the rules of Sanskrit grammar be followed?

(2) How far should Sanskrit words be preferred to their vernacular equivalents of non-Sanskrit origin?

These are questions that relate more to Language and Literature than to Education; and where the usage of language and literature has answered them in a certain way, the teacher has primarily to follow that usage. But where, as in the case of Indian vernaculars like Bengali, they have not been settled yet, the teacher must settle them for the purposes of his teaching. I shall not, therefore, be going outside the scope of my subject in offering a few remarks on them.

How far to follow rules of Sanskrit grammar.

A *vernacular language should primarily follow its own grammar*, and so far as declension and conjugation are concerned, the vernaculars have their own forms, and the rules of Sanskrit grammar do not and cannot interfere with them. So again, so far as the rules of *sandhi* or phonetic combination are concerned, there is equally little difficulty, though for an opposite reason, the rules applicable being exclusively those of Sanskrit grammar, and the reason being the absence of any rules in the vernacular. But the question arises, whether an adjective should take the gender of the noun it qualifies, as is the case in Sanskrit, or whether it should remain unaltered in form whatever the gender of the noun it qualifies may be, as is the case with words of vernacular origin. Usage is not consistent on this point, and opinions of the learned range between two opposite extremes.

I venture to think that the right course to adopt would be *to follow the Sanskrit rule only when both the noun and the qualifying adjective are Sanskrit words which have undergone no corruption.*

In regard to the formation of compounds and derivatives, the rules of Sanskrit grammar, which alone authorize the coining of such words, *should be followed,* except in cases where usage has clearly sanctioned an irregular form. The irregularly formed word সৃজন (*srijana*) is an instance in point, and it would be considered pedantic to use the regular form সর্জন (*sarjana*) instead.

How far we should use Sanskrit words.

Upon the second question stated above, there has been great diversity of practice and opinion. Some are in favour of using vernacular words whenever available, and would resort to Sanskrit words only if necessary, somewhat after the manner of those English writers who prefer words of Saxon origin to those derived from Greek or Latin; while others maintain that the relation of a Sanskritic vernacular to Sanskrit is very different from that of English to Greek or Latin, and that it would be provincialism, if not vulgarism, to use too many vernacular words in serious composition. Here, as in most other similar cases, the right course lies between the two opposite extremes.

The relation of an Indian vernacular like Bengali to Sanskrit, as regards both vocabulary and grammatical peculiarities, is of a very intimate character, and *it will serve no useful purpose to make a sustained effort to avoid using Sanskrit words*; and, on the other hand, *it would be equally unnecessary and unprofitable to aim at avoiding the use of vernacular words where approved usage has raised their status*. So long as simplicity and clearness together with force and elegance are secured, it does not matter whether the words used are of Sanskrit or vernacular origin. The subject-matter of the composition should determine its style and form.

> "For different styles with different subjects sort;
> As several garbs with country, town and court."

Translation of English into vernacular.

82. The translation of English into a vernacular like Bengali, is a work of some difficulty, by reason of the differences in idiom and in the grammatical structure of sentences in the two languages being so great.

Thus, words and phrases in each of these two languages have acquired *idiomatic meanings* in certain contexts which their dictionary equivalents do not convey, and in such cases, the latter cannot be correct substitutes for the former. Many instances of errors arising from this source have been pointed out in Rowe and Webb's Hints on the Study of English under the head of Common Errors (Chapter VIII).

Again, while in English a *preposition* comes *before* the word it governs, in Bengal it comes *after*. In English, adverbs follow verbs as a rule, in Bengali the reverse is the case. So also, *the order of words connected by "of"* in English has to be *reversed* in Bengali. Nor is there this reversal of the order of words alone (which may not cause much difficulty): but in complex sentences, the order of entire subordinate sentences has to be changed.

These differences should be carefully pointed out to the student, and he should be told to keep them in view so as to be able to avoid errors which by overlooking them he may fall into.

A translation should be literal, as far as it is possible to make it so, consistently with preserving the sense of the original; and the main rule to follow will be, first to *ascertain the meaning* of the original *as a whole*, then to find out *appropriate equivalents* of the *words and phrases* composing it, and finally *to string those equivalents together* in their *correct order* according to the grammatical rules of the language into which the translation is made.

History.

83. History being a literary subject, and in fact the only subject allied to language and literature, which a boy of twelve to fifteen years should read in addition to English, a classical language, and his vernacular, I shall offer a few remarks next on the teaching of History.

I have already said that in his eleventh year an Indian boy should be taught a few simple facts of the history of India from a suitable text-book in his vernacular. In his twelfth year he should read some simple and short history of Greece and of Rome written in English. Every student of English, and indeed every one desirous of having a liberal education, should know something of the history of the two great nations that have so largely influenced the literature and civilization of the West. I would recommend as a text-book that portion of Peter Parley's Universal History, which treats of Greece and Rome, on account of its simplicity and shortness, and also because it presents history as a continuous narrative of prominent events, instead of being, as many brief histories are, a mere table of crowded and disconnected facts.

Of Greece and of Rome.

It will be too early for a boy of twelve years to read history as it should be read, that is, in the words of Sir J. Herschell in his Preliminary Discourse on Natural Philosophy, "not as a record of tyrannies and slaughters, but as an archive of experiments successful and unsuccessful, tending to the solution of the problem, how the advantages of Government can be secured with the least disadvantage to the governed."

For him History is, as has been aptly said, only an outline *time* chart of the world's past, as Geography is a *space* chart of its surface. But though that is so, the teacher should still try, and he will do so not in vain, to awaken in the minds of his pupils the idea of a *political society*, that is, a society held together by common interest, restrained from causing internal disturbance by a governing power, and protected against external aggression by its combined strength guided by the same power. He should then point out that it is these societies, which, by the more powerful ones *absorbing* the less powerful, compose *nations*; and these last again, by further union, the result of conquest or concession, compose *empires*; and History is an account of the processes of these formations. Lastly, he should impress on them the idea that through paths sometimes straight and sometimes crooked, and with motions often backward, but generally forward, the human race, under the unseen guidance of a Higher Power, has been progressing on in the direction of what is good for all. And *the particular facts of the history of every nation should be dwelt upon as illustrating this general truth.*

Of England and of India.

In his thirteenth, fourteenth and fifteenth years, an Indian boy should read the histories of England and India in English, those being the two countries with which he is most intimately connected. But the teacher should bear in mind that what is wanted is a *general* and not a *minute* knowledge. *The learner's memory should not be encumbered with unnecessary names, dates or other facts.* There are many of these which may well be passed over, without affecting the continuity of the narrative, or impairing the student's appreciation of the sequence of events.

Geography.

84. Geography being connected with History, I shall speak of it next. From his twelfth to his fifteenth year, a boy should read Geography more systematically and more fully than he did when he first read it. He should begin with the shape, size, and motions of the earth, the way in which these have been ascertained being explained to him so far as he is able to follow the explanation. The points and lines of reference, namely, the Poles, the Equator, the Tropics, the Polar Circles, and Parallels of Latitude and Meridians, should be next explained and shown as marked on a Terrestrial Globe and in charts. The teacher should then explain to his pupils that the position of a point on the earth's surface is determined by its Latitude and Longitude, and he should teach them the mode of Drawing Maps by reference to the lines of latitude and longitude. The different zones of the earth, its divisions of land and water, the different races of men that inhabit its surface, the countries they are natives of, and their different degrees of civilization, should be next pointed out. And, lastly, the student should learn something of the natural and political divisions of the earth's

Drawing Maps correct to Scale and Compass.

surface, the Geography of India and of England being learnt in greater detail than that of any other country. The student should know also something about the flora and fauna, and arts and manufactures, of different countries.

Important Geographical proper names should, as far as possible, be explained. They are often significant, and when explained become interesting and easy to remember. If they are left unexplained, ingenious students sometimes fall into curious mistakes about their meaning. I was once asked to visit a school. During my visit, one of the classes was going on with its Geography lesson. I asked a boy to name the highest mountain in the world; his answer was, Mount Everest; and on my asking him why it was so named, he said, "Because it was *ever* covered with snow, and Everest was the superlative of ever."

Physical Geography and Physics.

85. I do not think it would be right to insist upon a systematic study of Physical Geography at this stage of the student's progress. That subject cannot be properly understood without a previous knowledge of several other subjects, such as Physics, Chemistry, Dynamics, &c., which it would be too much to expect from a boy of fifteen. Nor would I, with all my desire early to initiate the learner in the direct study of the great book of Nature, insist upon the systematic study of Physics before the student enters college. Studying Physics merely from books without the aid of experiments, is perhaps

worse than not reading it at all; and in the schools in their present condition, it is not possible to have the necessary arrangements for teaching science with the aid of experiments. We should, for a time, be satisfied with a less systematic study of Nature by means of Object Lessons.

An enthusiast in science might say, "A school which cannot afford to teach science experimentally should be abolished." An assertion like this assumes that the teaching of science is absolutely necessary at the stage of a student's progress, which we are now considering, and that it is better to have no education than to have education without science. But these assumptions are not correct. While it must be freely admitted, that the power of observing facts accurately and of drawing correct inferences from observed facts, and the habit of submitting our inferences to the test of experiment, should be cultivated early, it will be going too far to say that the cultivation of these powers and of this habit, is the whole or even the principal, part of education. On the contrary, as Sir J. Fitch,[1] speaking of the faculty of observation, remarks, "In the long run it is a less valuable factor in the intellectual life than the habit of reflection;" and this habit of reflection, the study of the other subjects mentioned above will evidently help to cultivate. Nor can observation and induction be absolutely ignored in any education, merely because the formal teaching of Physical Science is no part of it.

1 Lectures on Teaching, p. 200.

There are lessons in other subjects of study, such as the lesson in Geography on the shape, size and motions of the earth, the lesson in Sanskrit Grammar on the classification of letters according to the principal organs of speech by the help of which they are pronounced, and the lesson in Arithmetic on the origin of the Common System of Notation, which exemplify more or less the processes of observation and induction, to say nothing of other lessons which a good teacher may dwell upon as illustrations of one or other of those processes.

Mathematics.

86. It remains now to say a few words about the teaching of Mathematics, that is, Arithmetic, Geometry, and Algebra, these being the only three branches of it that a boy should learn before his sixteenth year.

Arithmetic. Reason for every Rule to be explained.

In regard to Arithmetic, as I have already remarked (see paras. 61 and 62), a boy should learn not only the *rules* of the subject but also the *reasons* upon which they are based, and he should once more go rapidly over the ground already traversed, to see if any point remains to be cleared up. In explaining the principles of the subject, the teacher should make use of illustrations and *graphic methods* to help the pupil in understanding them. Thus, in explaining the reason of the rule for finding the Greatest Common Measure of two numbers, he should take two straight lines to represent them (which they will do if they are supposed to contain as many units of length as the numbers contain abstract units); then *measure* the longer line by the shorter (which is the same thing as dividing the larger number by the smaller); and if the shorter line measures the longer exactly, that is, if the division leaves no remainder, the smaller number, which also measures itself, will evidently be the greatest common measure of the two. If the measuring leaves a remainder, then he should measure the shorter line by this remainder, and if there is no remainder in this case, the first remainder which measures the shorter line and also itself, and therefore also the longer line, is the measure required. But if there is a remainder at the second measuring, he should measure the first remainder by the second, and if there is no remainder left, the second remainder will be the common measure required.

The following diagram will make this clear, the numbers taken being 14 and 8: —

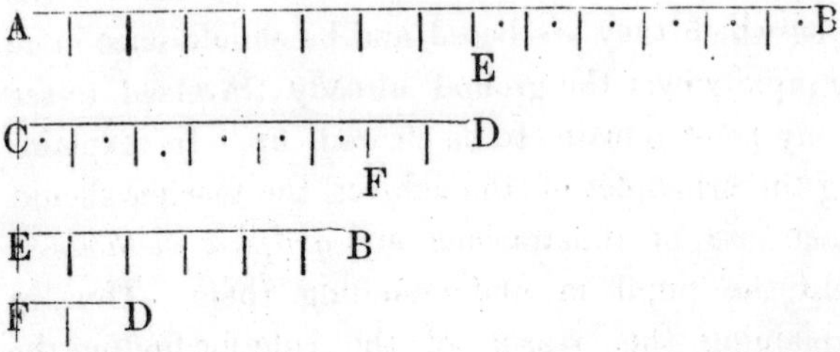

In treating of Fractions, the teacher should point out that Decimals, while in their *nature* they are fractions, being parts of unity, are in their mode of *representation*, an *extension* of the *common system of notation*, removal by *one* step to the *right*

involving a *reduction* in value to *one-tenth*, or conversely, removal by *one* step to the *left* involving an *increase* in value *tenfold.*

In dealing with Concrete Numbers, the teacher should carefully point out that though the relations between successive denominations in some of the Tables is *conventional*, in others they are *necessary.* Thus though the relation between an inch and a foot might or might not have been what it is, when once it is settled that 12 inches = 1 foot, it is *necessarily* settled that 144 square inches=1 square foot. This should be carefully shown, and in this connection, the teacher should also explain to his pupils what is meant by multiplying one length by another. A good deal of misconception often exists on this point. It is sometimes thought that to the rule that the multiplier must always be an abstract number, the case of a length is an exception. The truth is, that there is no such exception; that in performing a multiplication the multiplier must always be regarded as an abstract number, and then the product has to be *interpreted* according to the nature of the case: and that when the *two numbers* that are multiplied by one another, are those representing respectively the number of *linear* units in the *length* and in the *breadth* of a rectangle, it so happens from the nature of things, that the *product* represents exactly the number of *square* units or squares upon each linear unit, that the *area* of the rectangle contains.

Bengali Notation of concrete numbers of different denominations.

There is another matter connected with tables of concrete numbers, which may require to be explained. The notation of concrete numbers in Bengali is somewhat peculiar, and may not be known to a boy who has not attended an indigenous school or *pathshala*, or has not read the long tables given in books called Dharapat (ধারাপাত). To enable him to read Bengali accounts and documents involving concrete numbers, he should be told that the method followed is, to represent the *highest* denomination of any concrete number by the *ordinary figures*, the *quarters* of that denomination by the *vertical strokes*, ।, ।।, and ।।।, (written as ৸), and the quarters of the quarters or *sixteenths* by the *slanting strokes*, /০ //০ (written as ৵০) and ///০ (written as ৶০), and sometimes the *excess* of a number of subordinate denomination over a quarter by *ordinary figures* whose *position* determines the *denomination*. Thus, rupees being represented by the ordinary figures, Rs. 15 will be written as ১৫৲ (the sign indicating that the number represents rupees), and 15 Rs. 14 as. will be written as ১৫৸৵০. Again 12 maunds will be written as ১২মন, and 12 maunds 16 seers as ১২।৬.

The Rule of Three should be taught rationally, as being an application of the rule that where four quantities are proportionals, the product of the extremes is equal to the product of the means ; and the pupil should be asked to ascertain from the nature of the question, whether there is *any propor-*

tion subsisting among the numbers given and that required to be found, or among any combinations of these. If there is any proportion subsisting, it should be properly stated, that is, in its correct order, regard being had to the fact of the numbers involved being directly or inversely proportional, and the number required being represented by the usual symbol x; and then the rule above stated being applied, x will be easily found.

This avoids the unnecessary distinction between Single Rule of Three and Double Rule of Three, and the mechanical methods adopted for working out examples of the latter class. Boys sometimes fall into strange mistakes in applying the Rule of Three, where there is no proportion subsisting among the given and required numbers. I shall here give one instance. Many years ago when I was practising as a pleader at Berhampore, on one occasion I appeared before the Collector, in support of an application on behalf of the grand-mother of a ward under the Court of Wards for raising the amount granted by the manager of the ward's estate as the expense of her pilgrimage to Benares. The manager having stated in his report that he had allowed an amount equal to what the father of the ward had spent at Benares, I pointed out that the two cases were not analogous, and that the father of the ward went to Benares on a pleasure trip when he was a youth of 25 years, whereas the lady who was past fifty was going to the holy city on a pilgrimage, and had to perform many religious ceremonies there which her son did not care to observe. The learned Collector, who was an able officer and a man of strong common sense, appreciating the argument and being desirous of cutting short further discussion, remarked in a half serious way that he was willing to double the amount having regard to the fact that the lady was twice as old as her son was when he visited Benares. Though the process was arbitrary, the amount arrived at was considered reasonable, and there the case ended. Shortly after this, I was asked by the head of the Local College with which I was connected as Law Lecturer, to examine the Entrance class of the Collegiate School in Mathematics; and led by curiosity to see how far the view of proportion given effect to by the Collector was shared by the boys of his District, I asked the following among other questions :—

A gentleman goes to Benares at the age of 25 years and spends there Rs. 500. Can you say how much he will spend if he visits the holy city again at the age of 50 years?

And strangely enough, not a few of the boys applied the Rule of Three, and answered that the amount would be Rs. 1,000.

I have endeavoured to treat the subject rationally in my Elements of Arithmetic to which I may refer the reader for detailed explanation.

In treating of Present Worth, Discount, and Stocks, the teacher should explain the nature of the problems requiring solution, as the real difficulty in these subjects lies, not in applying Arithmetical rules, but in understanding the meaning of the question. The beginner not unnaturally finds it difficult to follow the abbreviated language of the questions in stocks, and the fact of stock of the nominal value of Rs. 100 or £100 being worth only Rs. 86 or £86 appears to him to be strange. The economic principles concerning the subject should be shortly explained, and the learner made clearly to understand that Government securities not being like currency notes, but being securities for money lent on interest, their real value must depend upon competition with other investments. I would here add that the multiplication of Miscellaneous Examples and Problems to be worked out arithmetically, is wholly unnecessary for students who intend to read Algebra. To them these problems, which can be sloved arithmetically only clumsily and with difficulty, abbreviated expressions such as " the number required " being used for the usual symbol x, would be much more easily and neatly solvable as problems on algebraical equations; and it would be waste of time to exercise them in working out such problems arithmetically. It would be a far more profitable employment of time, *to make a boy thoroughly familiarize himself with fundamental arithmetical ideas while reading his Arithmetic, instead of anticipating work which ought to be done algebraically.*

I have sometimes found students of the fourth year College class hesitating and making effort to realize the truth of the simple statement that the value of a fraction is raised or lowered according as its denominator is diminished or increased, which would never be the case if a boy learns Arithmetic properly, instead of wasting his time in the misdirected work of solving difficult problems.

There is one other important arthmetical notion, the necessity of a clear realization of which I may here refer to. It is connected with the subject of division. The word *divide* is used in two different but connected senses in the two questions—

(1) If you divide Rs. 20 among 5 men, how many rupees will each get? and

(2) If you divide Rs. 20 into groups of Rs. 5 each, how many groups will there be?

The answer to both questions is the same number 4, and it is obtained by going through the same process of dividing 20 by 5; but both the operation and its result have different meanings in the two cases. In the former, the operation is the determination of the magnitude of each part of the dividend when it is divided into as many parts as the divisor indicates, and the result is Rs. 4; in the latter, the operation is the determination of the number of times that the divisor is contained in the dividend, and the result is the abstract number 4. The distinction is simple, and when once stated, it is easily understood and never forgotten; but it is worthy of notice, and if not noticed early, the omission may affect the student's power of readily interpreting the results of complex processes in the solution of problems.

I have remarked upon only a few of the important points connected with the teaching of Arithmetic. To speak of them all would require the writing of a short treatise on Arithmetic; and I must refer the teacher for further directions to works on Arithmetic dealing at length with the principles of the subject, one of which I have already referred to, namely, the book written by myself.

87. Geometry should be commenced by a boy in his twelfth year. The subject is not really difficult, if it is properly taught. Boys should not be alarmed as they sometimes are, by having vague apprehensions raised about the difficulty of this branch of Mathematics. On the contrary, they should be encouraged, and should have their interest excited by being told that they are beginning the study of a subject which will enable them to solve many practical problems, and to explain many apparently strange things. As instances, they may have the following questions put to them:— Geometry.

(1) Find the length of a ladder that will just reach the top of a wall of known height from a point at a given distance from its base.

(2) If a man wants to go from a place A to a place B on the same side of a river RR^1, after taking his bath in the river, what is his shortest route?

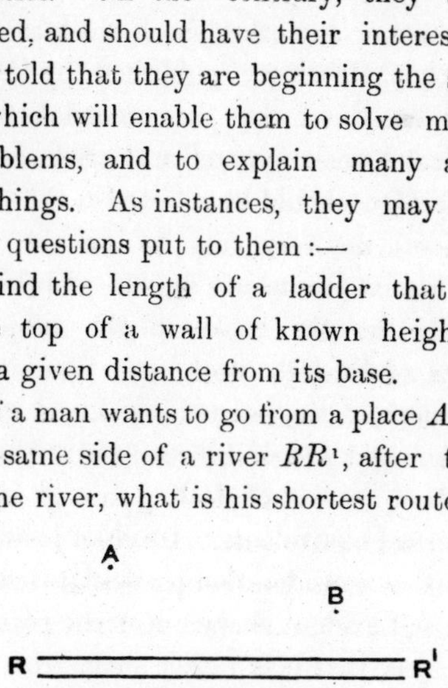

(3) If you stand on one side of a road and look at

the gas lamp posts or other posts placed at equal distances on the other side, why is it that the distances between the posts, which are really equal, appear shorter and shorter the further they are from you?

And they may be assured that after they have read Geometry for about six months, they will be in a position to answer these and many other similar questions. They should also have a short account of the origin of the science, to impress on them the fact that from the beginning of its study, it has been helpful to us in our practical concerns.

Whether Euclid's Elements should be the text-book.

The point that arises for determination at the very outset is whether in teaching Geometry, Euclid's Elements or any other book such as Hall and Steven's School Geometry published by Macmillan & Co., and based on the recommendations of the Mathematical Association and on the Schedule adopted at Cambridge, should be selected as the text-book. The question is not very easy to answer. Euclid's Geometry has its merits and defects, and the same is the case with the other books on the subject. The chief merits of Euclid's work are, that it is well known throughout the learned world, and its demonstrations are rigid and deal directly with the magnitudes involved, instead of dealing in any case with their numerical equivalents. Its chief general defect (leaving out of consideration particular defects such as the non-self-evident character of the truth of the 12th axiom,) is, that it is rather long, and some of the demonstrations are tedious. Several of the proposed substitutes for Euclid's Elements have the merit of being simple and short, but they all labour under the disadvantage of not being so well known and well recognized as Euclid's work, and some of them, in their endeavour to be concise, have failed to be as direct and rigid in their methods of demonstration as Euclid is. A learned countryman of mine, the late Babu Ram Kamal Bhattacharya, wrote a book on Geometry in which, in forty-three propositions, he gives all the important theorems in the first six books of Euclid's Elements. His view is that Mathematics is only the handmaid of Physics, and its study should be made as easy as possible, so that it may not prove a deterrent to the study of Physics; and in his letter to Mr. Woodrow, Inspector of Schools, appended to his book, he somewhat pathetically exclaims, "How many noble spirits, otherwise blessed with extraordinary gifts, have been forced to bid a distant and melancholy farewell to the ever alluring bower of the mistress on account of the stern and heartless frownings of the maid." His book may teach shortly the important truths of Geometry, but his demonstrations are not always rigid and purely geometrical, and they have not that disciplinary value that Euclid has. Geometry is read not merely for the important truths it teaches, but also for the mental training it gives.

The modern method of teaching Elementary Geometry, though different from the method of Euclid, keeps this object fully in view.

The points of difference between the modern method and the method of Euclid may be shortly stated thus :—

i. Euclid, from a strict regard for regularity, does not allow any construction, though required only for demonstrating a proposition, to be assumed as effected, without shewing previously how it is to be made ; whereas, according to the modern method, for convenience of treatment, simple constructions, such as the bisection of a straight line or an angle. or the drawing of a straight line parallel or perpendicular to another, are assumed to be effected, when necessary merely for the purpose of proving a theorem.

ii. Euclid, with a view to dispense as far as possible with the aid of instruments in effecting his constructions, grants only three things to be done, namely, the drawing of a straight line from one point to another, the production of a given straight line indefinitely, and the describing of a circle from any centre at any distance from that centre ; that is, he allows the use of only two instruments an ungraduated straight ruler for drawing straight lines, but not for taking any measurements, and a pair of compasses for describing a circle, but not for transferring, or for taking the measure of, any length from one position to another in any other way ; whereas, in the modern method, these things are allowed to be effected with the aid of instruments.

iii. Euclid deals with magnitudes directly, without resorting to their numerical equivalents in terms of any units of measurement, and is thus able to treat commensurable and incommensurable magnitudes alike, but at the same time, he is obliged to have recourse to a cumbrous and by no means obvious criterion of proportionality; whereas in the modern method, magnitudes, especially when considered with reference to proportionality, are taken to be represented by their numerical equivalents, the difficulty in the case of incommensurables being got rid of by the fact that they may be expressed numerically to any required degree of accuracy by adopting adequately small units.

iv. Euclid is content with merely demonstrating his propositions, without helping the learner much to see why a particular construction is made, or a particular series of steps in a demonstration is taken; and his propositions stand detached, without there being any attempt at generalisation of allied truths; while Modern Geometry seeks to indicate to the learner, and to help him in finding out for himself, the reasons for the processes of construction and demonstration adopted, and to present generalised statements and proofs of connected propositions.

v. Besides the above mentioned general points of difference, there are some particular points, such as those connected with the definitions of an angle, a diameter of a circle, and a tangent to a circle. Euclid's definition of an angle will exclude from consideration a re-entrant angle, and his definitions of a diameter and a tangent, though simple and sufficient for the circle, are inapplicable to many curves; whereas Modern Geometry, in order to make the definitions of those terms more comprehensive, introduces the idea of rotation of a line about a point into the definition of an angle, and regards the diameter as the locus of the middle points of a system of parallel chords, and the tangent as the limiting position of a secant.

It will thus be seen that Euclid's method, if it has the advantage of being more direct and more rigorous in form than the modern method, labours under the countervailing disadvantage of being less comprehensive and more cumbrous; while the modern method, if it is less direct and less rigorous in form, has the compensating advantage of being more general and less burdensome, and better adapt ed to help progress in mathematical study.

It should be noticed that Euclid has the advantage of being well known and well suited for easy reference.

The advantages of Euclid's method at one time seemed to me to outweigh its disadvantages, and induced me to think that his Elements of Geometry with suitable modifications, should be adopted as the text book in Geometry for the beginner. But it has since appeared to me to be necessary to lighten the labour of the student in acquiring a knowledge of Elementary Geometry, so that he may be able to spare time and energy for studying other subjects: and I am now of opinion that Euclid may well be replaced by Modern Geometry.

But if Euclid is to be superseded, our chief aim should be to help the beginner in the subject in learning, with ease and within a short time, all the important elementary truths of Geometry. In a little book written by me, I have accordingly omitted all unimportant propositions, and tried to give the substance of the first six books of Euclid in 50 Theorems and 25[†] Problems.

Even if Euclid's Elements be adopted as the text-book, I would not adhere to the text of Euclid as scrupulously as some mathematicians wish. I would accept Playfair's substitute for the twelfth axiom as being much more self-evident; I would substitute simpler modes of demonstration for some of the propositions, such as the mode of demonstration with the help of the 5th that has been given of the 8th proposition of the First Book, by placing one of the triangles on the opposite side of the base of the other; I would pass over the 7th and other subsidiary propositions, retaining them in the book but marking them as unnecessary; and I would add as an alternative proof of the 32nd proposition, the one given by Playfair, which is independent of the properties of parallels. Nor would I object to similar modifications being introduced in other places.

In teaching Geometry, care should be taken not to puzzle the pupil by creating needless difficulties. Thus, in explaining the definition of a point and a line, it will only confound the beginner to tell him that they are mere mathematical abstractions, words which are themselves mere logical abstractions conveying no more clear meaning to him than the definitions sought to be explained. It is quite true that it is not possible practically to represent on paper a point or a line as defined, as the one will always have some magnitude, and the other some breadth, however small; but the simple and sufficient explanation to give will be, to tell the student that the magnitude in the one case and the breadth in the other, are disregarded, because otherwise difficulties will arise. Thus, when we say that a straight line is bisected at a certain point, if the point has any magnitude, we shall have to add, to which half of the line that magnitude appertains; and so when we say that a figure is bisected by a line, if the line has any breadth, we shall have to add, to which half of the figure the breadth of the line appertains. I shall now make a few remarks on the definitions, postulates, axioms, and propositions of Elementary Geometry. I shall refer to Euclid's Elements as well known to all; but the remarks will apply to the corresponding matter in any book on Elementary Geometry according to modern method.

Euclid's definition of an angle, which is not very happy, requires explanation. An angle is neither a point, nor a line, nor an area, but is a magnitude of a peculiar kind, whose nature can be understood only by introducing the idea of revolution of one of the containing lines after coincidence with the other. This the student should be made to understand.

The other definitions I need not go through in detail, but I leave it to the teacher to ascertain after questioning his pupils, what their difficulties are, and to try to remove them as well as he can.

The postulates should be explained as showing that the only instruments of construction allowed by Euclid, are the ruler and compasses, to be used, the one for drawing a straight line, and the other for describing a circle, but neither of them for taking any measurement.

The axioms, though self-evident, require a few words of explanation which the teacher should offer. They are the only truths assumed by Euclid to prove his propositions. They are divisible into two classes: the *general* axioms which are true for *all measurable quantities,* and they are the first seven and the ninth axioms of Euclid, and the *geometrical* axioms which relate to *geometrical magnitudes,* and they are the eighth and the last three axioms. When the pupil commences to read the propositions, the teacher should explain that they are divisible into two classes, Problems and Theorems, the former requiring some *construction to be effected,* the latter, some *truth to be demonstrated*; he should also point out the different parts of which each is composed; and he should then briefly indicate the nature of deductive reasoning.

The teacher should also explain the symbolical method of writing out propositions, which will shorten very much the labour of writing; and he should insist upon the different steps in the particular enunciation, the construction, and the demonstration, being written in separate lines.

In Proposition I of Book I, the teacher should point out that the same construction gives two solutions, a second equilateral triangle being obtained by joining the lower point of intersection of the circles with the extremities of the given straight line.

In Proposition II, the pupil should be asked to note that there are three different cases according as the given point is—

(1) at either extremity of the given straight line;

(2) in the given line but not at either extremity of it; and

(3) outside the given line, as shown in the text book.

In (1) Euclid's construction will evidently fail, but the solution is easy, and is obtained by describing a circle with the given point as centre and the given line as radius, taking any point in its circumference, and joining it with the given point. In (2) the construction will be the same as that given by Euclid, with this difference that the given point being already joined with both the extremities of the given line, will not have to be joined with either extremity. One thing which puzzles some students, if the figure is slightly altered in appearance by shifting the position of the given point relatively to the given line, is, to determine which sides of the equilateral triangle should be produced, and what point and what straight line should be taken as the centre and the radius of the second circle. The teacher should point out that the sides produced are those other than the side joining the given point with an extremity of the given line, that the centre of the second circle is the angular point of the equilateral triangle opposite to the last-mentioned side, and that its radius is that portion of the produced side passing through the extremity of the given line which lies between the last mentioned angular point and the circumference of the first circle. And he should do a little more. He should endeavour to explain the reason why the sides of the equilateral triangle are produced and the second circle is described, and why the different steps of the construction are taken; and this will help the pupil not only in remembering the steps that are to be taken in this particular instance, but also in being put in the way of remembering the different steps taken in other instances, and gradually in discovering those steps for himself. In the instance under notice, the equilateral triangle is described to obtain a point from which two straight lines diverge, one passing through an extremity of the given line and the other through the given point, such that their portions between the point of divergence and the two last named points are equal; the first circle is described to obtain a radius for the second equal to the given line together with a side of the equilateral triangle; and then the second circle is described to obtain an intercept on the line through the given point equal to that radius, from which a length equal to a side of the equilateral triangle being taken off, a remainder is left equal to the given straight line and passing through the given point. This should be clearly seen by the student.

He should be further told that when one line is drawn through the given point equal to the given straight line, any number of such lines may be drawn by describing a circle with the given point as centre and the first drawn line as radius, and joining points in its circumference with the centre, the circumference of the circle being what is called the *locus* of the further extremity of all straight lines drawn from the given point equal to the given line.

The third proposition does not call for any remark; but Proposition IV of the first Book requires to be dwelt upon at some length. It being the first *Theorem* in Euclid that the boy reads, he should be made to understand what the facts *assumed* to be true are, and what the facts to be *demonstrated* to be true are, and how these latter facts are established. He may be told that of the six parts of which a triangle is composed, that is, the three sides and the three angles, if any three (except the three angles) in one triangle are equal to the corresponding three parts of another, it will be shown (subject to one qualification) that the two triangles are equal in every respect, and that the 4th Proposition of Book I is only one of these cases, namely, the one in which the equal elements are two sides and the contained angle. The equality of the remaining side involves no difficulty; but that of the remaining angles is subject to the qualification, that they are equal *each to each*, that is, *those to which the equal sides are opposite*. This should be clearly understood.

The method of demonstration in Proposition IV is that by *superposition*, that is, by the *immediate* comparison of the things whose equality is to be proved, and not by their comparison mediately through any third thing to which they are both shown to be equal. It is the simplest kind of proof possible, and the student should be exhorted to realize this, instead of feeling vague doubts and difficulties in his mind. To help him in doing so, two equal triangles on thick paper should be superposed as indicated in the text. There is one step in the demonstration which is sometimes passed unnoticed, but the full importance of which should be always pointed out. It is that in which it is said that one of the equal sides of one triangle coinciding with the corresponding side of the other, the remaining pair of equal sides must also coincide, *because the angles contained by them are equal*. The force of this reason should be made clear by showing that the side of the triangle having a greater angle will fall outside of the other, when the contained angles are not equal.

The difficulty of Proposition V, which has been called the Ass's Bridge, has been greatly exaggerated.

The first part of the enunciation may require a word of explanation, as it does not explicitly separate the hypothesis from the conclusion. Stated more explicitly, it should run thus—"If two sides of a triangle be equal, the angles opposite to them are also equal."

The construction effected, has for its object the obtaining of two pairs of triangles which are equal by Proposition IV; and the demonstration consists in applying Proposition IV to these pairs of triangles, and thence showing that the angles on the other side of the base, which are equal angles of the pair of small triangles, and the angles at the base, which are equal angles of the pair of large triangles diminished by equal angles of the other pair of triangles, are equal. The difficulty of the demonstration consists in its length, and in the fact of the pairs of equal triangles overlapping one another instead of being altogether separate from one another. A little practice will enable the student to get over these difficulties, the latter of which may be removed for the beginner by tracing along the sides of the two triangles of each pair differently coloured pencils.

Two other proofs have been given of the first part of the 5th Proposition, which are no doubt very simple. In one of these, the vertical angle is supposed to be bisected by a straight line which meets the base, and the triangles into which the given triangle is divided, being equal by Proposition IV, the angles at the base are shown to be equal. But this is open to the objection that it anticipates the construction which is effected by Euclid in Proposition IX. In the other proof, a second triangle with the same three sides the two equal sides being placed in the reversed order, is taken, and then by the application of Proposition IV, the angles at the base are shown to be equal. But this again is open to the objection that it anticipates the construction effected by Euclid in Proposition XXII. The second proof may be given in a somewhat modified form so as to avoid the objection, by regarding the given triangle as two triangles, one of which has its right and left sides as they are, and the other has for its right and left sides the left and right sides of the original triangle, this inversion being possible by reason of the two sides being equal; and then applying the 4th Proposition to these two triangles to prove the equality of the two angles at the base, which would be either the left or the right side base angles of the original triangle and the triangle obtained after its imaginary inversion.

Proposition VI being the first instance of a *converse* proposition, and the mode of demonstration in it being the first instance of *indirect* demonstration in Euclid, the teacher should explain the nature of converse propositions and that of indirect demonstration.

I have already remarked above that the 7th Proposition may be passed over, and the 8th proved independently of it, by placing one of the two traingles on the opposite side of the base of the other and joining the vertices, and then applying the 5th Proposition as indicated below.—

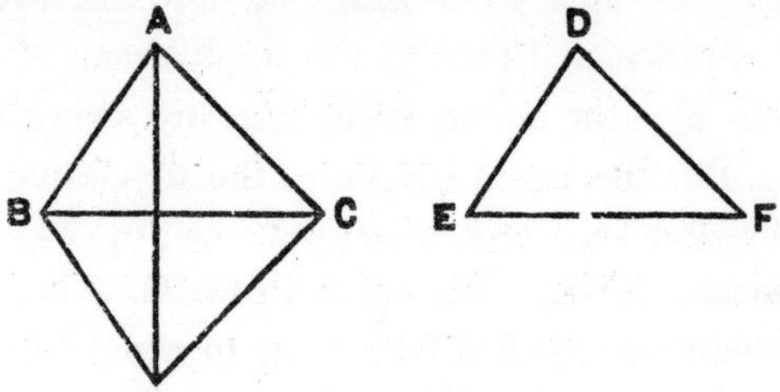

Proposition VIII is the second case of the equality of two triangles given by Euclid, and is in one sense the converse of Proposition IV, the hypothesis in the latter being that the two sides and the contained angle of the one triangle are equal to those of the other, and its conclusion being that their bases are equal, while the hypothesis in the 8th Proposition is that the two sides of the two triangles and their bases are equal, and the conclusion is that the angles contained by the equal sides are equal.

The next proposition requiring notice is the 13th, which is proved by proving that the two supplementary angles and two right angles are both equal to the same three angles, and thence showing by the application of the first axiom that they are both equal. But if Euclid had accepted the notion that angular magnitudes result from the revolution of a straight line about a point, and that they may equal or exceed two right angles, the two supplementary angles, would at once have been seen to fill up the angular space of two right angles, and the proposition could have been proved by *immediate* comparison of the given angles with two right angles, with the help of the 8th Axiom.

Proposition XVII, which has been rightly considered by Euclid as requiring proof, may be noticed as disproving the self-evident character of his twelfth axiom which is its converse.

Proposition XVIII deserves notice next, as being in the nature of a supplement to Proposition V, as is the converse Proposition XIX supplementary to Proposition VI. The four propositions may be taken together to embody the complete truth which may be stated thus:—

If one side of a triangle be greater than, equal to or less than another, the angle subtended by the former will be greater than, equal to, or less than that subtended by the latter; and conversely, if one angle of a triangle be greater than, equal to, or less than another, the side opposite to it will be greater than, equal to, or less than that opposite to the other.

Proposition XX is useful in proving that the straight line is the shortest distance between any to points.

After this proposition, the teacher may ask the pupil to turn back to the second and the third of the three questions stated to him at the outset, and help him to solve them, premising for the solution of the third, that the apparent distances referred to in it, depend upon the angles subtended at the observer's eye by the real distances, so that if these angles are shewn to become less and less, the distances will also appear to diminish gradually.

To answer the second question, t. e student should proceed as in the annexed figure,

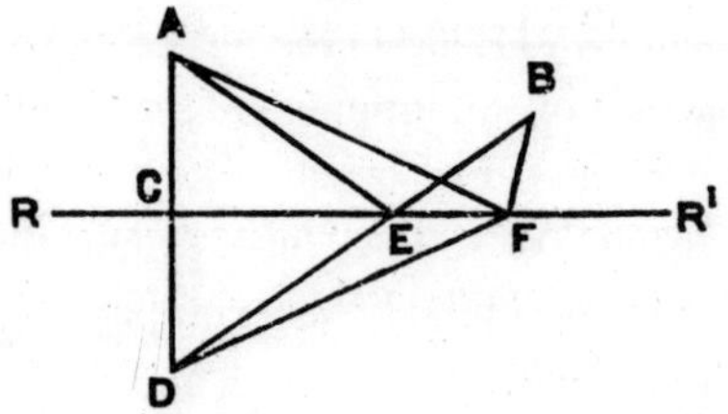

drawing A C perpendicular to R R,[1] producing A C to D so that C D = A C, and joining D B cutting R R[1] in E. Then A E B shall be the shortest route required.

For taking any other point F in R R,[1] and joining AF, BF, DF,

since AE = DE (Euc. 1. 4), and AF = DF,

$$\begin{aligned} AF + BF &= DF + BF \\ &> DB \text{ (Euc. 1, 20).} \\ &> DE + EB. \\ &> AE + EB. \end{aligned}$$

The third proposition may be proved by the application of Propositions XVIII and XIX with the help of the construction in the annexed figure, where O is the observer, and A, B, C, D, E, are the successive points, and OC=CF, so that from the triangles OCD and FCB, $\angle COD = \angle CFB < \angle COB$, because $OB < OD$ or FB.

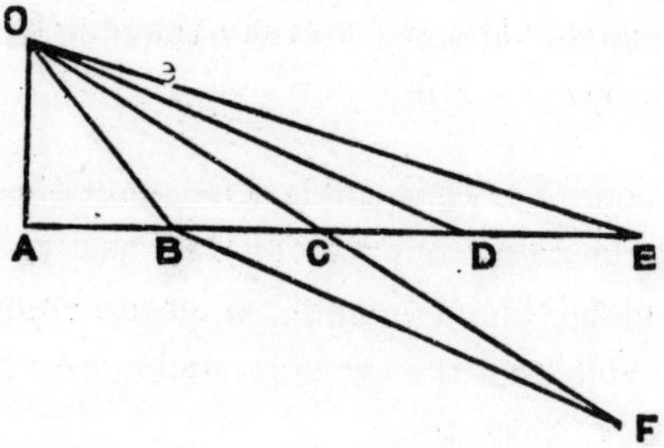

The condition that any two of the given straight lines are together greater than the third, in the enunciation of Proposition XXII, the learner should understand, is necessary, because the sides of a triangle must fulfil that condition as proved in Proposition XX. It is sometimes said that the condition is necessary because otherwise the construction fails. That is not the correct way to state the point. The necessity of the condition arises from the truth of Proposition XX, and the construction fails if the condition is not satisfied because of that truth.

Propositions XXIV and XXV should be explained as being supplementary to Proposition IV and VIII in the same sense as Propositions XVIII and

XIX are supplementary to Propositions V and VI. They may be enunciated together thus:—

"If two triangles have two sides of the one equal to two sides of the other, the base of the one will be greater than, equal to, or less than that of the other, according as the angle contained by its sides is greater than, equal to, or less than that in the other, and conversely.

Proposition XXVI is the last one about the equality of triangles given by Euclid. It has two cases, one in which the two equal angles are adjacent to the equal side, and the other in which one of them is opposite to that side.

The remaining case, namely, that in which the equal elements are two sides and one angle opposite to one of them, has not been considered by Euclid. It is true, subject to the condition that the angles opposite to the other pair of equal sides are either both acute or both right or both obtuse. This case should be proved for the learner, and the necessity of the condition explained.

The propositions relating to parallel straight lines I pass over, with the remark I have already made, that Playfair's 12th Axiom should be adopted in preference to Euclid's, as being more self-evident than the latter.

The corollaries to Proposition XXXII, and the algebraical formula deducible from the first corollary, namely, an $\angle$ of a regular polygon of n sides $=\frac{2n-4}{n}$ rt. $\angle$s

$$=(2-\tfrac{4}{n}) \text{ rt. } \angle\text{s}$$

should be clearly explained.

With the aid of Corollary 1, the student should be able to prove that the only regular figures, an integral number of which can exactly fill the angular space round a point are, the trigon, the tetragon, and the hexagon, their angles being respectively $\frac{2}{3}$ of a right angle, 1 right angle, and $\frac{4}{3}$ of a right angle, and 6, 4, and 3 of these figures being therefore just sufficient to occupy the angular space round a point, which is equal to four right angles.

An angle of any regular polygon of 7 or more sides being greater than $\frac{4}{3}$ of a right angle and less than two right angles, no other polygon by being taken an integral number of times can exactly fill the angular space round a point. The student should be asked here to note the fact, that bees build the cells of their hive in the shape of regular hexagons. There is thus no waste of space at any point. And the hexagon approaching more nearly in shape the cylindrical larva for the abode of which the cells are intended, than the other two regular figures mentioned above, further economy of space is secured. The science, an elementary knowledge of which enables the learner to appreciate interesting truths like these, should not be regarded as dry and hard study.

The last proposition of the First Book of Euclid that I would comment upon is the 47th. This is a very important proposition. It is of very great use in Mathematics. It enables us to express numerically the length of any side of a right angled triangle, if the lengths of the other two sides are numerically given, from the formula, $h^2 = p^2 + b^2$, where h, p, and b are the lengths of the hypotenuse, the perpendicular and the base.

Solution of Geometrical Problems.

88. While reading the First Book of Euclid, the student should be exercised in solving Geometrical Problems; and I may here offer a few remarks regarding the mode of teaching him how to proceed.

As Geometrical Problems are of unlimited diversity of form, it is not possible to lay down any detailed general directions for their solution. All that could be said by way of general direction, would be to tell the student to assume that the deduction, if a problem, is solved, or if a theorem, is proved ; then to examine the figure constructed to see what known lines or points, or what known truths or properties, the assumption can, stage by stage, lead to ; and lastly to retrace these steps, proceeding from given things to the required things, or from known truths to those required to be proved, so as to solve the problem or prove the theorem under consideration. But this direction is exceedingly vague, and will be of use, only after the student has had some practice in working out deductions ; and it will be for the teacher to help the pupil by leading him on in the solution of easy riders, that is, deductions upon particular propositions of Euclid, instead of solving hard problems for him. I cannot too strongly deprecate the practice of setting hard problems for exercise. It is based upon the idea that if students are trained in hard work, easy work will have no difficulty for them. I have already tried to controvert this notion in a previous part of these remarks. We do not learn to walk by being taught to jump, nor do we get the benefit of exercise by being carried on the shoulders of others from one place to another. It does the learner little good, to be waiting with despair until the teacher thinks that he has had sufficient trial, and then to copy with admiration the solution written on the black board. It is better that the teacher should begin with easy riders, and help the student on, so that he may have the satisfaction that he can do something, and the hope that by proceeding in the manner indicated to him, he will gradually be able to do more. To quote the words of Proctor whose "First Steps in Geometry" I would request all students and teachers of Geometry to read, "The average mathematical student requires to learn—not how to solve this or that problem, nor what construction will help him in any particular case; but what are the general methods which he must apply to problems in order to obtain solutions for himself. The mathematical teacher who simply solves the problems brought to him by his pupils, does little to show how such problems are to be treated. He should exhibit to his pupils the train of thought which leads him to apply such and such process to the solution of a problem * * * * * * * * One problem thus dealt with is worth a dozen which are merely solved."

But though difficult problems for exercise should be generally avoided, important propositions not proved by Euclid, should, even if somewhat difficult, be read, such as the propositions relating to the concurrence of the lines bisecting the angles of a triangle, of the lines bisecting its sides at right angles, of the lines joining the middle points of its sides with the opposite angles, and of the lines drawn perpendicular to the sides from the opposite angles.

The solution of problems by the intersection of loci is a method which should be explained to the student.

Remarks on Euclid Book II.

89. The student should finish the First Book of Euclid or the subject matter of it in his twelfth year, and commence Book II when he is thirteen years of age, and when he has read a little of Algebra. The teacher should explain to him the scope of Book II, which is to prove certain important truths relating to the areas of rectangles, and should teach him the mode of dealing algebraically with those propositions that may be so treated. As a necessary preliminary to this last mentioned course, the teacher should clearly explain to the pupil the fundamental proposition, that the area of a rectangle contained by the

lines a and b is equal to the product $a \times b$, the meaning of which is, that if the length and the breadth of a rectangle be represented by the numbers a and b, that is, if they are straight lines containing a and b linear units respectively, the area of the rectangle will contain $a \times b$ square units, each of such units being a square on the linear unit. He may also shortly explain here the ideas of unit and measurement of magnitudes as they have been explained in the introductory chapter of Dr. Mukhopadhyay and Mr. Basu's Arithmetic for schools and colleges.

Book II, Propositions IV and V expressed algebraically will be found to be the well known formulæ,

$$(a+b)^2 = a^2 + 2ab + b^2,$$
$$a^2 - b^2 = (a+b)(a-b).$$

Proposition V may be referred to as an instance of a class of questions known as *Maxima* and *Minima* questions, the nature of which may here be explained to the student.

As the square on half the line, which is the rectangle contained by its equal segments, is equal to the rectangle contained by the unequal segments, together with the square on the line between the points of section, it is clear that the rectangle contained by the segments of a line has the maximum value when the segments are equal; and there is no limit to its minimum value, the rectangle becoming less and less the farther the point of section is removed towards either extremity of the line.

This is the algebraical theorem $\left(\frac{a+b}{2}\right)^2 > a\ b$, unless $a=b$.

The teacher should explain to the pupil that as a line may be cut *internally* when a point is taken in it its segments being the parts into which it is divided,' so, by stretch of language, it may be said to be cut *externally*, when it is produced to any point, its *segments being the distances of its extremities from the point of external section*; and with this extended definition of *section*, and *segment*, Propositions V and VI may be enunciated together thus:—

If a straight line be bisected and also cut unequally, whether internally or externally, the rectangle contained by the unequal segments is equal to the difference between the squares on half the line and on the line between the points of section.

It is desirable that the learner should become accustomed early to *methods of generalization* like these. Propositions IX and X may be similarly expressed in one enunciation. This may be left as an exercise for the student.

The student should learn to solve Propositions XI algebraically, and should carefully note the lesson which the solution of this problem teaches as to the *method of applying Algebra to the solution of Geometrical problems.*

Assuming the given line to be a, and one of the required parts to be x, the problem will be reduced to the solution of the equation,

$a. (a-x)=x^2$ or $x^2 + a\,x - a^2 = 0$,

whence $x=\frac{-a+\sqrt{a^2+4a^2}}{2}=\frac{\sqrt{5}}{2}a-\frac{1}{2}a$, that is, the part $x=\frac{\sqrt{5}}{2}$ of the given line—half of the given line.

Now $\frac{\sqrt{5}}{2}\times$ any line = the side of a square which is $\frac{5}{4}$ of the square on the line;

and $\frac{5}{4}$ of the square on a line = square on the line + square on its half.

So that by Euclid I, 47, $\frac{\sqrt{5}}{2}\times$ a line is the hypotenuse of a right-angled triangle of which the sides are the line and its half.

Thus x is that hypotenuse diminished by half the given line. And this is exactly the way in which Euclid proceeds, E F, or E B in his figure being the hypotenuse, and A H or A F being E F—A E = E F—$\frac{1}{2}$ A B.

This instructive process, the teacher should explain to the pupil and ask him to remember.

Propositions XII and XIII supplement Proposition XLVII of Book I, and all these three may be enunciated together thus:—

The square on any side of a triangle is greater than, equal to, or less than the sum of the squares on the other two sides, according as the angle between them is greater than, equal to, or less than a right angle, the excess or defect being equal to twice the rectangle contained by either of those other two sides and the straight line intercepted between the foot of the perpendicular let fall upon it from the opposite angle and the angle contained by those other sides.

The student should be asked carefully to note this general enunciation of the three allied propositions, and to read the alternative proof, given in Dr. Casey's Edition of Euclid, of Propositions XII and XIII of Book II, which is similar to that given by Euclid of Proposition XLVII of Book I. The annexed figures will explain my meaning.

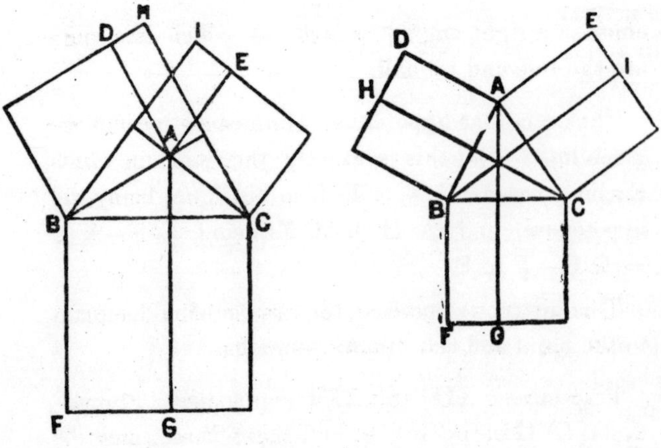

It may be shown as in Euc. Book I, Prop. 47, that rectangle B H = rectangle B G,

. . . . . . C I = ... C G,

and . . . A H = ... A I.

Books III and IV of Euclid or their subject matter should also be read by the student before entering college, and they are included in the Entrance or Matriculation Course in Geometry by the Indian Universities.

The end of the 4th Book marks an important point of division in Euclid's Geometry. Up to that point, Euclid is treating of the equality or inequality of *magnitudes themselves*; after that, he begins to consider the equality or inequality of *ratios* or *relations of magnitudes*.

As I have said a good deal with reference to the first two books of Euclid, I shall not take up the time of my readers with remarks on the next two Books, but leave teachers and pupils to refer to the notes in annotated editions like those of Casey, and Hall and Stevens.

I have gone into some detail, and occupied much time, in giving hints on the study of Geometry. My only excuse for doing so, is, that I feel with regret that a branch of study which is not very difficult in itself, and which is so full of interesting truths and so well calculated to exercise and invigorate the mental powers, should be made to appear repulsive, and should be unintelligently committed to memory as a burden, merely for want of proper teaching. I do not presume to think that the few brief and slipshod remarks I have made above, will remove the evil, and produce the wished for good. But they indicate the mode in which I believe Geometry may be made interesting to students, and they may put others, better qualified than myself, in the way of using more efficient methods.

Algebra.

90. Algebra is the only other branch of Mathematics which should be read to some extent by a boy of twelve to fifteen years, and on the teaching of which a few suggestions may be offered here.

The nature of the subject should be roughly and broadly indicated. It is true, it is not possible to give a boy of twelve or thirteen years who is just commencing the study of Algebra, any clear and complete idea of the nature and scope of an extensive subject like this; but still as every intelligent boy, when beginning any new branch of study, is anxious to know what it is about, the teacher should not leave this natural curiosity altogether unsatisfied, but should shortly explain, that one main object of Algebra is to reason about quantities by representing them, *not by numbers* which are necessarily *definite and particular* as in Arithmetic, *but by symbols* which are *indefinite and general.* And he may illustrate his meaning by a simple example like this:

The proposition that the product of two numbers is the same whether we regard the first as the multiplicand and the second as the multiplier or the second as the multiplicand and the first as the multiplier, is proved in Arithmetic by taking any two particular numbers, 3 and 5, and by showing that, as

$$3=1+1+1 \text{ and } 5=1+1+1+1+1,$$

$$\begin{aligned} \therefore 3\times 5 = &1+1+1\\ &+1+1+1\\ &+1+1+1\\ &+1+1+1\\ &+1+1+1 \end{aligned}$$

=5 horizontal rows of 3 ones
=3 vertical rows of 5 ones
$=5\times 3$.

But the same proposition will be proved in Algebra by taking two integral numbers represented by the letters a and b, which may represent any numbers, and showing that as

$$a = 1+1+1+\ldots\ldots \text{ to } a \text{ terms,}$$
and $$b = 1+1+1+\ldots\ldots \text{ to } b \text{ terms,}$$
$$\begin{aligned} \therefore a\times b = &1+1+1+\ldots\ldots \text{ to } a \text{ terms}\\ &+1+1+1+\ldots\ldots \text{ to } a \text{ terms}\\ &+1+1+1+\ldots\ldots \text{ to } a \text{ terms}\\ &+\ldots\ldots\ldots \text{ to } a \text{ terms}\\ &+\ldots\ldots\ldots \text{ to } a \text{ terms,}\end{aligned}$$

there being as many horizontal rows as there are units in b,

that is $=b$ horizontal rows of a ones each
$=a$ vertical rows of b ones each
$=b\times a$.

The rules relating to subtraction and negative quantities should be clearly explained to the beginner, care being taken not to discourage and bewilder him by making him think that there is something abstruse and difficult about the matter, but to encourage and enlighten him by telling him that the rules are based on a *useful and rational extension* of the *ordinary meaning* of subtraction. The simplest statement of the rules will be this:—

I. Rule for Subtraction:—Change the sign of every term of the subtrahend and then proceed as in addition. Negative Quantities.

II. Rule relating to Negative Quantities. Regard the sign $-$ *as a sign of operation*, when the quantity following it is connected with others preceding it; and regard it *as a qualification* of the quantity following it, when it stands alone, the qualification being that the quantity in question is of a nature which is the *reverse* of that of a similar quantity with a $+$ sign or no sign before it.

To prove Rule I, suppose we have to take $b-c$ from a. Then $a-b$ will not be the result, but will be less than the true result by c, as we have subtracted from a the whole of b, whereas, not b, but $b-c$, that is b diminished by c is to be subtracted. To get the true result we must increase $a-b$ by c,

so as to have $a-b+c$,

which shows that $a-(b-c)=a-b+c$.

To explain Rule II, we may proceed thus:— Suppose that a tradesman A has assets $=a$ Rs. and debts $=b$ Rs., so that his worth in money will be represented by

a Rs. $-b$ Rs.,

where the sign $-$ before b Rs. is a sign of the operation of subtraction, b Rs. being connected with a Rs., and the result we want being the difference between a Rs. and b Rs. But if $-b$ Rs. stood by itself, the quantity would be called a *negative* quantity, the sign $-$ before b Rs. indicating that the quantity $-b$ Rs. is of a nature the very *reverse* of what it would have been without that sign, that is, instead of being b Rs. *owned* by A, it is

b Rs. *owing* by him, and has the effect not of increasing but of diminishing his pecuniary worth.

So again, if b was greater than a as for example, if $a = 500$, $b = 800$, the expression a Rs. $- b$ Rs would be a negative quantity, -300 Rs., and would mean that the precuniary worth of the tradesman A is negative, that is, that instead of *owning* any money he is *indebted* to the extent of Rs. 300 which he has no means of paying.

So also, if *gain* is represented by a positive quantity, *loss* will be represented by a negative quantity. Thus if a person *gains* Rs. 50 in one month, and *loses* Rs. 20 in the next, his real *gain* in the two months is 50 Rs. $-$ 20 Rs. or 30 Rs.; and if the figures were reversed, his real *gain* would be 20 Rs.—50 Rs. or $-$ 30 Rs., that is, the result of his business in two months would be a *loss* of 30 Rs.

The student may be told that in the same manner if distance *measured in any direction* (generally from left to right) is represented by a *positive* number, that *measured in the opposite direction* will be represented by a *negative* quantity; and if time running *forward* from any given instant is represented by a *positive* number, time running *backward* from that instant will be represented by a *negative* quantity; he should be asked to wait till he comes to the solution of problems producing simple equations for illustrations of the last-mentioned *rules of convention*; and when he has read something about equations, he should have the problem known as that of the couriers worked out in Todhunter's Algebra, fully explained, and the *signs* of the values of x properly *interpreted*.

The multiplication of quantities by a negative quantity, and the identity $(-a)\times(-b)=+a\ b$, often puzzle the beginner, and the ordinary explanation deduced from the multiplication of $(a-b)$ by $(c-d)$ does not seem to be quite satisfactory. The difficulty might to some extent be removed by the following explanation :—

To multiply a quantity by a positive number is to take it as often as is indicated by that number, and to deal with the result as a positive or a negative quantity according as the multiplicand was originally positive or negative. To multiply a quantity by a negative number must therefore be to take it as often as that number regarded as a positive number would indicate, and to deal with the result in a way which is the *reverse* of that in which it would have been dealt with had the multiplier been a positive number, that is, to treat the product as a *negative* or as a *positive* quantity according as the multiplicand is *positive* or *negative*.

The meaning of the formulæ

$$a^m \div a^n = a^{m-n} = a^{-(n-m)}$$

$$= \frac{1}{a^{n-m}} \text{ if } n \, 7 \, m,$$

$$\text{and } a^0 = 1,$$

should be fully explained.

In connection with these formulæ, the student should carefully note that though a *new* symbol when *first introduced* in any Science may have *any* meaning, yet when a symbol *not altogether new* but connected with another symbol, comes to be used, it should not have an *arbitrary* meaning, but should, for securing consistency in our results, have a *meaning that is consistent with previous connected conventions.*

Algebraical conventions —should be consistent.

Thus, as a^m has a definite meaning and accordingly $a^m \div a^n = a^{m-n}$, the meaning to be given to a negative index, that is, a^{-n} must be consistent with our previous conventions.

In dealing with equations, the learner should have the distinction between an *identity* and an *equation* clearly explained; he should be thoroughly practised in applying the rules of *transformation* and *transposition,* as they are of frequent application; and he should be able to apply those rules correctly without any conscious effort.

In regard to Algebraical exercises, I would make the same remarks that I made with reference to deductions in Geometry. Difficult examples should be avoided at least in the earlier stages of a student's progress, as they do not afford any scope for the exercise of his mental powers, and are positively discouraging. It must also be borne in mind that it is not every student who can be expected to be a mathematician, or who intends to read mathematics more than as a branch of general education.

SECTION III. MORAL EDUCATION.

Moral education in early boyhood should be similar to that in infancy.

91. In the earlier years of boyhood, that is, from the sixth to the ninth year, moral education should proceed in the same manner as in infancy; and the remarks I have made on the subject in the preceding Chapter will hold good during that period.

From the tenth year moral education should be methodical and strict.

92. From the tenth year, moral education should be more methodical and more strict.

93. The methods I would suggest are the following:—

Methods to be followed Moral texts.

In the *first* place, for Hindu boys, simple and short moral texts selected from Sanskrit literature, sacred or secular, should be collected in a small book, and these should be read by boys who are intended to receive liberal education, and who in their tenth year are expected to have learnt a little Sanskrit, so as to be able to understand the texts when explained. For those who do not read Sanskrit, vernacular translations of the texts should be prepared.

In compiling the texts, the *Chanakya Sloka*, the *Moha mudgar*, and the *Bhagavadgita* may be largely resorted to.

My reason for insisting upon moral texts being read by Hindu boys in Sanskrit if possible, is, that apart from the inherent force and beauty of the texts, they have acquired a power and a charm from the hallowed associations clustering round them for ages past, the benefit of which we should not lose.

In the *second* place, short anecdotes teaching moral lessons, should be collected from biography, history, and even mythology, and should be read by boys, not merely as literature but also as illustrating moral truths. But the stories should be selected with care. Stories may teach morality by presenting heroic or striking examples of the discharge of duty under difficulties, or by showing that moral conduct ensures happiness, or by depicting the miseries of vice. Stories of the first sort are unexceptionable, but those of the second and third descriptions should be judiciously presented to the learner. For unfortunately for the world, in the common course of human affairs, and as judged by our ordinary rough standards, the good are not always happy, nor the bad always miserable. Moreover, though the hope of happiness and the fear of misery as motives for doing what is right and abstaining from doing what is wrong, may be availed of in due measure in the earlier stages of the pupil's progress, the moral teacher should aim at a higher object, and should endeavour to awaken in his pupil the desire of doing his duty regardless of consequences, adopting as his rule of conduct the sublime text of the *Gita*.[1]

Moral stories.

"अनाश्रितः कर्म्मफलं कार्य्यं कर्म्म करोति यः ।
स सन्न्यासी च योगी च न निरग्निर्न चाक्रियः ॥"

"He is a renouncer of the world and a seeker after salvation who does his duty regardless of its fruits;

1 Chap. VI, verse 1.

not he who has extinguished his sacrificial fire and renounced action."

Then, again, stories of the third description are not without the danger of sometimes teaching the boy the nature of a vice of which he was ignorant, while dwelling on the miseries it may bring on.

Moral truths from other lessons.

In the *third* place, the teacher should avail himself of every opportunity afforded by the lessons in the different subjects of study, in impressing on his pupils the moral truths they teach.

Teacher should have a moral ideal, self-abnegation to be its prominent feature.

94. As the moral texts, stories, and lessons deduced from other subjects of study, must, from their very nature, be detached and fragmentary, the teacher should, in the *fourth* place, keep in view *a connected and complete ideal of moral character*; and he should direct all his efforts at moral teaching towards moulding the character of his pupils after that ideal. In doing this he must not attempt to take his boys through a systematic code of ethics. If he does so, it will be impossible to avoid entering on debatable ground; and considering the age of his pupils, it will be too early, and perhaps also a little dangerous, to discuss controversial topics of morality with them. The ideal he is to keep in view, though connected and complete, should be delineated, without developing any delicate features of questionable grace, but merely by marking prominently those broad features which are agreeable to all tastes and feelings.

What then should this ideal be? For Hindu boys, and it is for them chiefly that I speak, I feel little hesitation in answering that it should be the ideal that is presented to the Hindu mind by the significant word *Brahmacharya*, the student life of rigid discipline in ancient India. In saying this, I hope I am not justly chargeable with disregarding my own direction, and recommending an ideal which may not be acceptable to many. I know it may be said that our respect for the past should not stand in the way of our progress in the future; that having regard to the altered conditions of society and the advanced ideas of men, what suited us three thousand years ago may be quite unsuitable now; and that a life of austere self-denial, however conducive to spiritual welfare, is poor preparation for improving our material condition and fighting the battle of life. While fully appreciating the force of these objections where they really apply, I venture to think that they have very little application to the point under consideration. I have recommended for boys of ten to fifteen years a life of *Brahmacharya*, not from any sentimental predilection, excusable as it may be, in a member, however unworthy, of the Brahminical class, but for practical reasons, being firmly convinced that a life of ascetic self-abnegation is a much better preparation than a life of luxury and frivolity, for all good work, whether it be spiritual improvement, or the improvement of our material condition. Not only in quiet peaceful work, but also in the stirring scenes of the now inevitable evil, war, it is those trained in rigid discipline and strict self-denial that bear privations and stand strain much better than those differently brought up. And as for the altered conditions of society and advanced ideas of men, they only render the enforcement of a life of ascetic discipline more necessary at the present day than it was before. For while material objects of comfort are being produced in greater variety, and our notions of comfort are being raised more and more, and the struggle for existence is becoming more and more severe, the discontent arising from unsatisfied supposed wants, is growing more and more alarming; and the only remedy against the evil is early training in self-denial. It must not be supposed that the present backward condition of India is due to the repressive influence of her early discipline. The truth is that our material progress has been retarded by the exclusive devotion of our forefathers to the cultivation of spiritual knowledge, to the utter neglect of the knowledge of the material world. Nor need we be under any apprehension that a few years of strict discipline in a life of *Brahmacharya* will repress all desire for material comforts and all ambition for honest fame, so as to make our boys, when they grow up, indifferent to action and devoid of emulation. The selfish instinct is too strong to be completely repressed; and the utmost that the proposed training can effect will be, the not undesirable result of restraining and regulating it so as to prevent its manifesting itself in those innumerable mischievous ways in which it often asserts its existence. It is no exaggeration to say that by far the greater part of the miseries we inflict upon others and upon ourselves, such as the evils of war, of crime, of civil wrongs, and of discord, disappointment, and discontent, arise from unrestrained or ill-regulated selfishness. Education, which aims at training our boys to be good men and good citizens, will fail in its main object if it does not do all in its power to enable educated men to curb and control their selfishness, the undoubted source of so much evil. I do not deny that the selfish instinct was implanted in us to serve useful ends. All I say is that *it requires to be restrained and regulated.* Its free exercise is excusable on the ground of necessity in the helpless condition of the child and the savage; but in grown up and civilized man, with his own reason and that of the members of his community to guide and help him, its sphere of action must become extremely limited.

Having made these remarks to meet the objections which might find favour in certain quarters, I would ask the teacher to exhort his pupils to live up to the old ideal of student life in India. He should tell them that while food should be sufficient and nutritive, it need not be excessive and rich; that dress, while it should be comfortable and decent, need not be costly and gaudy; that luxury in diet and dress should be avoided, and the money saved should be devoted to higher objects than the gratification of the senses—to relieve the wants of others. He should make them understand that physical exercise should be resorted to as being conducive to health, and not for the sake of following fashion or winning reward. He should impress upon them, on the one hand, the necessity of being firm in vindicating the right, and on the other, the no less paramount duty of being meek and forgiving even to an enemy. These are opposite virtues but not altogether incompatible with each other; and the skill of the moral teacher consists in training his pupils so that they may have humility without meanness, and they may be forgiving without being wanting in courage. Where meekness and a forgiving disposition proceed from want of strength, they are virtues of necessity; and where they are affected for the purpose of gaining an ulterior object, they are worse than the opposite qualities of arrogance and vindictiveness, which have the merit of being straightforward. For the former I have no commendation; the latter merits nothing but reproach. But where one having the strength to resent and not caring for anything except his adversary's feelings, is meek and forgiving, does he not deserve greater praise than the man who boldly resents an affront? We all admire the display of strength; and does not the self-restraint of the meek and forgiving when proceeding only from a desire not to deal harshly with a fellow man, imply the exercise of much greater strength than the excitement of the resentful? The truth is, that it costs much less strength to act on the impulse of the selfish instinct than to restrain that impulse, but the effort in the latter case is without display and is felt only by him who makes it. If the moral teacher explains all this to his pupils, he will awaken in them a due sense of the nature of true humility, and a wholesome desire to be meek and forgiving; and they will then realize the full import of the saying, "To err is human, to forgive, divine."

Morality should no only be learnt but should als practised.

95. Morality should not only be *learnt in theory* but should also be *reduced to practice.* If exercise is so necessary, as an aid to intellectual education, it is still more needed as an auxiliary to moral training. Happily for man, the cardinal truths of morality are so simple and well recognized that the humblest intelligence can easily understand them. But unhappily for him, the real difficulty lies in reducing them to practice; and the most resolute will often fails to do so.

We must not think that

"जानामि धर्म्मं न च मे प्रवृत्ति-
र्जानाम्यधर्म्मं न च मे निवृत्तिः"

"I know the right and approve it too;
I hate the wrong and yet the wrong pursue"

is an exclamation of affected humility.

A little self-examination will satisfy every one how true it is. The only way to remedy the evil is to endeavour by constant practice to acquire the habit of doing the right.

Just as we are talking prose every hour of our lives without always knowing it, we perform moral exercises every day and every hour without being always conscious of our doing so. When we discharge a duty, we perform our exercise correctly. When we fail to discharge a duty, or do something in violation of it, we still perform a moral exercise, only we fall into error in the performance. And the point for the moral teacher to bear in mind is, that he should watch the conduct of the pupil, ascertain where his weakness was that led to the slips, and try to guard against their repetition in future. If the errors are few and slight, they will in general be freely confessed, and the teacher will find it easy to correct them. But if they are many or grave, the sense of shame will stand in the way of their free disclosure, and the work of the teacher will be a delicate one. He should not, even if he be a near and dear relation of his pupil, try to be too inquisitive. *He should never press for a confession.* The sense of shame, which prevents a free confession being made, should not be weakened. For though it is reprehensible as leading to the suppression of truth and the suggestion of falsehood, it serves as a powerful preventive of wrong doing. The teacher should ascertain the truth from other sources where the offender is reticent, and then proceed on the assumption that he knows it. But *he should never be reproachful.* As his object is *reform* and not *punishment*, he must secure not only the *respect* but also the *love* of his pupil. He should be *stern* in *condemning* the *offence*, but *gentle* in *correcting* the *offender.* And then a second offence will be readily admitted, and his aid and advice voluntarily sought with a view to avoid slips in future.

Another important point to bear in mind, is, that errors, whether intellectual or moral, should never be allowed to pass unnoticed, even when they are of a trivial nature. *If slight errors go uncorrected, the habit of remissness is allowed to grow, and grave errors are gradually the result.*

Moral environment should be favourable.

96. The moral environments of a boy, like the physical, should be made as salutary as possible. But we should avoid the extreme of removing a boy from his home and the custody of his natural guardian, to a boarding institution, merely because the latter is situated amidst more favourable surroundings than the former. It is matter for serious consideration whether the gain by removal from the bad surroundings of a boy's home compensates for the loss by removal from salutary home influences.

SECTION IV.—RELIGIOUS EDUCATION.

Questions arising under this head.

97. The questions requiring consideration under this head are—

(1) Is religious education necessary?

(2) If it is, what should be its nature?

(3) How should it be given?

Is religious education necessary?

98. Religious education would be unnecessary, only if religion be either altogether useless, or perfectly easy to know and practise.

If religion consisted only in the knowledge of some irrational *dogmas*, or the observance of some unmeaning *forms*, it might be said to be useless. But that is not the true meaning of religion. In its proper sense it means, belief in God, that is, an intelligent and infinite Being, as the Creator and Governor of the universe, belief in the immortality of the soul, and the moulding of life in a manner such as these beliefs require. In this sense, religion concerns not merely a part of man's life but the whole of it; all that he is required to do is directly or indirectly his duty to God; and he must bear the consequences of his acts, both here and hereafter. Thus understood, religion is neither useless nor easy to know and practise. And religious education, so far from being unnecessary, embraces the whole field of education. For the improvement of our physical, intellectual, and moral nature, though directly a duty unto ourselves, is indirectly a duty to God; and physical, intellectual, and moral education must be regarded as a part of our religious education, and must be so given as to qualify us not only for this life but also for the future state.

Another reason why religious education is necessary, is, that if it is neglected, the greater truths of life which it teaches will be kept away from us by the lesser truths, which being more obtrusive in their nature, will soon occupy all our attention.

99. It becomes necessary then to consider what the nature of religious education for a boy should be.

Up to his ninth year it should proceed upon the lines of education in infancy as indicated in the preceding Chapter. In or about his tenth year, a Hindu boy belonging to one of the three higher castes, is formally initiated in his religion. The ceremony, though many parts of it might from a rationalistic point of view, be deemed unnecessary, has much that is, or at one time was, full of meaning, and there is hardly anything in it that is really objectionable. But I need not say more on this point, as with the observance of forms and formalities in religion, I do not here propose to deal.

The religious education of a boy of ten to fifteen years should consist in the *first* place, in the teacher's impressing on him the beliefs common to the principal religions of the earth, and they include belief in the existence of God as the Creator and moral Governor of the universe, and as a Being whose attributes are infinite, and also belief in the immortality of the soul. Though according to some psychologists the infinite is unthinkable, and though it can be conceived only by negation, the religious teacher should do well early to awaken the idea of the Infinite in his pupil's mind, as it is this idea that forms the central one in all religions.

The teacher should in the *second* place impress on his pupil the truth that all our duties are, either directly or indirectly, duties to God; that He sees where no human eye can see, and that every violation of His laws carries with it inevitable evil consequences which we shall have to bear.

The pupil should in the *third* place be taught the salutary lesson that everything happens according to the inexorable laws of God, and that if any evil befalls him, he should not fret and whine, but should proceed according to His laws to get rid of it, and if it is beyond his power to do so, he should submit to the inevitable, with calm resignation, taking proper precaution to avoid falling into similar evils in future.

The teacher should in the *fourth* place endeavour to awaken in his pupil's mind the consoling faith that as the universe is governed by an all-powerful and at the same time all-merciful Ruler, everything must lead to the good of all in the end.

Religion to be practised.

100. Religion, like morality, *has to be practised and not merely to be professed*, and practised not merely in the sense of observing certain forms and formalities, but in the sense of *moulding all action and the whole life according to it.* The pupil should be told with all the earnestness of which the teacher is capable, to remember that God is with him everywhere and at all times, and that everything is in Him. To the Hindu boy he may cite the well-known text of the *Gita*,[1]—

'यो मां पश्यति सर्व्वत्र सर्व्वञ्च मयि पश्यति ।
तस्याहं न प्रणश्यामि स च मे न प्रणश्यति ॥"

"He who sees me everywhere, and everything in me, never loses me and I never lose him."

---

1 Ch. VI, v. 30.

If a boy remembers this great truth, that God is omnipresent, he will never feel helpless, and will never go wrong. He will always be prayerful in the true sense of the word, and will find deliverance from evil. Of formal prayer I will say nothing except this, that if it consists in mere words, "Words without thoughts never to Heaven go." It is only when prayer is prompted by faith in the presence of God that it can have any efficacy.

Controversial points to be avoided.

The religious teacher of boys should avoid dwelling on controversial points. The intellect during boyhood is unfit to discuss questions upon which the highest mature intellects have failed to arrive at unanimity; and the result of discussion upon such questions will be to unsettle the minds of his pupils. Occasion may arise when such discussion might seem unavoidable; as, for instance, when a boy asks his religious teacher to reconcile any religious observance in his family with his notion of the fitness of things. Perhaps the simplest and safest explanation which the teacher can give, assuming of course that the observance involves nothing morally wrong (and happily most religious observances satisfy this condition), is, that as God is infinite in His attributes, things inconsistent with finite beings may be reconcilable in Him.

How should religious education be given.

101. The answer to the third question is not very difficult. Considering the diversity of the creeds professed by the people of this country, and considering the necessity of the religious teacher being of the

same persuasion as the pupil, it must be admitted that the home and not the school should be the place for direct religious education. But we should not object to a teacher (whatever his own creed may be) availing himself of every opportunity of indirectly inculcating on his pupils the truths common to all the principal religions of the world. Then again, as Sir J. Fitch very properly remarks,[1] where a school is a boarding institution exercising ontrol over the whole of a boy's time, it should provide for religious education.

SECTION V.—INSTRUMENTS OF EDUCATION.

Instruments of education in Boyhood.

102. The Instruments of Education in Boyhood are (I) Teachers, (II) Text-books, (III) Schools, and (IV) Examinations.

I. TEACHERS.

I. Teacher.

103. The aid of a good teacher, which is always useful, is absolutely necessary for education in boyhood. A boy, however intelligent he may be, requires the guidance of a teacher to learn any subject. Hence it is that the importance of the teacher is so much emphasized in the writings of our sages, and notably in the Institutes of Manu (Chapter II).

---

1 Lectures on Teaching, p. 427.

The qualifications of a good teacher are :

(1) that he should *know well the subject* he teaches ;

(2) that he should *know how to teach* it ;

(3) that he should have a *powerful voice* and *distinct articulation,* and be of *even temper* and of *high character ;*

(4) that he should have *liking for his work* ; and

(5) that he should have *love for his pupils.*

104. The first qualification is evidently necessary. The teacher must not only know his subject, but he must *know it well,* so as to be able *to meet any unexpected difficulty* that his puplis may find, and *to create in them an interest in the subject* by pointing out its importance in the advanced stages of their progress. **Should know his subject well.**

105. The second is equally necessary. For one may know a subject, and yet he may not know how to teach it. To teach a subject well, one must know how to present it shortly and effectively ; he must know what the different mental processes are by which minds of different degrees of acuteness can grasp it ; he must know what the different points are that present difficulties to the learner, and how they are to be removed ; in short, he must *know the science and art of teaching* which constitute a special branch of study. I may here name a few of the important books on the subject of Teaching which I would earnestly request every teacher to read, if he has not read them already. **Should know how to teach.**

They are:

Locke on Education.
Spencer on Education.
Bain on Education.
Sir J. Fitch on Teaching.
Landon's Principles and Practice of Teaching.
Rousseau's Emile by Payne.
Froebel's Education of Man by Hailmann.
Oscar Browning's Educational Theories.
Gill's System of Education.
Gill's School Management.
Thring's Theory and Practice of Teaching.
Laurie's Training of Teachers.
Raymont's Principles of Education.
Todhunter's Conflict of Studies and other Essays.
Harrison on the Choice of Books.

In recommending the study of these and other similar books, I must not be understood as requesting teachers to adopt the views, or follow the methods, approved in any of them, with implicit reliance on the authority of a great name. In adopting any definite views on any subject, and in following any particular methods in doing any work, every man must think for himself. To use a homely metaphor, 'a workman works best with his own tools.' But before adopting any particular views or methods relating to any subject, *it is always well to know what great minds have thought* about it, instead of relying solely on our own intelligence however strong and acute it may be.

The best way to ascertain whether the mode adopted by the teacher is the proper one, would be for the teacher to examine his pupils at the end of each day or week, with a view to see whether what he has been teaching is well understood. Such an examination by the teacher himself will test not only *his pupil's capacity to understand*, but also *his own ability to explain*, the lessons; and it will show where and how far the mode of teaching adopted requires modification. Every teacher ought to avail himself of this simple test.

Should have a strong voice and clear articulation, and be of even temper and high character.

106. Besides knowing his subject and knowing how to teach it, a teacher must also possess the third qualification, without which he will not be able successfully *to practise the art of teaching*, even if he is versed in the science of teaching. In the opinion of some psychologists, the apparent differences of intelligence in boys are often resolvable into differences of acuteness in their senses of sight and hearing. Now teaching for boys must be mainly oral; and if the teacher has not a strong voice and a clear articulation, his words with all the modulations of his voice, which must be distinctly heard to make his teaching effective, will fail to produce the necessary impression on boys whose apparent dullness proceeds from want of acuteness in the sense of hearing.

The teacher must further be of even temper. For if his temper is liable to be ruffled by any disturbing cause, as from the nature of his vocation many such causes must frequently arise, he will often find himself *unfit for the moment to teach* his pupils; and if his temper manifests itself in harshness towards them, he will find them for the moment equally *unfit to receive his teaching*. Locke has very rightly observed:[1] "It is as impossible to draw fair and regular characters on a trembling mind as on a shaking paper;" and we may add, "It is as difficult for a mind agitated with anger to convey clear ideas on complex topics, and it is for a hand trembling from palsy to make a neat copy of a complicated diagram."

Then again the teacher, not only of morality but of literary or scientific subjects as well, must be a man of high character. For in order to be able to engage the serious attention of his pupils, which he must do to make his teaching effective, he should *command respect*; and he cannot do so without possessing a high character.

Should have liking for his work.

107. The fourth qualification is equally necessary. For although a teacher may be physically and intellectually fit for his work, yet if he has no liking for it, but does it from a feeling of necessity, as, for instance, when he does it only to earn his living, or under a feeling of discontent owing to his emoluments not being as he wishes, he will not be *able to put forth his energies* in imparting his lessons with that effective zeal which love of the work alone can create. No doubt a man with a high sense of

[1] Thoughts on Education, § 167.

duty will rather not undertake any work if he does not like it, than do it in a half-hearted way; but as such men are rare, it behoves those who have to employ teachers, to see, not only that they are qualified for the work, but also that they will do it cheerfully.

There was a time in this country when teaching was considered the highest work of man, and was almost entirely gratuitous. But that was so, mainly because the knowledge most sought for was spiritual knowledge, the cultivation of which made its professors indifferent to their temporal wants, and partly also because men of wealth and rank vied with one another in honouring the learned and removing their wants. Those times are gone, and it will not be possible to recall them. *The State should therefore accord to the teaching profession due rank and adequate emoluments*; and modern society, instead of measuring the worth of a man by the wealth he can earn, *should show ill-remunerated teachers the respect which is their due,* if it cares for the welfare of future generations of men which must depend largely upon the efficient teaching of the present generation of boys.

108. The last qualification of a teacher, though not by any means the least in importance, is, that he should have love for his pupils. Without this, no teaching can be effective. This qualification in a teacher increases the efficiency of his teaching in two ways. In the *first* place, a loving teacher

And love fo his pupils.

sympathises with his pupils when they are in difficulty, and he tries to explain and remove it and to help their understanding, instead of chiding their dullness; and so *he makes their work easy.* And then in the *second* place, his love for them awakens in them a reciprocity of feeling which enables him to secure willing obedience and attention and increased receptivity for his teaching; and so *they in their turn make his work easy.*

On the other hand, the absence of this qualification in a teacher otherwise competent, will often reduce his work to the mere carrying out of dull routine, without that earnestness which the teacher's love for his pupils can alone inspire. I have heard it said that though a sentimental people like the Indians may like to have sympathy from everyone and in everything, other and more practical races would prefer to do their work as business men, purely from a sense of duty; and that is all that is needed. It is unnecessary here to examine this assertion in all its bearings. But so far as the subject of teaching is concerned, I must, with all respect for those who make the assertion, say that it cannot be correct. For teaching a subject does not consist in merely giving a course of lectures or a series of lessons in that subject, with such explanation as the teacher may think necessary; but *it requires that the pupils should learn the subject, and it is not complete until that object is attained.* But to attain that object, that is, to make the pupil learn the subject, the teacher must feel as the pupil does; he must know and appreciate his pupil's difficulties; and remove them as well as he can.

Want of sympathy in a teacher often leads to practical inconveniences. I have heard it said that no subject should be gone over a second time, as the prospect of revision makes pupils inattentive during the first reading. There may be some small truth in this, but it is only an unsympathetic teacher who will refuse to help his pupils in revising their lessons, for the purpose of enforcing attention, especially when it is a truth, well established by experience, that no subject of study can be thoroughly grasped in all its bearings at the first reading.

When the want of sympathy develops into a positive feeling of contempt for the mental inferiority of the pupil, it leads to evil in another way. The teacher by attributing the ill-success of his teaching to the want of capacity in the pupil to learn, and not to want of ability in himself to teach, *places himself in possession of a dangerous and often erroneous excuse which must unconsciously operate, to the detriment of diligent work.* The teacher should bear in mind that his function is to teach those placed under his care, however humble their powers may be.

The necessity of an educator's having sympathy for those whom he undertakes to educate is strikingly pointed out in a story I have heard related of the Prophet of Islam. Among his followers (so runs the story) there was a poor old man who had a son that was very fond of sugar; and the father with his scanty means found it very difficult to provide his son with that article of luxury. So he went with his son to the Prophet to be shown a way out of his difficulty. Mohammad after hearing them, directed them to come again after a fortnight. They did so. And Mohammad in a decisive tone commanded the son to give up the habit of eating sugar, pointing out to him that, though inconvenient, it was not impossible to do so, if he proceeded gradually by reducing the quantity of sugar he took day by day. They made their obeisance and took leave; but in a few moments the old man came back, and after begging the Prophet's pardon, asked him, how it was that it took him fifteen days to think out the simple direction that he had given. The Prophet smiled and said that it was because he himself was very fond of sugar, and he wanted to see if he could give up his own habit; for he did not think it right to give his followers any direction which he could not himself have carried out. The story may not be authentic; but the lesson it teaches is invaluable, namely, that *we should not give any direction to, or impose any task on, others which we could not ourselves have carried out.*

Teachers' Association.

109. Teachers should unite and form a Teachers' Association which would afford opportunities for their meeting together to discuss educational questions. Such an association is calculated to promote the interests of education in many ways. It would enable teachers to compare notes from time to time so that each may profit by the knowledge and

experience of his colleagues in the profession. It would foster friendly relations between different educational institutions. And it would raise the status of teachers by uniting them into an organized body, the dignity of which, unlike the strength of a chain which is measured by that of its weakest link, is estimated by the worth of its most respected member.

II.—Text-books

110. For the education of boys, the importance of text-books is next to that of teachers. In the earliest stage of a boy's progress when he is learning to read, a text-book of Alphabetical Primer is necessary to exercise him in reading. In later stages, after he has learnt to read, a text-book is of use, not much at first as a source of instruction, which must still proceed from oral teaching, but for recalling what the teacher has said at the previous lesson, and for preparing for what he will say at the next day's lesson. And as the boy progresses further, it will serve as a source of instruction, supplemented by oral teaching where necessary. In fact, the teacher does his work most efficiently, when he has trained his pupil early to be able to derive instruction from books with the least amount of aid from oral teaching. The habit of self-reliance is as necessary in study as in other concerns of life; and one of the great drawbacks to the formation of that habit is the appointment of bad or unsuitable text-books.

II. Text-books.

Text-books necessary for boys in English as in other subjects

111. There is great diversity of opinion as to the necessity and propriety of prescribing text-books in subjects other than literature in the higher stages of a student's progress. I shall revert to this point when dealing with education in youth. In regard to education in boyhood, the necessity of text-books in all subjects other than English is unanimously admitted; but there is difference of opinion as to whether English should be taught with the help of text-books, or should be learnt by the student from the reading of a wide range of books to be recommended but not to be regularly taught. With all respect for the opinion of those who support the latter alternative, I would venture to say that that view is not sound. It is based mainly on the ground that if text-books are prescribed in English, boys learn the text-books and not English, and they endeavour only to commit to memory keys and commentaries on the text. But is that so? And will boys learn English better if there be no text-books prescribed? I must answer these questions in the negative. For as ordinary language consists of repetition of a limited number of words and forms of expression, if text-books are well chosen and intelligently read, the reader will necessarily learn the language in which they are written, besides learning their subject-matter; whereas, on the other hand, if there are no text-books, and the student has to go over a wide range of books, he will necessarily have to read them hurriedly and superficially; and thus *notwithstanding that he may read more*

he will know less of the peculiarities of the language than if he had confined his attention to fewer books. An Indian boy of fourteen or fifteen years who has to read his other subjects through the medium of a difficult foreign language, has neither the time nor the ability to benefit by a wide range of rapid reading in English; and the indirect result will be to encourage the habit of superficial reading which is by no means desirable in a student. I am, therefore, of opinion that in the education of boys, *we ought to have text-books in all the subjects of study.*

Text-books should be carefully prepared.

112. But if text-books are of such great importance, they must be *carefully prepared and judiciously selected.* The preparation of text-books is always a difficult task, and the difficulty is much greater, when the book is to be written for the use of little boys, than when it is intended for more advanced students; for the former require more help, and have a smaller stock of words and ideas by the manipulation of which new ideas are to be expressed and explained to them, than the latter.

Points to be kept in view in preparing text-books.

113. I have already made some passing remarks about the requisites of good text-books, when speaking of alphabetical primers. I shall here make a few general observations on the points to be kept in view in preparing text-books specially for boys.

(1) A text-book should in point of *size* be as *short* as possible consistently with *clearness* and reasonable *completeness.*

A short book is likely to be less expensive and to be more encouraging to the reader from the prospect of being likely to be sooner finished, than a bulky one.

If the book is one of Reading Lessons in prose or poetry, either composed by the author himself or compiled from other authors, it should not be longer than what students for whom it is intended can go through in the course of one year, reading at a moderate rate and having time for revision. It is sometimes said that a long book of reading lessons is better than a short one, as it leaves room for selection of lessons by the teacher. I do not think that this is a sound view. While, on the one hand, the author's selection, if good, need not be supplemented by the teacher's selection, on the other hand, not only does a long book, a part of which alone could have been intended to be read, involve waste of time and energy to the author and waste of money to the readers, but the reading of a lesson here and a lesson there out of a book instead of reading it through, is *injurious to the formation of that habit of steady thoroughness, which is so essential in a student* and of such great value in after life.

If the book is one on Grammar, or Geography, or History, or Arithmetic, and is intended for students reading the subject for the first time, it should treat the subject in an elementary way, and so as not to require more than two or three years to finish it, care being taken *where the book is not likely to be finished in one year, to prescribe the same book for two or three consecutive classes.*

I think it necessary to say this, because I have sometimes found that different books on Grammar or Geography are prescribed for two consecutive classes, and students go on reading the same portion of the subject from two different books in two successive years, when they could have finished the subject if they had the same book prescribed for the two classes.

Text-books in Arithmetic, Algebra and Geometry should not have their bulk needlessly increased by the inclusion of too many or too difficult examples for practice, which, instead of giving the student encouragement for exercise, positively discourage him, owing to his inability to get through them.

(2) A text-book should in point of *form* be *neat* so as to create in the reader a liking for it; and all such *aids to attention* as the printing of *important* words in capitals, italics or antique letters, and illustration by *pictures* or *diagrams*, should be freely availed of.

In elementary text-books, directions for the teacher, if any, should be collected together either at the beginning or at the end of the book, and *things not intended to be read by the student, should never be interposed among those intended to be read by him.* Such interposition distracts attention.

(3) A text book, in point of *language* and *style*, should be *concise* and *clear*, *simple* and *attractive*; and *verbosity and indirectness of statement should be avoided.*

Unnecessary words in a text-book puzzle the reader who naturally expects that every word has a meaning; and want of directness of expression prevents him from understanding the meaning readily. Indirectness of expression, though sometimes a rhetorical beauty, is often a logical blemish, proceeding from ignorance or indecision. If the author has to speak on a point about which he is not clear, he should directly say so.

Text-books in Literature should avoid making selections from authors who are verbose or diffuse.

In early times in India, when the multiplication of text-books could be made only by the laborious process of copying, they used to be composed in the aphoristic style, and the following is given as the definition of an aphorism (*sutra*) :—

स्वल्पाक्षरमसन्दिग्धं सारवद्विश्वतो मुखं ।
अस्तोभमनवद्यञ्च सूत्रं सूत्रविदो विदुः ॥

"The wise understand an aphorism to be composed of the fewest letters, to be unambiguous, to relate to a material point, to deal with it in all its bearings, to be free from expletives, and to be unobjectionable."

The writers of text-books would do well to bear this in mind, though they must avoid the want of clearness which the brevity of the aphoristic writings involves.

(4). A text-book should in point of *matter* aim at teaching things *rationally* and not mechanically, but at the same time *avoid embarrassing and encumbering the student with help* in the shape of explanation. It should encourage him to think, but should not think out everything for him.

(5). A text-book should furthermore in point of *matter* deal only with those *broad* points of the subject which a general student can fairly be expected to retain in his memory; and it should not be encumbered with such *details* as can properly find a place only in books of reference or advanced text-books for those who intend to become specialists.

This is an important rule, but is often disregarded, owing to the ambition of authors to compress within their books all the learning on the subject, and to the anxiety of teachers to make their pupils learn at once all that can be said on the subject. This, I think, is a great mistake. The fabric of knowledge, like material fabrics, must be gradually built up, and it is vain aspiration to seek to raise it high all at once, without securing a proper basis. The capacity for knowledge expands gradually; and to force into the mind more detailed knowledge than it can assimilate, will be to spoil even the little it could have easily retained. Moreover, it is not right to compel a boy to encumber his mind with details which will be of little use to him, and which he will be little likely to remember when he grows up as a man. Mere exercise of memory, unlike the exercise of reason, has very little disciplinary effect. Nor is there any lack of really useful matter to exercise the memory.

Some are of opinion that it is only by making the memory retain many details at first, that we can insure its retaining in the end the few that are really important. No doubt it is well to have a higher aim so that at least a lower one might be reached; but it is no high aim to commit to memory unnecessary details.

Selection of text-books.

114. The selection of text-book is an important and not by any means an easy task. The simple rule to follow is, to select the best among the books that answer the required description. When among competing books there is one of decidedly superior merit, there is little difficulty in selecting it. But when that is not the case, and among the best available books there are more than one of nearly equal merit, a new principle comes into play, namely, that of distribution of patronage among authors of equal merit. That may be a good rule to follow; but as two books are seldom of exactly equal merit, the introduction of the second principle often makes us unconsciously err, and allow the second best book to share the patronage with, if not to displace, the best.

With regard to text-books such as those in literature, which are to be compilations from the writings of standard authors, and text-books in Sanskrit Grammar which are to be compiled from the aphorisms of standard authors according to a prescribed syllabus, the question may arise whether they should be selected out of those produced in the market, or should be prepared under the supervision of the prescribing authority. As books of these descriptions owe their large sale to the action of the prescribing authority, and as they do not exact any unusual exercise of intelligence in the compiler, I think it would be no undue interference with free competition to adopt the latter alternative, which has the further advantage of ensuring greater conformity with the prescribed requirements.

III.—Schools.

Schools. Day Schools better suited for little boys than Boarding Schools.

115. As in infancy, so in the earlier years of boyhood, that is, up to the ninth or at least the seventh year, education should be received at home and not at school. My reason for postponing the sending of a boy to school is not exactly that given by Locke,[1] namely, fear of spoiling the boy's manners by the bad example of the school fellows; but it is this, that a boy up to his seventh or his ninth year requires individual attention to be paid to him such as cannot be expected at school, and he is unfit to profit fully by listening to what is addressed to him in common with many others. Boys sent to school

[1] Thoughts on Education, § 70.

early, make much less progress than those of the same age who are taught at home. Nor do I think lightly of Locke's reason for not sending a boy early to school, though I do not go quite so far as he does. After the ninth year, I would prefer school education to home training, but I would send a boy to a day school and not to a boarding institution. My reasons for taking this view may be summed up shortly thus:—

In the *first* place, though a boarding institution may be a little more adapted for physical and intellectual education, it is much less adapted for moral and religious training, than a boy's own home, and the advantage in one respect is more than counterbalanced by the disadvantage in the other. The home where we live with those we naturally love and respect, must be more conducive to the growth of the unselfish and altruistic virtues, so necessary for our contentment and happiness, than the best boarding institution, where regard for fellow boarders and respect for superiors must be of an enforced character in the beginning at least. There is moreover another element of difference which cannot be eliminated, and which must operate to the disadvantage of a boarding school. Whereas all the comfort and convenience a boy may enjoy at home is obtained for love, in a boarding institution they are bought for money, and sometimes vary according to the fees paid. It was the absence of this element of difference which made the teacher's house where the student in ancient India used to reside, as good as his home. And then as regards religious education, in a country like India with its diversity of creeds, even the best regulated boarding school can be expected to make but very imperfect arrangements.

In the *second* place the large numbers of students with whom boarding schools have to deal, must make mechanical discipline take the place of personal supervision in a much greater degree there than in a boy's own home; and this must be a disadvantage with such institutions, especially in the case of boys who stand so much in need of personal attention.

Questions for consideration under this head.

Two important questions relating to schools require consideration here—

(1) What are the requirements of a good school?

(2) What should the mutual relations of one school with another be?

Requirements of a good School.

116. The requirements of a good school are, *first*, that it should have a commodious building and compound and should be located in a healthy and convenient place; *second*, that it should have a staff of teachers, in point of ability, competent to teach the different subjects of study, and in point of number, sufficient to enable them to give attention to the individual wants of the pupils; and, *third*, that it should work according to a set of simple but efficient rules and under proper supervision.

The first requirement is essential for the purpose of securing the health and comfort of the boys attending the school.

The second condition must be satisfied in order to ensure the efficiency of teaching. The teachers must not only *be able to teach the different subjects* of study, but they must also *have time to attend to the individual wants of their pupils.* To secure this latter object, no teacher should be placed in charge of more than forty pupils in the three higher classes, and more than thirty in the remaining classes, the demand for individual attention rising higher as we descend lower. Where a class consists of more than the allowable number of boys, it should be divided into sections, and the number of teachers must not be less than the number of classes, each section of a class counting as a separate class.

A rule limiting the number of boys in a class, is absolutely necessary for the teaching of boys, because their individual wants require to be attended to in a much greater degree than those of grown-up students. Such a rule exists in other countries. Thus we read in Mathew Arnold's Higher Schools and Universities in Germany, (p. 105), that it exists in that country. And it is necessary in this country much more than anywhere else, because here a boy has to read his different subjects of study through the medium of a foreign language, which increases the difficulty of his learning them, and makes him more dependent upon the teacher's help than he would otherwise have been. Moreover, a boy to be taught properly, must have regular and frequent exercises in his subjects of study; and the teacher will not have sufficient time to correct these exercises and set his pupils right where they go wrong, unless their number is reasonably limited.

One of the really beneficial changes (among others of perhaps doubtful utility) recently introduced by the Calcutta University, is the adoption of a rule limiting the number of boys in a class.

There is a practical difficulty in carrying out such a rule, which I do not lose sight of. Most of our schools are unendowed institutions which depend for their support on the schooling fees collected ; and it is not possible for them to employ good teachers and place them in charge of small classes, unless they can raise the schooling fee sufficiently high. But with the limits I have suggested as to the number of boys in a class, I think a fairly competent staff of teachers can be secured by fixing the fee for the last three classes at one rupee, that for the next three at two rupees, and that for the first three at three rupees.

The above consideration points to the rule for the maximum number of boys in a class as the natural and legitimate rule for regulating the minimum rate of fee which a school should charge ; and any other rule for regulating the rate of schooling fee must be artificial and arbitrary.

The third condition is necessary to secure efficient management of the school. There must be some controlling authority, whether it be a committee or a single individual, to see that the teachers work regularly ; and there must also be a set of simple and efficient rules for the guidance of teachers. The rules should be few and simple, to prevent difficulties arising as to their meaning and effect; and they should be efficient, that is, so framed as to ensure effective work. I would here suggest that for the latter purpose the two following rules should be observed by all schools :—

(*a*) The progress and conduct of each boy should be reported to his guardian once every month; and to save time and expense. the report may be noted in the receipt granted to the boy on the payment of his schooling fee.

(*b*) After the annual examination, a table should be prepared for the information of the public, showing the *average progress of every class* (that is, the average of the marks obtained by the boys of the class) in each subject; and for the encouragement of teachers, some mark of recognition should be shewn to the teacher whose class attains the highest average.

With regard to the desirability of the annual distribution of prizes to meritorious students, there is some difference of opinion, many educationists (among whom the late Pandit Iswara Chandra Vidyasagara was one) maintaining that it does more harm than good, as it gives encouragement to only a few of the best boys who will do just as well without it, while it has a discouraging effect on the majority. I am in favour of it, as a source of general encouragement, and I think the objection to it may be to a great extent removed by raising the number of prizes in each class from three, which is often the usual number, to half a dozen or more, so as to give boys of fair merit a chance of winning them.

117. As the multiplication of good schools within reasonable limits is conducive to the spread of education, such schools have a common object in promoting the welfare of society; and their relations ought therefore to be friendly and not hostile. But there is one reason why the opposite is not unfrequently the case, and it is this. As schools generally depend for their support upon the fees realized, when two schools are so situated that they can both draw their boys from a common area, in proportion as one of them succeeds the other must fail unless the number of school-going boys in the neighbourhood is large enough to support both. The course generally recommended and adopted to remedy this evil, is that the Universities and the Government Education Department should refuse to recognize any new school which is likely to be injurious to the interests of discipline and education.

Relations between different schools.

This is no doubt a sound rule in theory, but its practical application is not always easy and safe, owing to the indefiniteness and uncertainty of the tests to be applied. It is not always easy to say, judging from present circumstances, whether a new school may not exist without material injury to an old one, and with real benefit to it by relieving it of its excess of pupils; nor is it safe to predict whether

Recognition of new schools.

in future the co-existence of the two schools may not prove beneficial to the interests of education by drawing more students into them than would have otherwise sought for education, for though ordinarily supply should follow demand, it often happens also that supply increases and even creates demand. I would suggest that, with a view to moderate the operation of the rule stated above, a supplementary rule be followed to the effect, that when a school is started not for profit, it shall be presumed, until the contrary is shown, that it is not injurious to the interests of discipline and education.

Transfer of students.

A rule often advocated in the interest of education and discipline, is that no student shall be allowed to obtain transfer from one institution to another in the middle of a session, unless it be for special reasons. Such a rule, in my opinion, is not only attended with hardship on students but is calculated to impair the efficiency of schools. For, on the one hand, a student may ask for transfer by reason either of a favourable change in his circumstances enabling him to join a better institution, or of unfavourable change in the condition of his school rendering transfer to a better school necessary; and it is most undesirable that he should be compelled to state such a reason. And, on the other hand, a rule like this, lending artificial support to an inefficient school, may stand in the way of its exerting energetically to improve its condition. A school should retain its students not by the operation of a transfer rule to prop up its inefficiency, but through their spontaneous attachment to it resulting from its own merits. I think the only safe and sound rule to restrict transfer is, to disallow transfer when it is applied for to evade discipline.

IV. Examinations.

118. The questions that arise for consideration under this head are—

Examinations. Questions for consideration under this head.

(1) Whether our system of public examinations should be continued?

(2) If so, what should the standards of different examinations be? and

(3) How should examinations be conducted?

119. The results of teaching, that is, the acquisition of knowledge and attainment of culture by those receiving education, require to be tested before their education can be pronounced to be finished; and the test, before the development of the present system of examinations, was furnished in this country as in most others[1] by disputations conducted by advanced students in the presence of competent judges. With the progress of society, and the increase in the number of those coveting the distinction of being pronounced accomplished scholars, more compendious and exact methods of testing the merits of pupils became necessary, and thus our present system of examinations gradually grew up; and its importance was raised by a similar system

Necessity of examinations.

[1] See Latham's Action of Examinations, Chap. III.

being adopted for the selection of candidates for employment in the public service. The method of determining the merits of candidates by the marks awarded to answers to individual questions, helped to secure the integrity of examinations much better than the method of judging by the impression produced by an answer paper taken as a whole, by placing examiners beyond the possibility of being unconsciously swayed by unperceived influences; and, on the whole, the system of examination by marks had the effect of exterminating jobbery and favouritism in the distribution of academic and other public patronage, and was for a time looked upon as one of unmixed good. But in course of time, certain evil effects of the system as it has been working (such as the encouragement of cramming) came to be perceived, and a reaction has commenced, resulting in examinations being looked upon with disfavour more or less almost everywhere, and in an authoritative pronouncement in this country "that special competitions should, as a general rule, be dispensed with."[1] The question then arises whether our system of public examinations should continue.

Evils of the present system.

The evils of the present system of examinations that have been most loudly complained of are, that it fails to test real merit; that it demoralizes the student by making him study, not for gaining knowledge but for winning distinction; and that it makes

[1] Resolution of the Government of India, dated the 11th March 1904, para. 11.

teaching subserve the purpose of enabling students to gain transient success, losing sight of its higher aim of imparting sound knowledge.

If these evils be irremediable, then it would be matter for serious consideration whether the present system should be allowed to continue. But are they really so? I think not. They can be remedied, if not wholly, at least to such an extent as to make the advantages of the system far outweigh its disadvantages.

Are examinations necessarily no test for real merit?

The first mentioned evil, namely, the failure of examinations to test real merit, arises from our over-anxiety to exclude mediocrity, which has made us fix our standard so high that even the best competitors are unable to attain it by honest exertion and self-reliant study, and this has led to that system of coaching and cramming which artificially props up the weak, which often prevents the strong from exercising their strength, and which, except for a few of the best who are unaffected by the faults of the system, makes the result of an examination depend upon a retentive memory and the tact of showing to advantage the little knowledge that has been acquired. With our age limits,—and they must exist considering the shortness of life and the fact of the examination stimulus being unsuitable and injurious after a certain age,—what more can you expect, when you require a youth of not more than twenty years to be examined in the whole of English Literature, the whole of Mathematics, or a wide range of History, and sometimes on combinations of these? The qualities that these examinations test are no doubt valuable, but they are not always those that are most useful in life, namely, the possession of sound knowledge and not knowledge hurriedly acquired to be forgotten as fast, and the possession of an intellect, acute and not flashy but capable of sustained exertion. But considering the nature and origin of the evil, it is clear that the remedy lies in our own hands, and consists in our adopting a standard, high enough to exclude incompetency, but not so high as to make it unattainable by fair intelligence except through cramming.

Do examinations really demoralize students?

The second ground of complaint referred to above, is based upon misconception. It is true that the desire for gaining emoluments or distinction by passing examinations is the main motive for study with the majority of students, and it is only a few who study merely for gaining knowledge. It is true also, that it is most desirable that knowledge should be pursued for its own sake. But the pursuit of knowledge though not unattended with pleasure, requires labour; and it would be contrary to human nature that knowledge should be pursued for its own sake and without any extraneous motive, unless the pleasure of the pursuit over-balances the trouble inseparable from it; and it is only a few with whom that is the case in any society. How then can the abolition of public examinations or the weakening of the stimulus furnished by them, improve matters? If public examinations are abolished, or by some contrivance, the stimulus furnished by them weakened, its only effect will be to reduce the number of those who studied under the influence of that stimulus, without in any way increasing the number of those who pursue knowledge for its own sake. It is a mistake to suppose then that public examinations have any real effect in demoralizing students who would otherwise have acted under a noble impulse.

Do examinations necessarily affect teaching prejudicially?

The third evil, like the first, no doubt really exists; but like the first, it is the result of our erroneous endeavour to raise the standard of examination above the limit attainable by fair intelligence aided by ordinary teaching. The questions set at our examinations, moreover, serve by their crotchetiness and mannerism to enhance the evil. Teachers find that the natural mode of teaching in which the pupil must be left to work for himself with only general directions, and special aid in getting over difficulties, will hardly do, when the extent of work to be gone through does not leave the student time to think, and the nature of the questions which examinees will have to answer, requires special coaching; and they have accordingly been forced to subordinate teaching to examination. The remedy for the evil which is not necessarily in the system of public examinations, but arises from the mode in which it is worked, lies entirely in our hands. We have only to prescribe courses of study which can be gone through by the student with reasonable help within the time allowed, and to set searching but fair questions, instead of ingenious puzzles, at our examinations, and the evil complained of will soon disappear.

But even if any of the evils of the system of public examinations be irremediable, still the system must continue, because examinations are a necessary evil, as Huxley remarks,[1] and there is no other system that can well be substituted for it. The only substitute sometimes recommended is examination by the teachers. But that will not do, because a system of examination of pupils by their teachers will not inspire confidence in its results, nor will it ensure uniformity of quality in those pronounced successful by different teachers.

Standards of x aminations.

120. The standard of an examination should be fixed with due regard to the progress likely to be attained by the pupils at the stage of their career at which the examination is held. Thus in order to fix the standard of an examination we should settle the number of public examinations that a student should pass before completing his school education. I am of opinion that the number should not exceed two, and that of the two examinations, the first should be held five years after a boy has entered school, and stand about midway between the present Primary and Anglo-Vernacular examinations, and the second held at the close of the school course.

The former will test the completion of primary education, and the latter that of secondary school education. The intermediate Anglo-Vernacular ex-

1 Science and Culture and other Essays, p. 59.

amination needlessly increases the pressure of public examinations, without serving any really useful purpose, or marking any natural period in the boy's educational progress. If my suggestion increases the period of primary education, it does so most usefully, without producing any undue strain on the parents of the boys; and the increased period may be utilized by adding to the list of subjects a little English, without some knowledge of which one cannot get on well at all at the present day. The standard for this examination should be the course of study I have suggested in Section II, for a boy at the age of ten years, Sanskrit being treated as an optional subject (see paragraph 68).

The standard for the second examination, which is to test the completion of School education, that is, education completed at the age of fifteen years, as distinguished from College or University education, should be, on the whole, the same as that fixed for the Calcutta University Entrance or Matriculation Examination with some modifications.

The course of study for this examination should consist of –

I. English.
II. A Second Language.
III. Mathematics, that is, Arithmetic, Algebra and Geometry.
IV. History and Geography, that is, History of India, History of England, and General or Descriptive Geography.

The knowledge of English required should be a practical or working knowledge of the language sufficient to enable the student to understand the lectures of College professors and text-books in different subjects in that language, and to carry on the ordinary business of daily life through the medium of that language; but English literature should not be altogether excluded from the course, and the text-books prescribed in English should consist of selections in prose and poetry from the writings of standard authors such as are of perennial and universal interest.

The second language for Indian students should be either a classical language such as Sanskrit or Arabic with an allied vernacular, or an Indian vernacular.

The course in Mathematics should include the whole of Arithmetic, Algebra up to Quadratic Equations, and the first four books ef Euclid's Elements of Geometry or the substance thereof treated according to modern method. I have already stated my reasons for thinking that Euclid's Elements may well be replaced by modern works on the subject, and I need not repeat them.

The text-books in History should be such as give a broad general view of the past, with special reference to the manner in which the past state of things has led to the present, matters of detail which do not interest the general reader and are not likely to be retained long in the memory, being left out. It is not easy to find such books, but demand will create supply. Geography should include only general Descriptive Geography, Astronomical and Physical Geography being excluded from the course.

The subjects mentioned above are necessary for completing school education, and they should also be deemed sufficient.

I should mention that the course of study given above differs in some respects from that recently prescribed for the Matriculation Examination by the Calcutta University.

Two questions here arise for consideration :—

(1) Whether there should be an alternative course in which certain practical subjects such as Commercial Arithmetic, Shorthand, and Typewriting should take the place of a Second Language and Geometry ; and (2) whether the examination should have any connection with the University or should be only a School Final Examination.

Alternative courses not desirable.

The alternative course is suggested for the benefit of those students who do not intend to prosecute their studies in a College, and to whom a Second Language and Geometry are thought to be of much less use than the subjects proposed to be substituted in their place. I am not in favour of an alternative course. The object of ordinary school education is not only to impart useful knowledge, but also to train the mind ; and the student who desires to complete his school education should study a Second

Language and Geometry, which, to say nothing of their practical use, are valuable as means of mental training. If he does not wish to prosecute his study any further but is desirous of qualifying himself as a clerk in a Government or mercantile office, he may learn the practical subjects after leaving school, and there will be no difficulty in finding teachers or institutions for the purpose, whereas it would be difficult for an ordinary school to arrange for teaching two alternative courses.

Nor two separate Examinations, the Matriculation and the School Final.

The proposal for having a School Final Examination distinct from the University Entrance or Matriculation Examination is sometimes made with the object of relieving the latter from the numerical pressure upon it resulting from all students upon completion of their school course appearing at it, whether they intend to enter the University or not. It is thought that if there be two examinations, only those intending to enter the University will be drawn to the Entrance or Matriculation Examination. As there must be a separate machinery for conducting the School Final Examination, the proposed change will not effect any economy of labour; it will only at best reduce the number of candidates for the Entrance or Matriculation Examination. That may, perhaps, be an advantage, as the crowding of candidates for an examination is undesirable. But I doubt very much whether the expected result will follow. The Entrance or Matriculation Examination, from the fact of its qualifying a successful candidate to enter the

University, will be considered a higher test than the proposed School Final Examination, and will continue to attract candidates even though they may not intend to prosecute their study further. The remedy for the evil of numerical pressure is to be found in the multiplication of Universities with exclusive local limits, and not in the multiplication of examinations.

121. The question—How should examinations be conducted so as to make them real tests of merit ?—is not very easy to answer. As Huxley has well remarked, " Examination is an art and a difficult art which has to be learned like all other arts." It is a great mistake to suppose that every one who knows a subject is competent to examine others in that subject. I know of instances in which some of the most learned men in their respective subjects entertained rather strange notions about examination in those subjects. Thus, a learned lawyer once said that where a paper had to be set on three Acts of the Indian Legislature, the same number of questions, all carrying equal marks, should be set on each of the three Acts, though one of them consisted of more than 300 sections of great importance and no small difficulty, and the other two of less than 100 sections comparatively less important and less difficult, the reason assigned being that as they were three different Acts on three different subjects, they should be deemed to be of equal value. On another occasion, a learned mathematician was of opinion that answers to questions on Euclid's Elements of Geometry should

Examinations how to be conducted

receive no marks if they were written symbolically, that is, if the symbol $\angle$ was used for the word "angle," $\odot$ for "circle," and the like. This was carrying to an unwarrantable extent the Cambridge rule against the use of the symbol AB. BC for the "rectangle contained by AB and BC," which was cited in its support, but which is intended to prevent Geometrical demonstration imperceptibly gliding into Algebraical. On a third occasion, a scholar of great learning expressed the opinion that where a question consisted of several independent parts, a candidate was not entitled to any marks for answering it unless he answered correctly all the parts; and it was not until after a pretty long and elaborate discussion that he hesitatingly conceded that his view could be correct only when the different parts of the question were so connected by reason of their being dependent on one rule or principle that ignorance as to any one part indicated ignorance of the rule or principle. Many other instances might be mentioned; but it is needless to multiply them. The instances I have given are sufficient to show that the principles upon which examinations should be conducted are not so simple and obvious as one may at first sight suppose. But unfortunately, learned men, and in particular specialists, from their lofty standpoint generally look down upon detailed rules for the conduct of examinations as mere devices to help the incompetent to get through; and they would leave the determination of examination results to the unfettered discretion of examiners. The consequence has been that, though the matter has now and then attracted attention (see Latham's work on the Action of Examinations and Todhunter's Paper on Competitive Examinations published in a book entitled "The Conflict of Studies and other Essays") it has not received the consideration it deserves.

If all that we wanted to ascertain was whether a candidate was perfectly qualified or not, perhaps rules might be dispensed with, and everything left to the discretion of examiners. I say *perhaps* because even a mathematician like Adams, who is said to have obtained only 50 per cent. of the marks at the Mathematical Tripos Examination, could not have been pronounced perfectly qualified. But be that as it may, we cannot expect perfection. If examination is to be not only an absolute test of the worth of the intellect and acquirements of an individual candidate, but also a measure of the relative values of such worth in a number of candidates, it is nothing strange that principles have to be settled and rules framed for regulating the machinery intended for measuring things so difficult to evaluate, when machines and instruments for measuring much less subtle things are designed with so much care.

Points for consideration.

122. The matters requiring consideration here may be grouped under three heads,—

(1) the Selection of Examiners;

(2) the Settling of Minimum Pass Marks and the Setting of Question Papers; and

(3) the Award of Marks to the Answers.

A few general Rules suggested. (1) For selection of Examiners.

123. Much must always depend upon the proper selection of examiners, as notwithstanding all our rules and directions, it will be impossible to eliminate the result of personal equation.

The very first rule should, therefore, be somewhat to the following effect :—

RULE I.—An examiner should not only know his subject well, but he should be possessed of sound judgment, strong common sense, and even temper, and should be absolutely free from bias for or against the examinees or any class of them.

The necessity for the last qualification arises from the fact that candidates of different nationalities appear at our examinations, and learned men not unfrequently are of opinion that candidates of certain nationalities have inherent deficiencies in certain respects.

To preserve the fairness and integrity of our examinations in the strictest possible manner, there should be a second Rule as follows :—

RULE II.—No one engaged in teaching any of the examinees in any subject should be appointed to set questions in that subject.

The necessity for such a rule arises from the fact that otherwise the pupils of the teacher examiner, who would be likely to know his views on the subject he teaches, would have an undue advantage over other candidates. For if such an examiner teaches his subject properly, he must let his pupils know the relative importance and the peculiar bearings of the different portions of his subject; and if he examines properly, he must set his questions in accordance with his views as to such importance and bearings; so that his pupil will be likely to have an idea of the nature of his questions beforehand.

The reason for the rule is obvious. Nor does it imply any slur on the honesty of teachers. Mr. Todhunter, a distinguished Senior Wrangler and a teacher and an examiner of great experience, in his "Conflict of Studies and other Essays" (p. 57), says, "I am astonished to see how completely the necessity and the reason for such a regulation are overlooked or denied." A rule like this was adopted by the Calcutta University on the recommendation of educationists like Sir A. Croft and Mr. Tawney;[1] but I am sorry to say that some high authorities are opposed to its being retained. It has, however, been partially retained in the new regulations of the Calcutta University.

Rule III.—In cases where owing to the large number of the candidates, their answers to a question paper have to be distributed to several examiners, to secure uniformity of standard, a Head Examiner should be appointed in each subject, to ascertain from time to time, as the work proceeds, whether each examiner is examining according to the rules settled at the outset as to the method of awarding marks; but to avoid unnecessary friction and to

[1] See Minutes for 1890-91, p. 49.

overcome the disinclination of competent men with a sense of self-respect to accept examinerships, it should be an instruction to Head Examiners that they are to treat the examiners as colleagues and not as subordinates.

There should be a fourth rule relating to the appointment of examiners to the following effect.

RULE IV.—The appointing authority should, other things being equal, have regard to the representation of the different institutions that send candidates for examination, and give the professors of all colleges a fair share in the work of examination, to minimize the chances of complaint against the fairness of the work, and to make an even distribution of University patronage.

(2) For fixing marks and setting question papers.

124. The *maximum* marks to be *assigned* to each *subject* must be settled before the *minimum pass* marks in it can be properly fixed; and each of the two has to be determined with reference to the relative importance of the subject. Moreover, for an examination like the Entrance or Matriculation in which the number of candidates is large, it is desirable that these matters should be settled beforehand, instead of being left to the discretion of the examiners. So far there is perhaps no difference of opinion. But the difficulty arises in fixing the figures. Should English carry a maximum of 200 marks and mathematics 160? Should the minimum pass marks in the former be 33 or 40 per cent., and in the latter only 25? or should other figures be adopted? And

what should the maximum and minimum marks in the other subjects be? These are questions of some nicety and can be answered only roughly.

The inportance of a subject depends upon the amount of useful knowledge its study imparts, and the degree of mental training such study insures. Keeping this in view, it may roughly be estimated that of the four subjects for the Entrance or Matriculation Examination, the Second Language and History and Geography are almost equal in importance. Mathematics is a little more important than either of those two, as well by reason of the greater usefulness of the knowledge acquired by its study as by reason of the greater degree of the mental training secured, the excess in importance roughly speaking being more than a fourth and less than one half, or being taken at one-third as much again; while English for its additional importance as the medium through which Mathematics and History and Geography have to be studied, may be taken to be about a quarter more important than Mathematics. On this estimation, the four subjects should be valued thus:—

History and Geography	valued	at 3,	carrying	120	marks.
Second Language	,,	3,	,,	120	,,
Mathematics	,,	4,	,,	160	,,
English	,,	5,	,,	200	,,

The minimum pass marks in a subject might perhaps be not inappropriately fixed at one-third, making allowance of a third for the incompleteness of the candidate's knowledge in point of quantity, and of another one-third for the imperfection of his knowledge in point of quality, that is, for his want of precision and order in expressing himself. But as all students have not the same aptitude for all the subjects, this minimum should be insisted upon only in the all-important subject English, and in the other subjects, a lower minimum of one-fourth of the full marks may be accepted, provided a candidate makes up his deficiency in individual subjects by his proficiency in the aggregate; so that the rule for minimum pass marks may stand thus:—

A candidate in order to pass must obtain one-third of the full marks in English, one-fourth of the full marks in the other subjects, and one-third of the full marks in the aggregate.

This preliminary point being thus roughly settled, we come to the principal matter for consideration, namely, the framing of question papers. This is a very important function of examiners, as it influences not only the result of the examination, but indirectly also, the teaching of students. For while only a small minority of students, namely, the best, read regardless of the kind of test to which they may be subjected, the great majority regulate their reading so as to be able to come out successful at the expected trial. If then there is any mannerism or peculiarity in the question papers, it will not be without its effect upon teaching; and if we wish to have the teaching of students proceed uninfluenced by examination, the only way of securing that object will be by framing our question papers in such a manner that they may serve simply to test whether the candidates have been taught properly and have understood their subjects, and to enable intelligent and painstaking students to get through without much mechanical and ingenious coaching. It is quite true that an examination must aim at testing not only the knowledge of a candidate but also his readiness in doing things, and his quickness of intelligence; but for this latter purpose too, straight forward questions would serve quite as well as ingenious and puzzling ones. Nor must we show any feverish anxiety for avoiding everything which a candidate would be likely to be prepared for, as if the object of an examination was to take him by surprise. Of course, a candidate must not be allowed to have any idea of the particular questions that are going to be set, as in that case he will not read his subjects but will only get ready with his answers to the expected questions. But though that is to be avoided, it does not follow that the question paper must be a surprise on the candidate. Indeed one test of a question paper being a good and proper one, is, that it does not take intelligent and hardworking students by surprise.

Another point requiring consideration here is, whether it is right to expect from examinees, in subjects other than Mathematics which is studied more for the mental training it gives than for the useful truths it teaches, knowledge of minute details such as no general scholar is expected to carry in his head in after life. I would answer the question in the negative. It might be urged that unless a subject is so read that minute points are remembered for a time, its broad points will not be likely to be retained in the memory long. I do not consider this argument sound. If a subject is *carefully* read with due *appreciation* of the *relative* importance of its *different parts*, its broad points will make an impression likely to last much longer than if it is *hurriedly* gone through, as a *whole*, without due *discrimination* of the *more* important parts from the *less*, out of an anxiety to retain them all in the mind.

If the papers set are, as a rule, either too long or too difficult for the candidates to answer, you drive them to shifts and contrivances, such as laying hold of groups of what are called model questions, and committing to memory the answers to them, in the hope of finding some of these prepared answers to be of service in the examination hall. It is in this way that the setting of unduly stiff papers tends to encourage cramming.

The rules deducible from the foregoing considerations may be formulated thus:—

RULE I.—The questions in each subject should be fairly distributed over the whole course in that subject.

This rule is intended to insure the reading of the whole course by the student.

RULE II.—The questions should be framed with a view to test a general but intelligent knowledge of the subjects, and questions that are very minute and difficult should as a rule be avoided; but one or two difficult questions may be set in each paper to discriminate the best among the candidates from the rest.

RULE III.—The papers set should be such as can reasonably be expected to be answered fully by intelligent and well prepared candidates within the time allowed.

RULE IV.—The full marks assigned to each question should be indicated by its side.

Some educationists are against this rule, which in their opinion is calculated to make examination too much of a mechanical nature, very little scope being left for the examiner to exercise his judgment. I do not see much force in this objection. I think a rule like this is helpful to the examiner rather than the contrary. It requires the examiner to assign to each answer its proper value; in doing this his judgment has full and unfettered scope; and the value of a whole answer paper is arrived at by adding together the values of the parts. If this does not agree with the value the examiner would assign to the whole from his general impression, as it is called, the error lies in my opinion, not in the method of marking the answers separately, but in the distribution of the marks to the different questions, or in the awarding of the marks to the different parts, or in the general impression being incorrectly formed by reason of any marked excellence or defect in some one answer.

(3) For awarding marks to answers.

125. The awarding of marks to answers is a task of considerable nicety and difficulty. The thing to be valued does not admit of any exact weighing or measuring. Perhaps the best mode to adopt would be for the examiner to have before his mind a model answer to each question as entitled to full marks, and to frame a few rules for regulating the deduction to be made for every material defect, such as bad spelling, bad grammar, bad reasoning, bad conclusion or error of fact. Touching each of these points, nice questions may arise. Thus, it may be asked, whether the deduction for bad spelling should be repeated every time that one and the same word is similarly misspelt in an answer; or whether any credit is to be given for an answer to an arithmetical question, which is slightly incorrect, though the process has been correct throughout except at the last and a comparatively unimportant step. Some will answer the former question in the affirmative, while others (and they seem to form the majority) will make only two deductions. To the second question the majority will return a negative answer, though there are some who are in favour of giving partial credit to the examinee. In these doubtful cases, the best course for the examiner will be to regard for the moment the particular answer as the only work of the examinee before him, and to see whether the examinee ought, in view of his work,

to be declared to have passed, and to determine the marks to be awarded accordingly.

The two rules indicated above may be shortly stated thus:—

RULE I.—Before proceeding to award marks to the answers, an examiner should set down in writing with reference to each question, the point or points to be noticed in the answer, and other conditions to be satisfied in order to entitle the answer to full marks; and he should also note what deductions should be made for errors in spelling, in grammar, in reasoning, and in the statement of facts.

RULE II.—Upon doubtful points, the examiner should see, if the particular answer giving rise to the doubt had been the only work upon which the result depended, whether the candidate should be entitled to pass, and in what division; and the examiner's answer to this question should determine the marks to be awarded.

Re-examination of answer papers to guard against chance of error.

126. When an examiner has to go through a large number of answer papers within a limited time, there is some chance of his falling into arithmetical or clerical error, in adding or noting the marks awarded. To guard against errors like these, it is desirable that when a candidate is found to have failed in one subject only, his papers in that subject should be re-examined, to see whether there has been any such error in his case. No such re-examination is necessary when a candidate fails in more than one subject,

as the chance of two different examiners falling into similar error in the case of one and the same candidate must be exceedingly small. The University of Calcutta adopted[1] in 1890, on my suggestion, this rule of re-examination, and has followed it since; and the general opinion, so far as I am aware, is, that it is a useful rule, and works well.

Vivâ voci Examination a very efficient test, but impracticable when number of candidates large.

127. A *vivâ voce* examination well conducted is a very efficient test of merit; but it is impracticable when the number of candidates is large.

1 See Minutes for 1889-90, p. 32.

CHAPTER III.

EDUCATION IN YOUTH.

INTRODUCTORY REMARKS.

128. On completing his fifteenth year, a boy should cease to be treated as a boy; and if he has made such progress as he should, he is no longer a school-boy, but takes rank as an undergraduate and a college student. The distinction is well marked and well-recognized. Indeed, some educationists go so far as to object to a school and a college being located in the same building, for fear of overlooking that distinction, and of making school-boys and college students indiscriminately mix with one another. While encouraging the distinction, I must say, I do not share such extreme views.

Education in youth.

Length of the period from sixteen to twenty years.

The first question for determination is, what should be the length of the educational period we are now considering, that is, the period of education in youth. The answer to this question depends upon the kind of education which we consider appropriate for youth. If it is, as I think it should be, only general education, ending with the course of studies for the M. A. or M. Sc. Degree, as distinguished from professsional or technical education, the period should cover five years from the sixteenth to the twentieth.

Professional and technical education.

129. Professional or technical education must be different for different students, varying according to their aptitudes and their circumstances. Technical education of an industrial or a mechanical type should commence immediately after school education is over. So also, professional education need not always be preceded by any course of general education at college. Thus a course in Engineering, if the student does not aspire for a degree, but is content with a license, may be commenced immediately after he has finished his school education and passed the Entrance or Matriculation Examination. A course in Medicine for a degree, can be commenced at the Calcutta University only after the student has gone through his college education for one year after passing the Matriculation Examination; while the study of Law has to be commenced after the student has gone through his college course for four years and obtained the degree of Bachelor of Arts or of Science. And this is perhaps, as it ought to be, the necessity of general education being the greatest for a lawyer, and the least for an engineer, while the case of a medical practitioner is intermediate between those of the other two in respect of this necessity.

I do not wish to say anything more now about professional or technical education. The few remarks I intend to make here, will relate to general education, and will be divided under the same five heads of Physical Education. Intellectual Education,

Moral Education, Religious Education, and Instruments of Education, as in the last Chapter.

SECTION I.—PHYSICAL EDUCATION.

130. I need not say much under this head, as a youth of sixteen years may be expected to be able to understand his physical wants, and to take care of himself. I shall only touch upon points on which he may be likely to go wrong.

Much need not be said on this head.

A simple and spare diet is more conducive to health and strength than a sumptuous and rich one, and this must be so. For if more food is taken than is necessary, a certain amount of energy, which might have been utilized in other ways, is needlessly spent in assimilating the excess of food and in eliminating its products from the system.

Diet should be simple and spare.

Occasional partial fasting, such as having a reduced evening meal on Sundays, is a good thing, as it destroys the germ of many a disease.

A student's clothing should be decent and elegant but not fashionable or foppish.

Dress decent and elegant, not fashionable or foppish.

In regard to sleep, students generally err on the side of defect rather than of excess. They read hard at night, forgetting that at their time of life, sleep for at least eight hours is necessary to give the system rest enough to make it fit for the next day's work.

Time spent in sleep is time well spent, as the succeeding day's work will thus be done with fresh vigour and so will be better done.

Sleep.

Exercise.

The physical exercise of a student should be regular and hard, but not strained and violent. It should be gone through cheerfully, but not under the influence of any strong stimulus such as competition for a prize or the like; for in the latter case it ceases to be a recreation, and is attended with considerable strain on the system, which is not always wholesome. Risky games and exercises should be avoided. Perhaps the best form of exercise for youths in this climate is walking at a rapid pace.

There is one point in connection with exercise which college authorities should not lose sight of. They must avoid making exercise irksome and painful. It sometimes happens that a student does not take any food at college, and his house is not near enough to enable him to go home, refresh himself there, and return to college for exercise. In such a case, to insist upon his going through a course of exercise at college is often attended with positive physical discomfort which is far from being conducive to health. Another matter worthy of consideration is, that we must not allow love for sports to run into excess. There are, I fear, already indications of this. Students not unfrequently take to games and sports to the neglect of their studies. The Calcutta colleges, which at one time used to have the largest share of the higher places in the lists of successful candidates at the different examinations are losing their position in that respect; and the result is attributed by many to the greater attraction of the recreation grounds in the metropolis.

The training of the body and the training of the mind should each receive due attention in proportion to its relative importance; and both the student and his trainer should bear this in mind.

SECTION II.—INTELLECTUAL EDUCATION.

131. The questions requiring consideration under this head are:—

Intellectual education. Questions for consideration.

(1) What should the graduated courses of study for youths from their sixteenth to their twentieth year be?

(2) How should those courses be taught and learnt?

132. By the time a young man completes his twenty first year, he should finish the courses of study for the degrees of Bachelor and Master of Arts or Science, the course for the Bachelor's degree extending over four years, and that for the Master's degree over more than a year and less than two years. The question then arises, whether the four years course for the Bachelor's degree should be an uninterrupted course, or whether it should be broken up into two, namely, an intermediate course of two years followed by a public examination, and a final course of two years.

What should be the courses of study.

I am of opinion that an uninterrupted course of four years would be far too long, and that it should be broken up into two courses of two years each, with an examination at the end of each course. This will insure the testing of study with sufficient but not troublesome frequency.

The next question is, how should the two courses of study be arranged, or, in other words, of what subjects should each course consist?

Let us consider the two courses separately.

Intermediate Course.

133. We shall consider first, the course of study for the Intermediate Examination.

The fixing of the course must depend upon the object we ought to have in view.

In my opinion our object should be, to insure a little deeper study in those subjects which are important but have been only meagrely read for the Entrance or Matriculation Examination, and to add such new subjects as are important and ought to be known to some extent by every general scholar, but are not likely to form subjects of voluntary reading. Under the former description will come:—

(1) English Language and Literature;

(2) A Classical Language (Sanskrit for Hindus and Arabic or Persian for Mohammadans) with an allied Vernacular;

(3) Elementary Mathematics (Euclid Books VI, and XI, or the substance thereof treated according to modern method, Algebra and Trigonometry).

And under the latter class should come—

(4) Physics and Chemistry;

(5) Logic;

(6) Elementary Physiology.

Of the six subjects mentioned above, the first is the only one about which opinion is unanimous

Against the second there is the high authority of Herbert Spencer, while many Indian experts think the amount of Sanskrit learnt by the First Arts or Intermediate Examination candidates is almost worthless. On the other side we have the well-reasoned opinion of Bain. My main reason for retaining it, is, that the knowledge of a classical language is the only key for direct access to the rare treasures of thought locked up in the ancient literatures of the world; and if the knowledge acquired at college is small, it is sufficient as a groundwork for further progress, and is just the portion that is least likely to be learnt by voluntary effort.

In regard to Mathematics, the adverse argument is, that it is a stumbling-block to many, and not being necessary for all, it should be made an optional subject for those who like it and who intend to pursue the study of Physical Science. I would retain Elementary Mathematics in the Intermediate Course, partly on account of its disciplinary value as a subject of study, and partly also for the value of the useful knowledge it imparts; and I would dispense with options at this stage altogether, as the too early exercise of option in study is not conducive to mental discipline

With regard to Physics and Chemistry, there is less difference of opinion, it being conceded that a scheme of general education would be incomplete without these subjects. In my opinion, every educated man ought to know something of them, as much for the value of the truths they teach as for the importance and usefulness of the methods of reasoning and investigation they illustrate.

Logic, as the science of the laws of thought and as dealing with the rules of correct reasoning in every science, ought to be read by every student; while Physiology, the science that deals with the laws regulating our physical frame and our senses, the gateways of knowledge, should be studied by everyone engaged in the pursuit of knowledge.

The only important subject, the omission of which in the above scheme will be matter for criticism, is, History; and my apology for this omission is as follows:—

The number of subjects is become too large to admit of any addition; and the only subject which it may possibly be allowed to displace is Physiology; but that is a subject of much greater importance, and is moreover, one which, unlike History, cannot be properly read without aids and appliances not easily available in private study. Besides, the histories of India and England are read, though meagrely, by the student when preparing for the Entrance or Matriculation Examination; while the histories of the Greeks and the Romans, the two great nationalities that have influenced the thought and civilization of Europe, will also be read, though very briefly, in the school course as indicated by me in Section II of the preceding Chapter.

I have shortly stated my reasons for adopting the above scheme. They are qualitatively good; but I am free to own that their quantitative strength, measured against the reasons in favour of a different scheme, must be matter of rough estimation and not exact calculation. That is the chief difficulty in all reasoning in such matters, different minds making different estimates of the relative strength of the same sets of reasons on opposite sides. I may add that my guiding principle has been to avoid bifurcation, options, and unnecessary complications, at an early stage, and to have a scheme fairly reasonable and practical, though not absolutely perfect.

I should here add that the University of Calcutta has now introduced bifurcation immediately after the Matriculation stage, and framed two parallel courses of study, one for the Intermediate Examination in Arts, and the other for the Intermediate Examination in Science, having some subjects common to both the courses, and giving plenty of option in regard to the other subjects in each course. The scheme is a complex one. I make no comments upon it at present. It has come into operation recently, and so let us wait and watch the results of its working. I will only observe that the importance attached to the study of Indian vernaculars is a satisfactory feature of the new scheme, and is likely to lead to salutary results.

The remarks which follow, though made with reference to my scheme, will apply more or less to that of the University, as the nature and extent of the subjects of study, taken singly, do not differ much in the two schemes.

Extent of subjects and mode of teaching them.

134. Touching the extent of each subject and the mode in which it should be taught and learnt, I shall offer my remarks as I proceed, premising at the outset that with such a multiplicity of subjects, the extent of each must necessarily be limited.

Extent of reading must be limited to give the student time to think.

I have kept in view the old definition of a scholar, namely, that a scholar is one who knows something of everything and every thing of something. A broad general knowledge is a good groundwork for specialization at a later stage when the student reads for his M. A. or M. Sc. Degree. One strong reason for limiting the extent of each subject in a pretty long course like that I have recommended, is, that otherwise the student will not have much time to think. *It is a mistake to suppose that we raise the standard of education by merely increasing the extent of study.* On the contrary, *the standard is really raised by making the extent moderate, so as to give the student time for reflecting upon what he reads.* One should read less and think more in order to profit by his reading. What we want is the maximum result; and that does not necessarily correspond with the maximum height of the course of study with a narrow basis of thoughtful reading, any more than with the maximum basis of careful reading and a low course of study.

English Course how to be selected.

135. The course in English for the Intermediate Examination should consist of Poetry and Prose, selected from the writings of standard authors. As the extent of the course must be limited, the

selections should be carefully made so as to include only the best pieces.

In selecting the course in English the following rules may be observed :— **Points to be kept in view.**

(1) The pieces selected should be taken from the writings of standard authors, and should be of universal interest, so that a foreigner may not find much difficulty in understanding and appreciating them ; pieces illustrative of the peculiarities of the English character, English humour, and English sentiments being reserved for the M. A. Course.

(2) Pieces abounding in obscure allusions or in literary criticism of works which have not been read by the students for whom the course is intended, should be avoided. Writings of the latter description are objectionable, not only by reason of the difficulty of understanding them, but also by reason of their encouraging cramming and the habit of dealing with matters not known or only imperfectly known.

(3) A good course being once selected, should be retained for a number of years, instead of our having frequent change.

It is said that a change in the course becomes necessary, as the good questions that may be set upon it become soon exhausted. This is one of the results of that nervous apprehension in examiners of being anticipated by examinees, which has created a corresponding apprehension in the examinees that an examination cannot be passed by honest and diligent study, but necessitates recourse to devices and cramming. If a student is prepared to answer all the good questions that can be set on a given piece, where is the harm? He should in that case be held to have studied that piece to full advantage.

(4) The selections should, in point of quantity, be such that they may be gone through and revised without difficulty within the time allowed.

One of the first four books of the Paradise Lost, selections from Byron's Childe Harold, or Scott's Introduction to Marmion, or one of his shorter poems, and Pope's Essay on Criticism, and selections from the Spectator and Blackie's Self-culture, will form a fairly good course in English. I leave out the drama which should properly find a place in a higher course, namely, that for the B. A. Examination.

English Course how to be studied as language and literature.

136. The Intermediate Course in English should be read for learning the English language and for studying the English literature. For the former purpose, the exact meanings of the words, phrases, idioms, and allusions, and the true construction of sentences, should be carefully understood; while for the latter object, entire sentences and groups of sentences, ideas and groups of ideas, should be attentively viewed, as a whole, from different points of view. If for learning language by reading a literary composition, you must break it into its parts, for appreciating its beauty, you must view it as you should view a painting or any other

work of art, as a whole. Both these modes, the analytic and synthetic, are legitimate modes of viewing things, only each has its appropriate object, each its proper purpose. If language has to be studied minutely and critically with a view to learn the nice differences of sense in different forms of expression, literature has to be studied with no less attention in order to comprehend and appreciate the sublime, the beautiful, and the good that it presents. And it is when thus studied that literature, in the words of the Sanskrit work on Rhetoric, the *Sahitya Darpana*, becomes a means for the easy attainment of the fruits of life by ordinary intelligence.[1] By making us appreciate and take pleasure in appreciating the good and the beautiful, it gradually leads us to love goodness and beauty. The student of literature should have this idea impressed on him.

To understand this he must rise above the words and sentences, and realise the things and thoughts they embody. He may read criticisms only so far as they have a meaning for him, and not merely as well written sentences; and he must never think of committing them to memory. If he wishes to commit anything to memory, it should be the immortal productions of master minds, and not the ephemeral comments on them by second and third rate men. Harrison in his Choice of Books justly complains that we read a whole library about the Paradise Lost,

1 चतुर्वर्गफलप्राप्तिः सुखादल्पधियामपि ।

but the Paradise Lost itself we do not take good care to read. That should not be so. If the student has got by heart any portion of the Paradise Lost, he has in his possession an inexhaustible source of refined entertainment which will help him to beguile his time if it ever hangs heavy on him. Nor must he think that such study will not pay in the examination hall, and that for the purpose of passing his examination he must learn to reproduce the comments of well-known critics. If he has studied his subject well, and can write thoughtful comments on it, no examiner will prove so unappreciative or unkind as not to give him full credit for his work.

To learn to write English correctly, the student must practise writing. Theoretical knowledge of the rules of Grammar and Composition and general directions from teachers are useful; but they can never be sufficient without practice in writing.

General directions for composition.

Of general directions for composition the following may perhaps prove useful :—

(1) Before you commence to write, think about what you are going to write, and arrange your thoughts in some order.

If you write without thought, your writing will be only words, words, words.

(2) Express your thoughts always in simple language and with the fewest words possible. Many are the advantages arising from this. In the first place, you avoid the chance of falling into unnecessary

errors of expression. And in the second place, you avoid making yourself ridiculous by clothing trite ideas in pompous language. For as the poet says,

> "A vile conceit in pompous words expressed,
> Is like a clown in regal purple dressed."

And if your thoughts are good, they will be all the more welcome in their simple garb. If perchance any noble thought finds expression in noble language, retain it by all means; but let your aim and ambition be to find out good thoughts rather than brilliant forms of expression.

(3) Say what you have to say directly and pointedly. A master of style may occasionally have recourse to indirect expression for greater effect. But oftentimes indirectness of expression is only a subterfuge for concealing ignorance or vagueness of thought.

(4) Avoid conceit and mannerism on the one hand and servile imitation on the other; and never try to gain credit which is not your own, but be content to pass for what you are, whether in relation to your literary composition or in relation to your ordinary conduct.

(5) In writing a Descriptive or a Narrative Essay or even a Didactic one, observe the difference between two well-marked modes of presenting the subject, one of which I may call the *scientific*, and the other the *literary* mode. The former proceeds with explicit regularity, touching upon every part of the subject

according to some order, dwelling on each in proportion to its importance, and viewing the subject from different points of view if that is necessary to give a complete view of it. But the latter mode selects a few broad and essential features of the subject, and delineates them, in due order no doubt, but without making any display of order, by bold and effective touches, the brightness of the broad points helping to disclose the apparently unnoticed finer points of the picture. To illustrate my meaning, let us suppose the subject of description to be a landscape. The scientific mode of presentation will give in detail the shape, size, and elevations of the tract of country; the rivulets, ravines, ridges, and roads by which it is intersected; any lakes, towns, cornfields, and hamlets it may contain; the character of the buildings standing on it; the nature of the trees growing and the animals dwelling on it; the density of its population, and other similar matters. But the literary artist will present the scenery to you more compendiously by taking you as it were to the top of a tower, and asking you to look at it as a whole at a glance. If the former mode presents you a *chart* with full details to be *worked out,* the latter presents you a *picture* which has only to be *looked at.* The former mode is available to all who will exercise diligence and care; the latter, only the gifted few can employ.

Course in Sanskrit.

137. The remarks I have made above will apply more or less to the course in Sanskrit.

The student, instead of wasting his time and energy in learning by rote pages of commentary and grammatical notes on Kalidasa, will do better if he were to commit to memory the immortal verses of the poet. And he should try to understand their meaning and find out with his own eyes their beauty, instead of merely following the words of others. Those verses are an inexhaustible mine of beauty, and no honest searcher will come back disappointed. I may be permitted here to refer to a small incident which occurred in my own knowledge.

I was reading with a friend that portion of the second canto of the Raghuvansa, where the poet speaking of the sacred cow returning to the hermitage with the king behind and the queen before her, compares her to the evening between day and night. With reference to this passage[1] my friend remarked, "We have heard a good deal about the beauty of Kalidasa's similes; but where is there any beauty in the present instance? The poet might as well have said that the sacred cow between king and the queen appeared like Sunday between Saturday and Monday or like any intermediate thing between the two things before and after it." I asked my friend to pause for one moment and mark what the point of time was when the cow returned to the hermitage. The cow described as of a bright-brown colour, was returning to the hermitage just at evening, with the

1 पुरस्कृता वर्त्मनि पार्थिवेन प्रत्युद्गता पार्थिव धर्मपत्न्या
तदन्तरे सा विरराज धेनुर्दिनक्षपा मध्यगतेव सन्ध्या ||

valiant king coming behind, and the gentle queen approaching to welcome her; and the poet's imagination naturally saw a counterpart of the interview between the king and the queen with the sacred cow between them, in the opportune conjunction of the moment between the bright departing day and the soft approaching night with the dusky evening twilight intervening. This remark quite satisfied my friend who expressed sincere regret for his irreverent banter.

Course in Mathematics.

138. The Intermediate Course in Mathematics should consist of —

Geometry, that is, Euclid, Book V, Definitions,
Book VI, Props. 1-19 and 33,
and Book XI, Props. 1-21;
or the same propositions in any book on Modern Geometry; Geometrical Conic Sections, Sections of the Cone and Elementary properties of the Parabola, Ellipse and Hyperbola;

Algebra up to the Binomial Theorem and Logarithms;

Plane Trigonometry up to the Solution of Plane Triangles.

In Euclid, I have omitted a portion of the Sixth Book as comparatively unimportant, in order to make room for a little of Book XI, that is, solid geometry, some knowledge of the geometry of three dimensions being absolutely necessary for the understanding of the conics as sections of the cone, and of many portions of Mechanics and Physics. In Conics I have included the part relating to the sections of the cone, as in my opinion no student should be made to go through the properties of the conic sections without knowing how they are obtained as sections of the cone.

How to be studied.—Geometry.

189. In the Fifth and Sixth Books of Euclid, quite a new and important set of ideas has been introduced and worked out. In the first four Books the equality or inequality of magnitudes is treated of; in the next two books what is dealt with is not so much the equality or inequality of *magnitudes themselves* as the equality or inequality of the *relations of magnituaes* to one another. Thus while in the First Book we have it proved that triangles upon equal bases and between the same parallels are equal to one another, it is proved in the Sixth Book that triangles upon equal bases and between the same parallels are related to one another in the same way as their bases, or, in other words, that the relation between the unequal bases is equal to the relation between the triangles on those bases when they are between the same parallels. This is a point which the student should clearly see.

Another point worthy of note is the peculiarity of Euclid's definition of proportion as compared with the ordinary algebraical definition. While the latter makes four quantities proportional when the first is the same multiple part or parts of the second, that the third is of the fourth, the former definition requires that any equi-multiples of the first and the third being taken and any of the second and the fourth, the multiple of the first is to be greater than, equal to, or less than that of the second, according as the multiple of the third is greater than, equal to, or less than that of the fourth. The reason for the difference is this, that whereas the algebraical definition primarily applies only to commensurable quantities, Euclid's definition applies to all magnitudes, whether commensurable or incommensurable. That the two definitions come to the same thing and that either is deducible from the other, may be easily explained in the manner shown in most works on Algebra. The student should clearly understand this.

The propositions of the Sixth Book (4—7) relating to the similarity of two triangles, resemble those of the First Book about the equality of triangles. This resemblance should be clearly seen by the student.

The 19th Proposition of the Sixth Book, which is a very important theorem, may be stated otherwise thus :—The areas of similar triangles are as the squares on their homologous sides. And this must evidently be so if we compare the numerical representatives of the magnitudes. For the area of a triangle in square units is represented by half the product of the numbers of linear units in the base and the altitude : and these two lines being both proportional to the homologous sides, the products of the numbers representing them must be as the squares of the numbers representing the homologous sides. This should be explained to the student.

The fundamental ideas of the Geometry of three dimensions require to be realized fully by the student.

He should, for instance, see clearly that whereas at least three straight lines are required to enclose superficial space, at least four planes are required to enclose solid space; that straight lines may never meet and yet they may not be parallel, as when they are lines in parallel planes; and that a straight line may be at right angles to two or more straight lines not all in the same plane with it.

In Geometrical Conics, only the simplest and most elementary properties of the curves should be all that ought to be required to be read.

140. In Algebra, the generality of formulæ, the interpretation of a formula according to the forms it assumes, and the meaning of a negative quantity are matters which the student should clearly understand, and which the teacher should lay hold of every illustration to elucidate. One simple problem beautifully illustrative of these matters, is the well-known problem of two couriers which may be stated thus: If two persons A_1, A_2 proceeding in the same direction at the rates of r_1 and r_2 units of length per unit of time respectively, pass by two points P_1 and P_2 d units of length apart at the times t_1 and t_2 reckoned from a certain initial instant, when will they meet? **Algebra.**

Let t be the time of meeting reckoned from the same initial instant;

then $$(t-t_1)\, r_1 = d + (t-t_2) r_2,$$

whence $$t = \frac{d + r_1 t_1 - r_2 t_2}{r_1 - r_2}.$$

In this value of t_1 if $r_1=r_2$, $t=\frac{F}{0}$ (writing F a finite quantity, for the numerator) $=\infty$, as it ought to be. For if $r_1=r_2$, A_1 and A_2 are walking at the same rate, and if they are separated by any interval of space, neither of them can overtake the other; that is, they will never meet or meet after an *infinitely* long time. If again $r_1=r_2$, $t_1=t_2$ and $d=o$, $t=\frac{o}{o}$, an indeterminate quantity, as it ought to be. For A_1 and A_2 are now together at P_1 or P_2 and walking at the same rate, and so they must be together all through. Next let $r_1>r_2$, $d=o$, and $r_1 t_1=r_2 t_2$ then $t=\frac{o}{r_1-r_2}=0$, as it ought to be. For in this case, A_1, who walks faster, being in advance of A_2 when he passes by P_1 or P_2, if they met they must have done so before coming to P_1, and as $r_1 t_1=r_2 t_2$ that must have happened at the initial instant. Lastly suppose $r_1>r_2$ and $r_1 t_1<r_2 t_2$ and $d=o$, then $t=-\frac{r_2 t_2-r_1 t_1}{r_1-r_2}$, a negative quantity as it ought to be, the time of A_1 and A_2 being together, if they ever met, having preceded the initial instant.

To make the subject interesting, and to illustrate the enormously rapid increase of quantities in Geometrical Progression, the farrier's demand of 1 farthing for the first nail, 2 for the second, 2×2 or 2^2 for the third, and so on to the 24th nail; the landlord's demand of 1 grain of wheat for the first week, 2 for the second. etc., etc., and 2^{51} for the last or 52nd week; and the demand by the inventor of the chess-play as his reward from the king, of grain of rice for the first square, 2 grains for the second, 2^2 grains for the third, and so on to 2^{63} grains for the 64th square of the chess-board, should be noticed as shewing how apparently modest demands rise to incredibly large quantities. That an infinite series of numbers, $1+\frac{1}{2}+\frac{1}{4}+\frac{1}{8}+\ldots\ldots=2$, is also another beautiful illustration of the sum of an infinite geometric series beinga finite quantity. The fallacy of Achilles and the Tortoise argument is also an instance of the same kind and may be stated thus:—If Achilles moving twice as fast as the tortoise, is behind the latter by any small distance, by the time he passes over it, the tortoise must pass over half that distance, and as Achilles passes over this last mentioned distance, the tortoise passes over half of it again, and so on. And as this process will go on *ad infinitum*, the inference is sought to be drawn that Achilles can never overtake the tortoise. But this inference is evidently false, because the process of Achilles passing over successive distances, each being half of the preceding one, though it may be supposed to go on without limit as to the number of steps, does not go on without limit either as to time or as to space, but must come to an end as soon as Achilles has passed over a distance equal to twice that between him and the tortoise at staring, and the tortoise has passed over a distance equal to half of that gone over by Achilles or equal to the initial distance between the two; and the two must meet at that distance.

The fallacy in the argument results from our overlooking the fact that the successive distances which are $\frac{1}{2}$, $\frac{1}{4}$, $\frac{1}{8}$, etc., of the initial distance, are rapidly decreasing, and the times of passing these, rapidly diminishing in amount.

The meaning of the expression Harmonical Progression should be explained to the student. If he does not feel the curiosity to enquire why quantities the reciprocals of which are in Arithmetical Progression, are said to be in Harmonical Progression, his curiosity should be aroused and satisfied. He should be told that the name of the series is derived from the fact that the lengths of three strings of the same material and thickness and under the same tension, that produce a note, its fifth and its octave, which are in harmony, are found to be such that their reciprocals are in Arithmetical Progression, these lengths being respectively as the numbers 1, $\frac{2}{3}$ and $\frac{1}{2}$.

Mathematical Induction.

Before dealing with Permutations and Combinations and the Binomial Theorem, works on Algebra generally devote a short chapter or section to Mathematical Induction. The student should understand what ordinary *Induction* is, and wherein it differs from Mathematical Induction. He should be told that while ordinary induction is the inferring of a general law from particular instances, and the possibility of the law not holding good in any particular instance is not absolutely eliminated, in Mathematical Induction no such possibility can exist, it being shown, not only that the law holds good in a number of instances, but further, that if the law is true in any one instance, it must be true also in the next.

Thus, it is found by trial that $a^n - x^n$ is divisible by $a-x$ if $n=1$ and also if $n=2$; it is further seen that $\frac{a^n - x^n}{a-x} = a^{n-1} + x. \frac{a^{n-1} - x^{n-1}}{a - x}$, so that if $a^{n-1} - x^{n-1}$ be divisible by $a-x$, $a^n - x^n$ will also be so divisible.

The conclusive inference therefore is that $a^n - x^n$ is always divisible by $a-x$ if n is a positive integer. The fact that a certain thing has been true in a number of instances, is no reason why it should necessarily be true in the next. This was strikingly illustrated by the fallacious assumption made upon repeated trials, that $2^{2^n} + 1$ is always a prime number. Though that is so for values of n from 0 to 31, the next trial disproved the inference.

The fundamental proposition about Permutations, namely, that ${}^np_r = n(n-1)(n-2)\ldots(n-r+1)$, may be proved in either of two ways, that is, by regarding the different permutations to arise either from our taking the n things, 1, 2, 3, etc., at a time, or from our filling, 1, 2, 3, etc., places with 1, 2, 3, etc., of the n things. The latter is the better mode, as it can leave no lurking doubt in the mind, such as the other mode might leave, as to whether we have got all the possible permutations and no more.

wo modes of proving Mathematical proposiions.

The two modes, in which the proposition, that the number of combinations of n things taken r together is equal to the number of combinations of n thing taken $n-r$ together, is generally proved, give rise to certain reflections which have an important bearing on the teaching of Mathematics.

One of these which is the common mode, is this :—

$$\overset{n}{\underset{r}{C}} = \frac{n(n-1)(n-2)\ldots\ldots(n-r+1)}{\underline{\lvert r}}$$

$$= \frac{n(n-1)(n-2)\ldots(n-r+1)(n-r)\ldots 1}{\underline{\lvert r}\,\underline{\lvert n-r}}$$

$$= \frac{\underline{\lvert n}}{\underline{\lvert r}\,\underline{\lvert n-r}};$$

$$\text{and } \overset{n}{\underset{n-r}{C}} = \frac{n(n-1)(n-2)\ldots\{n-(n-r)+1\}}{\underline{\lvert n-r}}$$

$$= \frac{n(n-1)(n-2)\ldots(r+1)\,r\,(r-1)\ldots 1}{\underline{\lvert n-r}\,\underline{\lvert r}}$$

$$= \frac{\underline{\lvert n}}{\underline{\lvert n-r}\,\underline{\lvert r}},$$

$$\therefore {}^nC_r = {}^nC_{n-r}.$$

The other mode may be shortly stated thus :— Suppose the n things to be contained in a basket or other receptacle. Then every time you *take* r things *out of* the receptacle, you *leave* $n-r$ things *in* the receptacle ; so that corresponding to every combination of r things out of the n things there must be a combination of $n-r$ things ; and there must necessarily be just as many different combinations of n

things taken r together as there are combinations taken $n-r$ together.

The first proof is perfectly sound and fairly simple, but it requires some previous knowledge of Algebra to follow it; and though convincing from the correctness of the reasoning employed, it does not enable the student to see that the proposition must, from the nature of things, be true. The second proof, on the other hand, requires no antecedent knowledge of Mathematics to follow it; and it makes the proposition clear to the mind as a matter which must, from the nature of things, be true. The one mode proves the proposition to be true by an elaborate process of reasoning, the other makes its truth almost self-evident. The superiority of the latter mode is shown not only by its simplicity, but also by the insight it gives into the nature of the thing to be proved.

Every teacher of Mathematics, and every author of a mathematical text-book, ought to try his best to bring home to the mind of the learner the truths of the fundamental principles of the subject, so as to enable him to have an insight into them as it were, and to feel that they must be true, instead of merely extorting his assent to them as proved to be true by elaborate and complicated processes of reasoning, and by skilful and intricate manipulation of long series of signs and symbols. Of course it is not often possible to avoid the latter mode; but our endeavour should be to use the former wherever practicable. In proportion as this is done, Mathematics will cease to bear that stiff and repulsive look which it has for many students. Not that there is any royal road to learning; but the aim of the teacher should be to remove all unnecessary obstructions from the ordinary road to it. Eminent Mathematicians have shown their anxiety to do so. I shall here quote a passage from Sir G. Airy's preface to his popular work on Gravitation. "The utility of a popular explanation of profound physical investigation is not," says he, "in my opinion to be restricted to the instruction of readers who are unable to pursue them with the powers of modern analysis. Much is done when the interest of a good mathematician is excited by seeing in a form that can be easily understood, results which are important for the comprehension of the system of the universe, and which can be made complete only by the application of a higher calculus. That such an interest has operated powerfully in our Universities I have no doubt. ....The exercise of the mind in understanding a series of propositions where the last conclusion is geometrically in close connection with the first cause, is very different from that which it received from putting in play the long train of machinery in a profound analytical process. The degrees of conviction in the two cases are very different." (Page iv.) I may illustrate my meaning by one or two examples from Geometry. The 4th Proposition of the First Book of Euclid may be shewn to the student to be evidently true, if he considers that where two triangles have two of their sides and the contained angles equal, their third sides, that is, the bases joining the ends of the first two must be equal, because the first two sides having the same amount of divergence in both the triangles, their ends, that is, points in them at equal distances from the vertices must be equally distant in the two triangles. So also the truth of the 5th Proposition, notwithstanding the complexity of Euclid's demonstration which has earned for it the name of 'the Asses' Bridge' may be made to appear almost self-evident, if the student considers that the angles subtended by the sides of a triangle at the opposite angular points, depend upon the magnitudes of those sides, and must be equal when the sides are equal. The symmetry of the figure will also lead to the same result.

To the student who has read the propositions of the Sixth Book of Euclid relating to similar triangles (which are proved independently of Prop. 47, Book I) the truth of the 47th Proposition of Book I may be made manifest in the following way, assuming that the area of a rectangle is equal to the product of its base and altitude, that is, that the number of square units in the area is equal to the product of the number of linear units in the base and the number of linear units in the altitude.

From the similar triangles ABC and HBA, CB : BA :: AB : BH,

i. e. CB > BA in the same proportion as BA > BH.

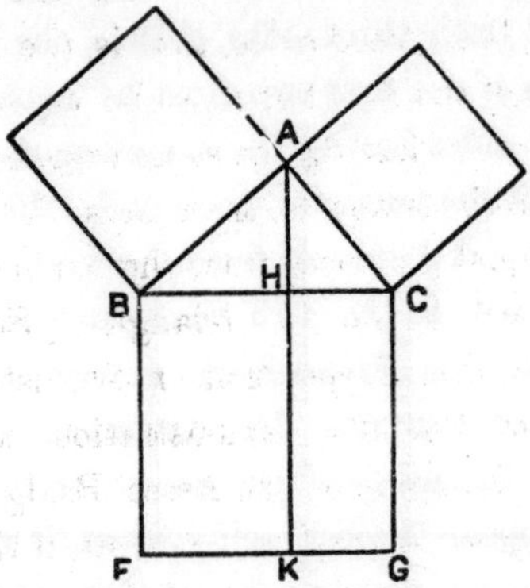

So that CB. BH = AB. AB

or the rectangle HF = AB^2.

Similarly rectangle HG = AC

And therefore $BC^2 = AB^2 + AC^2$.

The Binomial Theorem being the first instance that the student comes across of the expansion of an algebraical function into a series, he should study it with care. The proof of the Binomial Theorem for any index is based upon the principle known as the Principle of the Permanence of Equivalent Forms.

Principle of the Permanence of Equivalent Forms.

The student should be made to understand and realize it thoroughly; and for that purpose he should be asked to verify the principle by actual multiplication of a few of the terms of the two series,

$$f(m) = 1 + m\,x + \frac{m\,(m-1)}{1\cdot2}x^2 + \&c.,$$

$$\text{and } f(n)=1+n\,x+\frac{n\,(n-1)}{1\cdot2}x^2+\&c.,$$

and see that—

$$f(m)\cdot f(n)=1+(m+n)x+\frac{(m+n)(m+n-1)}{1\cdot2}x^2+\&c.$$

$$=f(m+n)$$

Another point which the student should notice in connection with the Binomial Theorem when the index is negative or fractional, is, that the equality of the Binomial expression with the series into which it is expanded, is *formal* equality and not necessarily *numerical* equality in every case.

The Chapter on Logarithms should have the special attention of the student. He should see that the invention of logarithms not only simplifies the operations of Multiplication, Division and Involution by reducing them to Addition, Subtraction and Multiplication, but also enables us to extract any root of a given number by reducing the operation of Evolution to one of Division. The practical importance of logarithmic and exponential series, the student should note, consists in their enabling us to construct Tables of Logarithms of numbers, without which logarithmic computation cannot be possible. I may here observe that much of what I have pointed out above as worthy of note in teaching Algebra, is noticed in all good text-books on the subject of which I may refer in particular to one, namely, that by Babu Mahendra Nath Ray.

Trigonometry.

141. In commencing the study of Trigonometry, the student may inquire what the object of the study is. In answer, the teacher should explain that it is useful remotely as a branch of analysis, and immediately as helpful in the solution of triangles. The real meaning of the first part of the answer the student must wait to understand; but as regards the second part of the answer, he may naturally ask what the use of an additional mode of solving triangles is, when geometrical methods are sufficient for the solution of triangles. In answer to this question, the teacher should explain that though geometrical methods may be sufficient for the *theoretical* determination of the *actual magnitudes* of some of the parts of a triangle when certain other parts are given, it does not help us to determine the *numerical values* of the unknown parts from the given numerical values of the known parts, and that this is what is necessary for *practical* purposes. The mode of connecting *angular* with *linear* magnitudes through the trigonometrical ratios is a beautiful device, the full import of which the student should carefully realise.

Distinction between Geometrical and Trigonometrical methods.

A given angle can have only certain definite trigonometrical ratios; but a given trigonometrical ratio may correspond to an indefinite number of angles differing from one another by multiples of two right angles. This the student should clearly understand; and he should carefully study the general expressions for angles having given trigonometrical ratios. These general expressions are instructive as illustrating the method of reducing *different* allied forms of expression to *one general* form.

Where different angles have *numerically* the same trigonometrical ratios which differ only in having the lines which enter into the fractions representing the ratios drawn in different directions, a *convention* has been adopted to express these different directions by different signs. The student should not only understand the convention, but he should mark the beauty and utility of it as he proceeds; and the teacher should call his attention to the generalisation of different truths into one form of expression which it enables him to effect. As an illustration, I may refer to the formula

$$a^2 = b^2 + c^2 - 2\, b\, c \cos A$$

(where a, b and c are the three sides of a triangle and A the angle opposite to a),

which embodies in one statement Euclid's Bk. I, Prop. 47, and Bk. II, Props. 12 and 13, according as cos A is zero or is a negative or a positive quantity, that is according as A is a right angle or is an obtuse or an acute angle.

142. The courses for the Intermediate Examination in Physics and Chemistry, should include an elementary knowledge of the fundamental principles of every branch of those two subjects. Courses in Physics and Chemistry.

Experts are extremely unwilling to reckon any knowledge in their own subjects as worth any thing, if it is not thorough knowledge of *principles* and *details*; but they forget that everyone does not intend, nor can he hope, even if he were to intend, to become an expert in every subject. Of course what is called *popular* knowledge is not what a college should be content to teach, or a student should be satisfied with acquiring. Whatever he learns he must learn systematically and precisely. But there is a clear distinction between a systematic and precise knowledge of *principles* and a knowledge of *details*. The former is what I would insist upon, but not the latter. Thus, one who does not intend to become an Electrical Engineer may not know the details of the method of actually laying out and working an electric tramway; but every general scholar ought to know how eletromotive power is generated, and how it is applied to the moving of machinery generally. So, one who does not intend to become a Chemist may not be able to give in detail the properties of all the different compounds of Nitrogen and Oxygen or of Hydrogen and Carbon; but no general scholar ought to be ignorant of the laws of combining proportion, and of their bearing upon the atomic theory, or of the distinction between metallic and non-metallic elements or between an acid and a base.

The Course in Physics should therefore include an elementary knowledge of Mechanics, Hydrostatics, Acoustics, Optics, and of Heat, Electricity and Magnetism; and the course in Chemistry should include a general knowledge of the laws of chemical combination and the atomic theory, the properties and principal compounds of the non-metallic and some of the important metallic elements, and of the distinction between organic and inorganic compounds.

143. The student preparing for the Intermediate Examination reads Physics and Chemistry for the first time, and perhaps also for the last time if he intends to take up a literary course afterwards. Considering the importance of the subjects, as well by reason of the amount of useful knowledge their study imparts, as by reason of the training of the mental powers and of the hands and the organs of sense which such study insures, the student should devote special attention to them. The truths that are learnt from these sciences are likely to be of use in the daily concerns of life, while the training that is received by their study, consisting in the exercise of the powers of observation and manipulation, prepares one for the daily work of life better than Mathematics. The subjects should be studied with earnestness and patience, and with the object of gaining knowledge, and not merely of passing the examination, it being borne in mind that if the former object is attained, the latter also is sure to be accomplished. It should be impressed on the mind of the student that he should acquire a knowledge of *the things themselves* and not merely of *their equivalents in words*, and that he should endeavour to *understand* the principles instead of merely *learning them by rote.* He should

How to be studied.

understand that *the facts of science are to be gathered and gathered, first hand as far as possible, by observation and experiment made by himself, his books being followed only as guides*; the principles are to be inferred by induction; and the deductions made from the principles are to be verified by experiment and observation.

The teacher should explain the nature of *induction*; and he may with advantage read out to the student Bacon's Novum Organum Bk I, Aphorism 19, and Newton's Rules of Reasoning in Natural Philosophy from Bk. III of the Principia.

Course in Logic.

144. The Intermediate course in Logic, which from its limited extent, ought to rank as a half subject, should include an elementary knowledge of Concepts, Judgments, and Reasoning, that is, of Terms, Propositions, and Syllogisms, of the Canons of Deductive and Inductive reasoning, and of Fallacies in reasoning. The subject should be learnt intelligently and not mechanically.

Course in Physiology.

145. The Intermediate course in Physiology, which also should rank as a half subject, should include an elementary knowledge of the processes of Digestion, Respiration, Circulation, Secretion, and Excretion, and of the functions of the brain, the Nervous System, and the Organs of Sense.

The remarks made above as to the mode of studying Physics and Chemistry, apply equally to this subject. The structures of the several organs and tissues should be shown by dissection of animal bodies.

146. When a student has gone through the two years' course of study prescribed for the Intermediate Examination, and has passed that Examination, he may be considered to have arrived at a stage of his progress at which he should be allowed some freedom in the choice of his subjects of study. Up to a certain standard, not very high, every student of sound mind ought to study something of every important branch of learning, partly for acquiring knowledge of important truths, and partly for receiving useful mental training. But when that standard is attained, as I think it is, after a student has finished his Intermediate course, it is unnecessary, as it is unprofitable, to compel him to study any subject further against his inclination. It is a well-known fact that different subjects of study have different degrees of attraction for different students. And a subject studied against one's inclination is not likely to be studied to much profit. The question then is—

The course of study after that for the Intermediate Examination is finished.

Whether an unlimited freedom of choice should be allowed, or whether there should be any limitation ?

Now it is clear that unlimited freedom of choice cannot be given at this stage, because in that case, most students will choose a single subject, and it is not desirable that a student should confine his attention to a single subject until a higher standard is attained. Nor will it do to impose a simple condition like this, that a student should take up any three out of a given number of subjects, as in that case so many different combinations of three subjects might arise as to make the work of teaching impracticable for any college. There must, therefore, be some well-defined limits within which the student's freedom of choice should be restricted, and we come to the question, what those limits should be.

The Calcutta University at one time answered this question by dividing the B. A. course into two, namely, the A course and the B course, the former consisting of three subjects—

1. English,
2. Mental and Moral Science, and
3. One of the following :—
   A Second Language,
   History and Political Economy,
   Mathematics ;

and the latter, also of three subjects—

1. English,
2. Mathematics, and
3. One of the following :—

Physics and Chemistry,
Physiology and Botany or Zoology, and
Geology and Mineralogy or Physical Geography.

And later, it instituted another course of study for a co-ordinate Examination, namely, the

Bachelor of Science Degree Examination, consisting of six subjects—

1. English,
2. Mathematics, that is, Statics and Dynamics.
3. Physics,
4. Chemistry, and

5. } Any two of the following :—
6. }

Physiology,
Botany,
Zoology,
Geology,
Mineralogy,
Mathematics, that is, Hydrostatics and Astronomy.

There was good reason for the division of the B. A. course into the A course and the B course; but the introduction of a third parallel course, namely, that for the B. Sc. degree side by side with the B course for the B.A., was an arrangement which, speaking with all respect, one must say, was neither quite logical nor quite convenient.

The only difference between the B. Sc. course and the B course for the B. A. consisted in the former having one additional subject and a short practical course. The number of subjects in the B. Sc. course was no doubt six; but subjects 3 and 4, that is, Physics and Chemistry, constituted one subject in the B course for the B. A. Examination, while subject 2, that is mathematics, of that course, was spilt up into two in the B. Sc. course. So that for a student who took up the optional Mathematics of the B. Sc. course, there was only one subject to be taken up in addition to the subjects of the B. course. With this small difference between the two, it was not quite logical to call the one course a course for a Science degree, while the other course was a course for the degree of Bachelor of Arts. There was no more reason for calling the B. Sc. course a Science course than there was for calling the B. course by that name. Moreover, even with the A course, the second compulsory subject, Mental and Moral science, is more a Science subject than an Arts or literary one : while of the three optional subjects, one, namely, Mathematics, is clearly a science, and an important portion of another, that is, Political Economy, comes also under that description. The truth is that the distinction between Arts and Science in the academic sense is more historical than logical, the subjects constituting the Trivium and the Quadrivium being called Arts Subjects.[1]

Nor was it practically convenient to have three parallel courses running side by side, when two of them differed very little form each other.

This anomalous state of things has been removed by the new regulations of the Calcutta University, under which there are now only two courses of study, one for the Bachelor of Arts degree examination and the

1 *See* Latham on the Action of Examinations, pp. 84—86.

other for the Bachelor of Science degree examination. But the distinction between Arts and Science, so far as one can judge from the subjects included in the two courses, is not very clear and well defined.

In my opinion the proper mode of fixing the different courses of study would be that which keeps in view three things, namely, (1) the importance of the different subjects to the student, (2) the differences in the taste and inclination of students, and (3) the connection of the subjects with one another.

Regard for the *first* matter would require that English should be a subject in a course of study for Indian students reading for the B. A. or the B. Sc. degree, because English is of such great importance to them for many purposes of life, that they should know a little more of it than what they learn in preparing for the Intermediate Examination.

The *second* matter involves delicate and difficult points for consideration. On the one hand, it is said that a powerful imagination is incompatible with a tenacious memory and an acute reason, or in the words of the poet,

> "Thus in the soul where memory prevails,
> The solid power of understanding fails.
> Where beams of warm imagination play,
> The memory's soft figures melt away."

And it is supposed that a taste for literature is incompatible with one for science. On the other hand, it is urged that the best scientific mind must be gifted with vivid imagination to catch distant glimpses of unknown truths, and frame bold hypotheses which are afterwards proved to be correct. That may be true for intellects of a superior order; but with ordinary minds, it is a well observed fact that some are inclined to be speculative, to take pleasure in reflecting and elaborating upon their own forms of thought and upon the phenomena of the moral world, while others show an inclination to be practical, and to delight in observing and gathering the truths of the material world. To the former, Literature and the Abstract Sciences such as Logic and Metaphysics and even Mathematics, and Concrete Sciences like Economics, Sociology and Politics are peculiarly agreeable, while the latter take pleasure in Concrete Sciences like Physics, Chemistry, and Physiology. Regard for differences in taste and inclination of students thus leads to the grouping of Literature, Mental and Moral Science, History and Political Economy and Mathematics under one head, while Physics, Chemistry, Physiology and other Concrete Sciences should come under a different head.

The *third* consideration should lead to our grouping Mental Science with Pure Mathematics, Physics with Mixed Mathematics, Physiology with Zoology and Botany, Geology with Mineralogy and Physical Geography.

The foregoing considerations lead to the grouping of the important subjects of study under the two heads of Speculative and Practical, or Literary and Scientific subjects in the following manner :—

Speculative or *Literary* subjects.

1. English,
2. Mental and Moral Science,
3. A Classical Language, and an allied Indian Vernacular for Indian Students,
4. Mathematics, and
5. History and Economics.

Practical or *Scientific* subjects.

1. English,
2. Mathematics,
3. Physics and Chemistry,
4. Physiology, Zoology and Botany,
5. Geology and Mineralogy, and
6. Physical Geography.

Two more points remain to be settled before the courses of study can be definitely fixed. These are, *first,* how many subjects should form a complete course under each head ; and *second,* which of the subjects should be compulsory and which optional under each head.

To the first question it would be a convenient answer to say that having regard to the time allowed and to the extent of the subjects, the number should be three, students of superior parts being allowed the option of taking an Honours course, that is, a higher course, in any one or two subjects.

In answer to the second question, every one will agree to make English a compulsory subject under both heads. Moreover, at least one subject of special disciplinary value ought to be a compulsory subject under each head. Now Mathematics and Mental Science including Logic are the subjects that answer that description; but as Mathematics is not agreeable to all literary tastes, Mental Science must be the second compulsory subject in the Literary course, while Mathematics should have a similar place in the Scientific course. It is the opinion of some leading educationists that as Mathematics is not attractive to all minds of a scientific turn and is not necessary for the study of any scientific subject except Physics, instead of Mathematics it would be better to make Physics and Chemistry the second compulsory subject in the Science course. I am unable to concur in this view. In the first place, the Mathematical subjects which should form part of the course are chiefly Mechanics and Hydrostatics; and they are not likely to prove unattractive to any scientific taste, if they are properly treated, that is, if they are not encumbered as they are in ordinary text-books, with an unnecessary mass of purely trigonometrical or algebraical matter. And in the second place, some knowledge of the above mentioned branches of Mathematics, that is, Mechanics and Hydrostatics, is necessary for the study, not only of Physics, but also of Physiology (when dealing with locomotion, respiration, and circulation) and of Geology and Physical Geography.

The complete scheme should therefore make subjects 1 and 2 under each of the two heads compulsory, leaving the student free to choose as his third subject, any of the remaining three subjects under the literary group, or any of the remaining four under the other group, and to take an Honours course in any one or two of his three subjects.

B. A. & B.Sc. Courses.

147. The two courses may each be called the B. A. course; or if there be any charm in a name, that name may be confined to the Literary course and the other course may be called the B. Sc. course.

We have now in the Calcutta University two courses of study, one for the B.A. and the other for the B. Sc., Examination. They are different in many respects from the two courses sketched above. I refrain from making any detailed comments on them for the present. The scheme being a recent one, we should wait to see how it works. I feel bound to say however, that I deeply regret the exclusion of Language from the B. Sc. course, and the making of Mathematics an optional subject in it.

The few remarks that follow, are made with reference to my scheme; but they will be found applicable to the University scheme so far as individual subjects are concerned.

The definition of subjects and mode of studying them.—English.

148. The B. A. or B. Sc. course in English should be of a slightly higher standard than that for the Intermediate Examination. It should include a drama (one of Shakespeare's plays) and some short poems of Milton and of Byron or Wordsworth or Tennyson, some of Bacon's Essays (omitting those in which he speaks irreverently of the Prophet of Islam), one on two of Macaulay's Essays (omitting ose on Clive and Hastings) and selections from the writings of DeQuincey or Carlyle or Ruskin. There should also be some work on English Literature giving a general account of it, such as Shaw's English Literature.

The Honours course should include an additional play of Shakespeare and a few poems and prose pieces in addition to those for the Pass course. Books of typical selections, though as presenting specimens of the writings of different standard authors, they may be useful for the study of the English language, are, from their fragmentary nature, not of much value for the study of English literature, and they should form a small part, if any, of the B. A. or B. Sc. course in English.

In excluding some of Bacon's Essays and two of Macaulay's, I have been influenced not merely by sentiment, excusable as it is, but also by reason. Writings which are offensive to the religious or the national feeling of the student can hardly be conducive to his literary or æsthetic culture, however high their literary merit may be. An author or a teacher, who is offensive or unsympathetic to the student, must repel instead of attracting him ; and a repellent attitude provoked in the student is incompatible with his imbibing any instruction from the book or the teaching.

The course in English should be studied by the Indian student for the two-fold purpose of learning the English language and attaining literary culture. Writing essays on the subjects of the course in English and on other subjects, must form an important part of such study ; and the essays written should consist not merely of *words* and *sentences* but of *thoughts* and *sentiments* reasoned out and felt *by the student.*

149. The course in Mental and Moral Science should include Psychology, Logic Deductive and Inductive, and Ethics ; and the Honours course should further include Natural Theology and History of Philosophy. And the extent of the subjects should be defined not only by a syllabus but also by well-selected text-books. Many experts on this subject, as in other subjects, are generally opposed to the prescribing of text-books, their reason being that what the student has to learn is the subject and not any particular book, and that the prescribing of text-books encourages cramming. Speaking with all respect, I must say these reasons are not valid, and the conclusion drawn from them is not sound. Mental and Moral Science Text-books.

It is quite true that what has to be learnt is the subject and not any particular text-book ; but how is the subject, to be learnt and how is it to be taught? If you discard text-books and depend entirely upon lectures or oral teaching, the result will be that the student will have nothing to prepare himself from previously, for the purpose of being able to follow the lectures; and he will have only an imperfectly retained recollection of the lecture or imperfectly taken notes of it to fall back upon, when revising the subject, to see if he has thoroughly grasped the substance of a lecture. Moreover you do not really dispense with text-books, but make the lectures take the place of a text-book so far as the teacher is concerned, and the notes of the lectures serve the purpose of a text-book so far as the learner is concerned; and the substitute must be an imperfect one, unless the teacher is a better master of the subject than the best and the latest author upon it, and the learner, gifted with a highly retentive memory or a rare power of taking down full and correct notes of the lectures while listening to them.

The importance of oral teaching should never be ignored; indeed, it can never be overstated; but it should serve as a supplement to, and not as a substitute for, text-books.

The view I take is in accordance with the opinion expressed by Bain in his "Education as a Science."[1] Speaking of the teaching of grammar, he says: "The suggestion is often made and is probably acted on by some teachers to teach grammar without a book

---

1 p. 344.

in the assumption that the difficulties are not inherent in the subject but come into being when it is reduced to form and put into the pupils' hands in print. There must be some fallacy here. What is printed is only what is proper to be said by word of mouth, and if the teacher can express himself more clearly than the best existing book, his words should be written down and take the place of the book. No matter what may be the peculiar felicity of the teacher's method it may be given in print to be imitated by others and so introduce a better class of books; the reform that proposes to do away with books entirely thus ending in the preparation of another book."

And as for the objection that text-books encourage cramming, I do not think that it is well founded. The intelligent reading of a good text-book, to understand and remember its substance, is not cramming; it is only the mechanical reading of a book to learn by rote its contents that is really objectionable. With a good text-book which is easier to understand than to get by heart, the evil sought to be avoided will never arise. It is only when an ill-arranged verbose and lengthy book is prescribed, that students finding themselves unable easily to grasp its substance, feel forced to get by heart its contents. Books which are mere compilations of discordant philosophical doctrines without evincing much attempt at reconciliation of differences, should never be prescribed as text-books.

But if the subject is to be defined by text-books, the student should be emphatically told, and he must distinctly bear in mind, that they are intended to be intelligently understood and not mechanically read, and that their *substance* is to remembered instead of their *language* being memorised. And the best mode of carrying this out is for the student, as he proceeds, to make condensed abstracts of his text-book in his own language, using the technical terms of the book where it is not easy to find their exact concise equivalents, and adopting a fixed rate of condensation of, say, ten pages of the text-book to one page of his note-book, which it should be his aim not to deviate from. This plan, the merits of which I have repeatedly tested, though it may take a little time and seem rather troublesome in the beginning, will soon be found to save time on the whole, and to become easy. It will not only help the memory a great deal more than the use of abstracts and notes made by others, but will be of immense aid to the clear understanding of the subject, and will serve as an effective check against superficial reading and the forming of erroneous or inexact notions.

The same plan may be followed in the reading of History, Physics, and even Mathematics, and indeed of every subject of study, with suitable modifications which the nature of the subject may suggest.

Sanskrit.

150. The course in Sanskrit should consist of a portion of Kalidasa's Kumara Sambhava and of a

drama such as Sakuntala or Uttaracharita, and the Honours course should include a portion of some standard work on Sanskrit Grammar as a specimen of the method of treatment of the subject by Sanskrit grammarians, and a short work on Comparative Grammar.

151. The B. A. or B. Sc. course in Mathematics should consist of elementary Statics, Dynamics, and Hydrostatics, that is, such portions of those subjects as may be studied without the help of the Calculus, and elementary Astronomy. The Honours course should in addition to these include Analytical Geometry and the Differential and Integral Calculus. **Mathematics.**

The subjects should be defined by syllabus as well as by text-books, especially so far as Astronomy is concerned. Parker's book, which is now prescribed by the Calcutta University, is perhaps as good a text-book as any that is now available.

152. In teaching Mechanics and Hydrostatics, the teacher should distinguish the Mechanical principles from those of pure Mathematics involved in the different propositions; he should point out that while the latter are necessary truths the contradictory of which cannot be conceived, the former are empirical, and inferred by induction from experience; and he should show that the latter are introduced either for the exact statement of mechanical truths or for the purpose of demonstrating them. Thus taking as an instance the proposition known as the Parallelogram of Forces, it should be **Statics.**

pointed out to the student that the mechanical principle involved in it is that a certain single force is exactly equivalent to two different forces; and that that principle, though proved apparently by a chain of deductive reasoning (I am referring to Duchayla's proof) is really different from any proposition of Pure Mathematics, as the proof is based upon axioms of which one at least, namely, that which asserts that the transmission of two forces in directions parallel to their original directions to any point in the direction of their resultant rigidly connected with the original point of application does not produce any change in the result, and which often puzzles the beginner, not being a self-evident truth in the mathematical sense of the expression, is an induction from experience. The "principle of sufficient reason" assumed in that part of the demonstration which says that the resultant of two equal forces must bisect the angle between them, may perhaps be accepted as a self-evident truth on the hypothesis that there are no disturbing forces in action from any other source. The teacher should further point out that the mathematical idea of a parallelogram is introduced to state the mechanical principle in exact language, and that the geometrical properties of parallel straight lines are made use of to prove the truth of the proposition as regards the magnitude of the resultant.

The other mode of proof, which deduces the truth of the proposition from Newton's Second Law of

Motion, is evidently an induction from experience, the Second Law of Motion itself being inferred from experience.

The student should in the first instance be taught to have a clear conception of mechanical principles, instead of being troubled with difficult problems of that description which are exercises more in geometry and trigonometry than in mechanics. The importance of having a clear idea of mechanical principles is most strikingly illustrated by the instance given by Whewell[1], of the strange error into which an acute mathematician like Pappus fell in attempting to solve the problem of equilibrium of a body on an inclined plain. The following is the solution given by Pappus:—

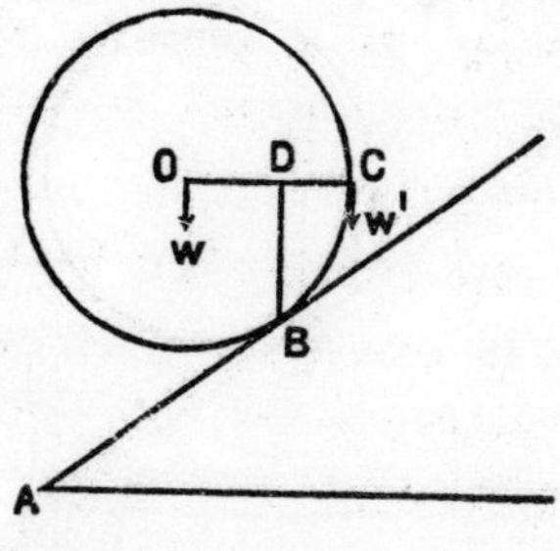

Let the body for simplicity's sake be supposed to be a sphere resting on the inclined plane A B in contact with it at B, and having its weight W acting at its centre O vertically downwards.

Draw the horizontal radius O C and the vertical line B D meeting O C in D.

Then O C may be supposed to be a lever having the weight W acting at its end O and having its

1 Mechanical Euclid, p. 176.

fulcrum at D, and the problem is reduced to one of equilibrium of this lever, which will be obtained by having a weight w^1 acting at C such that $w.^1$ DC $=$W. DO.

The solution arrived at is to the effect that to support one weight on an inclined plane we have to add another weight to it. This strange error arises from the wrong assumption that a sphere on an inclined plane can fall only by tilting over, that is, by rolling, and will be kept at rest if this titling is prevented; it being forgotten that the body may slide as well, and that the friction at B is not an unlimited quantity.

An important statical principle upon which I wish to say a word, as students often find a difficulty in grasping it thoroughly, is the principle of Virtual Work. It is generally worked out as a principle of *geometry*, its full *mechanical* import not being clearly realised.

The principle may be shortly stated thus:—

If a system of forces acting on a rigid body be in equilibrium, the algebraic sum of the total virtual work done in any small displacement consistent with its geometrical relations is zero; and conversely, if such sum is zero for all such displacements, the forces are in equilibrium.

The principle is called that of *virtual* work or *virtual* velocities, because the displacements are *not actual* but are *hypothetical* only, and are supposed to result from the simultaneous motion of the points of application of the forces; and the displacements are supposed to be small in order to keep unchanged the geometrical relations of the body, that is, the configuration of the system.

The student should be helped to understand that what the principle asserts is, that when any forces are in equilibrium, no work is done by them in any small displacement, and conversely, if the forces are such that no work is done by them in any small displacement, they are in equilibrium.

The teacher should see that the student clearly understands the two fundamental propositions relating to the composition of forces, namely,

(1) that when several forces act at a point they have a single resultant, and

(2) that when several forces act at different points on a body, they may or may not have a single resultant; and in the latter case they are reducible to a single force and a single couple,—from which the conditions of equilibrium for any forces are deducible.

The statical machines, though simple in their construction, should be shown to the student, and he should have an opportunity of handling them instead of being left to form an idea of them from mere diagrams. It is not until a machine is actually seen and handled that the student gets a clear idea of its construction and action.

The teacher should explain to the student how the knife is an instance of a wedge, and how an ordinary screw binds two pieces of wood through which it is driven. He should also explain the general principle of compensation applicable to all statical machines, that the gain in power is proportional to the loss in time.

ynamics.

153. In Dynamics the distinction between the pure geometry of motion and the motion of a material particle under the action of force should be clearly explained, and the student should understand how Newton's Laws of Motion have been inferred by induction from experience, how they have been verified, and how the conditions of motion under the action of forces are deduced from those Laws.

The teacher should take good care to see that the ideas of *matter* and *force*, and the relation of force to the *quantity* of matter or the *mass* of a body in the production of velocity and acceleration of velocity, are clearly understood; and he should illustrate his remarks by experiments with Atwood's Machine.

In Dynamics as in Statics, both teacher and pupil should bear in mind that a clear understanding of mechanical principles is of much greater importance than solution of problems of that class which are exercises more in pure mathematics than in mechanics. Problems which illustrate mechanical principles without involving much unnecessary geometrical or algebraical difficulty, should be copiously worked out.

154. The foregoing remark applies equally to Hydrostatics. Hydrostatics.

The student of Hydrostatics should bear in mind a point which is sometimes liable to be overlooked, namely, that though certain propositions, such as that relating to the equality of pressure in all directions at any point in a fluid, appear to be established by *deductive* reasoning and seem to be necessary truths, that is so only with reference to the *hypothetical* fluids as defined by us ; and the question whether they are true for *actual* fluids such as water, must be determined by *induction* from observation and experiment.

I may here mention an instance that I recently noticed, illustrating the necessity of a student's using with his own hands instruments of which he reads in his books. During the last summer vacation I was taking a student of fair intelligence through his text-book on Hydrostatics. He read the description of the Mercurial Barometer and the nature of the *correction for capacity* which I cursorily explained to him ; but it was not until I gave him a barometer tube and asked him to fill it with mercury and fit it up, and he began to think of graduating a scale for it, that he realised the necessity of the correction for capacity and the reason for it, by seeing that the surface of the mercury in the cistern or the open end of the siphon tube from which the height of the barometer is to be reckoned, varies with the rise and fall of the mercury in the tube.

I do not say that he could not have fully understood this from a diagram; but he had missed it. The reason is that, when the description of an instrument and the mode of its action are read in a book, there are so many things to be attended to and understood, that there is much chance of some of them being missed; whereas if the instrument and its action are actually observed, everything relating to them is so clearly seen, makes such a vivid impression, and is presented in association with so many other connected matters, that there is little chance of anything being missed afterwards.

Astronomy.

155. In studying Astronomy, one of the chief difficulties which the student feels, arises from his inability to comprehend figures in space in three dimensions from diagrams on a plane surface. To remove this difficulty, the teacher should refer to a globe wherever necessary. He should also explain the construction and use of Astronomical Instruments by actually showing them, and not merely by referring to their diagrams, and he should point out to the student the different heavenly bodies of which he reads, and ask him to familiarize himself, so far as he can, with the appearance of the heavens, so as to be able to say which groups of stars constitute what constellations. The Bengali student should be taught to be able to find out the planets in the heavens with the aid of the Bengali almanac. This may be easily done. The almanac gives a diagram of the zodiac for every month, showing the positions

of the sun and the planets by the initial letters of their Sanskrit names, the numbers indicating the *Nakshatras* or successive 27th parts of the zodiac. For an observer at the latitude of Calcutta, the zodiac may be roughly taken to be a broad belt of the heavens from west to east about midway and a little to the south; and each sign of the zodiac being one-twelfth of 360° or 30°, the sum may be taken roughly to go over 1° in a day. With these rough data, if on any day at sunset you reckon from the sun eastward along the zodiac allowing 30° for each sign till you come to the place of any particular planet as shown in the diagram of the zodiac for the month, and look about that place, taking care to distinguish a planet from the stars by the absence of twinkling, and further to distinguish Venus and Jupiter by their brightness and Saturn by its purplish light, you will be able to find out all the planets. They may not all or any of them be visible at the time of sunset, either from their dimness or from their not being then in the visible half of the heavens; but you can easily imagine their places below the horizon and estimate the time when they will rise, allowing 15° to the hour, and look at the heavens again at the expected hour. When a planet is in view, you can ascertain whether you have pointed to it correctly by looking at it through a telescope; and if it is a planet it will then appear as a disc.

The student of Astronomy, after he has had his text book explained, should be asked to verify what he reads by actual observation whenever possible.

That will not only make the subject interesting to him, but will remove many difficulties which he may feel, and clear up many points which may appear obscure at first.

Analytical Geometry.

156. In the Honours course, Analytical Geometry should be read first. The student will naturally ask the question, and if he does not of himself, he should be encouraged to ask, why he should read this subject when he already knows the truths it teaches from Euclid and Geometrical Conics. One simple answer to this is that Analytical Geometry teaches a great deal more than Euclid and Geometrical Conics. Another answer is that the student must restrain his curiosity and be satisfied with being told what the mother of Sir W. Jones used to tell her son when he applied for information, namely, "Read and you will know." Both of them are quite pertinent answers; but I would beg of the teacher to give a third answer, not indeed to satisfy the pupil's curiosity, which is not possible, but on the contrary to raise it from the lower level of ignorance to the higher pitch of imperfect and dimly foreshadowed knowledge, so as to make him seek for fuller knowledge with greater eagerness; and my proposed answer will be something like this: Analytical Plane Geometry makes the simpler, because more certain, methods of Algebra applicable to Geometry *by representing geometrical figures by algebraical equations*; and this is done by representing a point by its co-ordinates, and a line which is

a continuous series of points, all subject to certain conditions, by an equation involving two unknown variables, successive corresponding pairs of values of which represent the successive points of the line. This method, the learner should be told, was invented by Des Cartes, and with modifications and amplifications subsequently introduced, it has revolutionized Mathematics and augmented its power as an instrument of investigation almost beyond measure, by making it applicable to every science.

Differential Calculus.

157. The Differential Calculus should be studied next; and here too, the student should at the outset have some idea given to him as to the nature and scope of the subject, by being told that though Algebra is sufficient for dealing with uniform quantities, a new calculus is necessary for dealing with quantities that are variable, such as the direction of a curve which changes from point to point, the curvature of a curve other than a circle, the velocity of a point moving with changing speed, the motion of a body under the action of a variable force, and the like; that the Differential Calculus serves this purpose; and that it does so primarily by finding out the limiting values of the ratios, called differential co-efficients or derived functions, of the increments of different functions of a variable to the corresponding increment of the variable when this latter increment becomes indefinitely small; and these remarks should be illustrated by examples such as that of the changing direction of a curve.

Integral Calculus.

158. The Integral Calculus should be explained at the outset as having for its object, either the finding of the original function of which a given function is the derivative or differential co-efficient, or the finding of the sum of a series of products of successive values of a given function as the variable increases by small increments between two given values, each multiplied by such increment, when it is decreased without limit, it being pointed out that the two objects come to the same thing, by reason of the sum being obtained by successively substituting the two given values in the original function of which the given function is the derivative, and taking the difference between the two. The B. A. or B. Sc. student of Mathematics should, for his own information and not for passing his examination, read Ball's interesting books on the History of Mathematics and on Mathematical Studies at Cambridge.

History, Political Economy and Political Philosophy.

159. The B. A. course in History should consist of the History of India, including the History of Hindu and Mahomedan civilization, and the History of England, and the elements of Political Economy, the Honours course including in addition the History of Greece and Rome and Political Philosophy.

That the Indian Student of History should study the history of the Hindus and of the Mahomedans and the history of England is reasonable enough. That the Honours course in History should further include the history of the Greeks and the Romans, the two great nations whose civilization has influenced that of Europe, is equally reasonable. That Political Philosophy should form part of the History course is also reasonable, as History deals chiefly with the political events of the world. It may not, however, be equally clear why Political Economy should be part of the course in History. But it has been so here for a long time; and perhaps one good reason for this is, that History properly treated, is the subject that deals with the economic conditions of the world at different periods.

The B. A. student should read History in a scientific method; and if it is not possible to read the entire course in that way, at least the history of India should be so studied.

The scientific method of studying History.

The scientific method of studying History should include—

(1) An enquiry into the materials upon which the history is based, and an examination of their authenticity by the rules of historical evidence;

(2) A division of the history into distinct periods marked by characteristic differences;

(3) An arrangement of the events of each period under distinct heads such as political, social, economical, and religious;

(4) An investigation into the action and inter-action of the antecedent events of the different groups in determining subsequent events.

Physics and Chemistry.

160. The B. Sc. course in Physics and Chemistry should be somewhat wider in extent and fuller in details than the course in these subjects for the Intermediate Examination, and should be defined as well by text-books as by syllabuses; and the Honours course should include in addition Organic Chemistry.

Other subjects.

161. With reference to the other subjects I have no detailed remarks to make. I will only observe that they should all be studied with the help of observation and experiment, and the student should verify so far as possible the statements contained in the text-books.

The M.A. or M. Sc. Course.

162. The B. A. or B. Sc. course should be followed by the M. A. or M. Sc. course, which should be a specialized course in a single subject to be selected by the student, the study extending over about two years.

In Mathematics and Physics, considering the great extent of those two subjects, there should be a sub-division, a full course in the former consisting of either Pure Mathematics as principal subject, with Mixed Mathematics as subsidiary subject; or Mixed Mathematics as principal subject, with Pure Mathematics as subsidiary subject; and a full course in the latter consisting either of Heat, Electricity, and Magnetism as principal subjects and Light and Sound as subsidiary subjects, or of Light and Sound as principal subjects, with Heat, Electricity, and Magnetism as subsidiary subjects.

In Philosophy, Kant's Critique of Pure Reason as translated by Max Muller should be read instead of the second hand information furnished by works on Kant; and the Vedanta Sutras with Sankara's Bhashya as translated by Thibaut should form part of the course.

The D.Sc. and D. Lit. or Ph. D. Degrees.

163. If there is to be a doctor's degree in Science, there should, for symmetry's sake, also be the Doctor's degree in Literature or Philosophy; and bearing in mind the undesirability of having too many examinations and of extending examinations beyond a certain limit of age, I would suggest that there should be no examinations for those degrees, but that they should be conferred on M. A.'s and M. Sc.'s, upon their producing works of substantial merit characterized by originality of matter or method in their special subjects.

The stimulus of examinations which works upon our love of praise, is an inferior incentive, the operation of which should be kept within proper limits. As Dr. Martineau forcibly observes:[1] "The extravagant trust reposed upon the system of examination and rewards implies a cynical disregard of the natural craving of Reason for enlargement and lucidity of thought, and mischievously forces to the front motives intellectually cramping and morally inferior."

1 Types of Ethical Theory, Vol. II, p. 240.

SEC. III. MORAL EDUCATION.

Moral education in youth.

164. Moral education in youth should be more systematic than that during boyhood.

Its importance is much greater than that of intellectual education. For while deficiency in the latter may disqualify a man only for certain purposes, defective moral education will disqualify him for all; and the highest intellectual culture will fail to make him good and happy, if his moral culture has been neglected.

The teaching should be divided into two parts,—theoretical and practical, the former consisting in the inculcation of precepts, the latter in the regulation and examination of conduct; and each should proceed upon a definite plan.

Theoretical moral teaching.

165. For theoretical moral teaching, the precepts or doctrines to be inculcated should be arranged according to some method. This is work of some difficulty, but it must be done. For the student has now arrived at a stage at which unmethodical teaching is undesirable, and is not likely to be acceptable. The difficulty I have spoken of arises partly by reason of different views being maintained as to the method of determining right and wrong, and partly also from the fact that systematic moral teaching, though it does not mean a regular course of lectures on Ethics, must involve the discussion of many controversial matters, such as the question of Freewill and Necessity. But the difficulty should

no longer be shirked. We must meet it in the best way we can

166. The different points which systematic theoretical moral teaching should embrace may be shortly stated as follows :—

The points it should embrace.

(1) There is a moral sense in man for distinguishing between right and wrong.

(2) What is right is good, what is wrong is evil. The former is a source of pleasure, and the latter of pain. The distinction between right and wrong in the abstract is universally acknowledged, though opinions may differ as to whether any concrete acts under given circumstances are right or wrong. The conduciveness to pleasure is only a test, but is not a definition of what is right.

(3) Man must earnestly strive to attain moral progress, and to do what is right, whether his will be absolutely free or wholly determined by antecedent circumstances and dominant motives.

Reason serves to favour the view that our will is determined by circumstances and motives; the theory of a self-determining power of the will would make the phenomena of volition an exception to all other phenomena; and the testimony of consciousness relied upon by the libertarian, appears, on close cross-examination of the witness, to support the opposite view. On this point I would recommend the student to cousult Fowler and Wilson's Principles of Morals, Pt. II. Chap. IX, which gives a brief but lucid summary of the views of all the great writers on the subject. But if our will is determined by antecedent circumstances and dominant motives, it is of the utmost importance that we should so endeavour to conduct ourselves as to make our antecedent circumstances and dominant motives helpful in determining our volition so as to enable us to do the right.

The thorough-going determinist may ask "Why should I exert myself and how can I do so, when everything that I am to do is predetermined?" One answer to him is, "You do not know what your predestination is; go on exerting so far as you can, to do what you deem to be right."

Belief in determinism need not make men indolent and apathetic, nor need it lessen our moral approbation of what is right and disapprobation of what is wrong.

For the distinction between right deeds and wrong deeds must remain unaffected by the conditions under which the agent acts. And the effect of the former in making him happy and of the latter in making him miserable, apart from the satisfaction and remorse from doing them respectively, must also remain unaffected by those conditions. So that the agent, whether he believes in liberty or necessity, must be equally anxious to do what is right, and to avoid doing what is wrong; and must equally long for a state of mind in which he will do only what is right; the libertarian seeking so to train his will that by its self-determining power it may bring on that state, while the necessitarian would seek to bring it about by so training his mind and placing himself with reference to his environments that the dominant motives may be of such a nature as to lead to right actions. And if belief in the doctrine of necessity does away with the remorse of wilful transgression and is so far likely to prove disadvantageous to moral progress, it has the compensating advantage (which is of no small value) of doing away with the elation and conceit resulting from taking personal credit for goods acts. Nor is determinism inconsistent with punishment for wrong doing, if punishment is regarded, as it ought to be, preventive and reformatory, and not punitive and retaliatory.

(4) In a conflict of duties or of motives, the lower or those of an egoistic nature must yield to their altruistic rival.

(5) Self-abnegation and the doing of the right act regardless of its fruits, should be a man's guiding principle.

167. The giving of directions for the regulation and examination of conduct constitutes practical moral teaching. **Practical moral teaching.**

These directions (I do not profess to give them exhaustively) should be something like the following:—

(1) Tell the truth, the whole truth and nothing but the truth.

(2) Render to every one his due.

(3) Avoid giving pain to any one.

(4) Do the right act regardless of its fruits

(5) Learn to restrain yourself, and never do anything upon mere impulse without thinking of its consequences.

(6) Judge yourself strictly; judge others indulgently.

(7) Render before demand the dues of others; do not pressingly demand your own. Remember that payment put off inures to the benefit of the creditor and not of the debtor.

(8) Be self-reliant; and while thankfully receiving help if given unasked, avoid seeking for it.

(9) So train yourself as to make your happiness depend upon your own acts and not upon those of others.

(10) So conduct yourself as to avoid giving others any opportunity of doing you harm, and giving yourself any occasion for demanding retribution.

(11) Exert earnestly to get rid of avoidable evil, but accept the inevitable with calm resignation.

(12) Have firm faith in the operation of moral laws; do not entertain the false notion that they are uncertain in their operation and may be evaded. Never try to deceive others: they who do so only deceive themselves.

(13) Examine your day's acts and omissions before you go to sleep. Self-examination is the best scrutiny because there can be no concealing. Close the day's account before the day is over; and go to bed with a firm resolve to mend to-morrow what you have done amiss to-day.

168. The question who is to impart moral instruction is an important one. It will be enough to say that not only the professor of Moral Philosophy but also the Professors of Literature and History may, if they feel so inclined, instruct the pupil in morality.

The question who is to impart moral instruction.

SECTION IV. RELIGIOUS EDUCATION.

169. Religious education in youth, like moral education, should be more systematic than it can be in boyhood; and controversial points should no longer be avoided altogether, but should be met so far as possible.

Religious education in youth should be systematic.

Considering the tendency of the age, the question that presents itself for determination at the very outset is, whether the truths of religion are real truths or are mere phantoms of overworked enthusiastic brains conjured up for the consolation of humanity in its hours of affliction. To determine this question, we must first answer the question, What is religion and what are its cardinal truths?

Questions for consideration. Are religious truths real? What is religion?

It should be here premised that when I speak of religion, I mean Natural Religion, that is, *religion as it can be understood by the ordinary human mind unaided by revelation or inspiration*, as distinguished from Supernatural Religion, which is religion either revealed by supernatural process or apprehended by supernatural inspiration. Now, without attempting to give a philosophical definition, I think it will be enough for my present purpose to say, that Religion is a belief in a Supreme Being, infinite in His attributes, as the Ruler of the universe, and in a state of existence after death, accompanied by conduct in accordance with such belief. Religion differs from Metaphysics or a system of Philosophy in its practical aspect as influencing conduct; while it differs from Ethics or a system of Morals in its theoretical aspect as involving belief in God and a future state, as the guiding rule of conduct. *The two cardinal truths of religion then are, the existence of God, and the existence of a future state*; and the question is whether they are real truths or mere delusions.

The question has occupied the attention of the highest minds in all ages and countries ever since the dawn of human intelligence, and I do not profess to discuss it here at length for the purpose of convincing any one of the truth of my views. I intend only to suggest the simplest way of stating the question to, and of answering it for, the young student who, we may assume, approaches it with an unbiased mind.

Having regard to the object just stated, I think question whether the existence of God and tha of a future state are real truths, may be answered shortly thus :

(1) The universe of matter and mind could not have come into existence except from a cause that could produce not only material but also intellectual and moral phenomena, that is, a cause intelligent and moral, existing eternally and infinite in his attributes. God is therefore at least as great a reality as the universe itself. Indeed, He is a greater reality, for He transcends the universe which is only his manifested energy. If it is said that this reasoning about the infinite cannot be sound, as the infinite is unthinkable by us, the answer is, that though it is impossible for our limited intelligence fully to comprehend the infinite, it is equally impossible for us to avoid the conception of the infinite ; and that when we think of space or time or causality, it is impossible for us to stop at any finite limit.

(2) Belief in a future state is a natural consequence of our belief in our individuality as revealed by consciousness. The being we are conscious of as the self or Ego, is not the living body but something independent of it. The body is *mine*, but *I* am not the body. It does not follow, therefore, that the Ego should cease with the cessation of the body, but on the other hand its continued existence is much more consistent with our conception of it than the contrary. (The advanced student should be advised by the teacher to read in this connection the

Chapter on Death in its Metaphysical Aspect in Martineau's Study of Religion.)

Whether such continued existence is to be for all time, or whether the self when it attains perfection, will merge in the Infinite Self out of which it came, are questions in connection with which I may refer the student to the *Vedanta* system of Philosophy.

Religion the ultimate basis of morality.

170. The teacher should impress on the pupil the truth that *religion is the ultimate basis of morality.* No doubt there are instances of highly moral men who do not believe in the existence of God or of a future state. But though that may be true of a few among the highly cultured, what about the uncultured many? Besides, the religious sentiment of the majority cannot be without its effect in determining the moral standard of the few who have no religious belief. An eminent judge, who was a positivist, on one occasion in the course of a discussion on religion asked "When a man is tempted to do a wrong act and is hesitating, does he look above or does he look around?" implying that it was fear of public opinion and not that of God which kept men straight. The answer is, that many look around because there are at least some who look above. If religion disappears, public opinion will be sure to deteriorate.

Then again, though in ordinary cases the moral sense unaided by religious sentiment may enable us to distinguish between right and wrong, and the pleasurableness of righteous acts may suffice to induce us to do the right, yet in cases involving severe conflict of duties or serious sacrifice of interest, faith in an all powerful beneficent moral Governor and in a future state of existence, seems to be the only guide of unswerving duty, and the only refuge of suffering virtue.

The poet enunciates a great truth when, after describing the wintry appearance of

> "The ivy round the leafless oak
> That clasps its foliage close,"

he adds,

> "Thus Virtue diffident of strength
> Clings to Religion's firmer aid.
> So by Religion's aid upheld,
> Endures calamity."

The conquest of egoism by altruism possible only by the aid of Religion.

171. The teacher should next point out to the pupil the necessity of religion to complete the conquest of egoism by altruism. If the first encroachment on self-love is by the love of our nearest domestic relations, its final conquest can be effected only by the love of God. Neither the love of one's nation, nor even the love of humanity, can suffice, as they are in reality self-love transformed into higher phases. I love my nation because it is my nation. I love mankind because it is my kind. Not so however with the love of God. I love Him not because He is mine, but because I am His; and I should love His creatures because they are His.

Again, no *human agency*, however powerful or wise, can *reconcile* the complete happiness of any one human being with the complete happiness of all. The *world* has not *space* enough, and *human life* is not *time* enough, to enable us all to work so as to attain our highest aim. It is only an all powerful and all wise beneficent Intelligence that has the *power*, and a state of existence untrammelled by the limitations of *time* and *space*, that can afford the *conditions*, of working out the complete happiness of each consistently with the complete happiness of all. It is, therefore, the religious sentiment alone that can inspire us with a genuine disregard of self for the sake of others, and a true devotion to duty regardless of its fruits.

To remove any apprehension of such self-abnegation leading to inaction, it should be explained that the religious man's disregard for self arises, not from indolence or apathy, but from a genuine regard for the interests of all the creatures of God; so that he must do his duty, only he should do it not because it will benefit him, but because it is his duty.[1]

Religion must influence conduct.

172. The teacher should above all things make his pupil understand that religion should not merely be believed in, but should also influence conduct. Indeed, if the two cardinal truths of religion, that there is a God, and that there is a future state, are

---

1 Compare what the Gita says :—

अनाश्रितकर्म्मफलं कार्य्यं कर्म्म करोति यः ।
स सन्न्यासी च योगी च न निरग्निर्न चाक्रियः ॥

adequately realized, they cannot but influence conduct every moment.

The practical direction of the religious instructor to his pupil should therefore be, always *to realize the presence of God, and the nearness of the future state.* If one does so, he will not only never go wrong, but will go right amidst all the difficulties in his way, with the pleasing assurance that there is a beneficent Almighty Power ever present to help him on, and that the land of promise, where all the wrongs of this world will be set right, is not far off.

Here may be offered a few remarks on prayer, to remove any doubts that a rationalistic mind might feel as to its efficacy. It may be said that as prayer is an application to Heaven for some good which is to come to us either by supernatural intervention or by the operation of natural causes, and as it is unreasonable to expect such intervention, and unnecessary to supplicate for what natural causes will by their own operation bring about, prayer can be of no use to us. The answer to the objection is simple. Granting that no supernatural intervention can be expected, it is not correct to assume that the operation of natural causes will be the same without prayer as with it, when prayer itself must favourably affect one of the natural causes in operation, namely, our own exertion for obtaining the good prayed for. The man who seeks for any good in a prayerful spirit, is Prayer.

sure to put forth in an honest manner all his energies in obtaining it, and is not likely to be deterred by any difficulties in his way. And when what is asked for is strength to bear the evils of life with patience, or its blessings without elation, the very spirit of prayerfulness brings with it the patience wanted in the one case, and will exclude the elation sought to be avoided in the other.

Toleration.

The religious teacher should impress on the pupil the necessity of abstaining from showing irreverence to what is held as an object of worship by others. All men worship the Supreme Ruler of the universe, though they may do so in different ways.[1] Nor is this to be wondered at. The Supreme Being is infinite in his attributes and incomprehensible by us, and has been conceived and symbolized by different races and sects in different ways.

A word about pantheism.

Another point which sometimes puzzles the mind may here have a word of explanation. The Vedantic Pantheism which makes God include and transcend the universe, and is considered by many as giving the best conception of God, is yet felt to involve the difficulty of making our acts the result of the Divine energy in us, and of thus destroying the sense of personal responsibility and weakening the foundations of morality. The

---

1 See the Gita,

येप्यन्यदेवता भक्ता भजन्ति श्रद्धयन्विताः ।

तेऽपि मामेव कौन्तेय भजथन्त्यविधिपूर्वकम् ॥

IX. 23.

teacher may help his pupil out of the difficulty in the following manner. The belief that our power of action is only a part of the Divine energy that is in us, if it is not merely lip deep, but is really felt, will of itself be the best foundation of all morality, and will not require to be propped up by any sense of personal responsibility. For the man who feels that the very energy that moves him is a part of the energy of the Great and Righteous Being who rules the universe, cannot do anything that is mean or wrong. And if in an unguarded moment he does anything wrong, belief in Pantheism cannot lessen his remorse, as he must feel that until his belief takes such firm hold on his mind as to make wrong doing impossible, until his finite self is completely purified, he cannot have his salvation or final bliss, whether such salvation or bliss consists in the pure infinite Self-absorbing, or in its being more fully revealed to, his finite and impure self.

The inquiring student should be referred to the Vedanta Sutras with Sankara's Commentary, and to the Chapter on Pantheism in Martineau's Study of Religion, for further elucidation of the matter.

By whom should relig ous instruction be imparted.

173. To the question who is to impart religious instruction, the answer is not very easy, and the difficulty of the question is enhanced by the fact of there being the followers of so many different creeds among our students, and the Government having, wisely no doubt, adopted the policy of excluding religious education from institutions under its con-

trol. I shall in answer to the question only say this, that private colleges are free to make their own arrangements for religious teaching.

SECTION V. INSTRUMENTS OF EDUCATION.

Instruments of education in youth.

174. The instruments of education in youth may be arranged under the following heads, namely,

(I) Universities.
(II) Colleges.
(III) Professors.
(IV) Text-Books.
(V) Libraries.
(VI) Examinations.

I. UNIVERSITIES.

I. Universities.

175. While it is the College to which a student belongs that directly influences his education, the University with which the College is connected exercises an indirect influence through the control it has over its affiliated Colleges. Such control is desirable and useful for three purposes, namely, (1) to increase the efficiency of Colleges; (2) to secure their uniformity of action within certain broad limits, leaving their action free within the narrower sphere of internal management; and (3) to guarantee the soundness of the teaching of affiliated Colleges by granting degrees and diplomas to students who are proved by its examinations to have received good education.

No College can be expected to be able to enlist the services of all the best experts available; but the University which should be an association of the most learned and the best educated men in a large area, may give all the Colleges under it the benefits derivable from the united wisdom of the best men in the province, in the shape of well and progressively arranged courses of study, and well regulated methods of discipline. Again, while different Colleges, if left to themselves, might adopt courses of study and methods of discipline so widely divergent as to be embarrassing to students in their choice of a College, University control reduces such diversity to uniformity, leaving each College free at the same time in its internal management. Then again, while a certificate of proficiency granted to a student by the authorities of his College would be received with hesitation as the testimony of an interested witness, a degree or a diploma of a neutral body like the University must naturally be accepted without doubt or diffidence.

Constitution of Universities.

176. As the University thus exercises a potent though an indirect influence on education, the question of its constitution becomes an important one.

Representation of different interests.

A University must derive its authority from, and be constituted by, the State; and the different interests that require to be represented in it are those of learning, that is, of learned men, the custodians of learning; those of learners, and their guardians, that is, the general public; and those of Colleges, which are to be controlled by the University. Besides these three, there are the interests of Government which also require representation, Government being responsible for the peace and prosperity of the country, and being therefore interested in seeing that no revolutionary or mischievous doctrines are inculcated to the youth of the country, and that education such as is calculated to help the development of its resources is not neglected. Some are of opinion that a simple power of vetoing the regulations of the University is enough for Government, without its having any representatives in the University. It is however more satisfactory that Government like the general public should be represented; but that representation should not be of such a nature as to give it a standing majority, which would have the effect of destroying the independence of the University, and making it a department of Government. As the different interests overlap, the representation of one may secure a partial representation of another. Thus men of learning may be officers of Government and professors of Colleges, so that the same individual may represent three of the four interests mentioned above.

We need not regard the graduates as a body distinct from the educated public, and requiring separate representation, when they come under and indeed form the most important part of the general public in connection with educational matters. But if the general public cannot be conveniently represented, the graduates as a body should take its place.

Here arise certain important questions of detail as to what should be the number of members on the governing body or Senate of a University, in what proportions the different interests should be represented, and in what manner the members of the Senate are to be appointed or elected. There is another question of a delicate nature incidentally arising, which cannot be ignored, and which may with perfect fairness be freely dealt with as a question of principle; and it is this, namely, in what proportion should Indians and Europeans represent the different interests indicated above. The University being a Western institution, the active sympathetic co-operation of learned Europeans in its administration is at the present moment absolutely necessary, and will at all times be most welcome. But as the Indian Universities work for the training of Indian youths, educated Indians also ought to have an effective voice in their management, so as to adapt their working to the wants and habits and the sentiments and susceptibilities of Indian students.

I need not dilate upon these questions here at any length, as I have expressed my views upon them in another place (see my Note of Dissent from the Report of the Indian Universities Commission), as they have recently been discussed fully in connection with the Universities Bill, and as they must be taken to be settled for the present by the passing of that Bill into law.

The Syndicate.

There is another question which was much discussed, but which too must be taken now as settled, namely, whether in the Syndicate, that is, the executive committee of the Senate, there should be a statutory majority of teachers. No one objects to teachers forming a majority of the Syndicate; but what one would like to secure is that they should form a majority not *merely* because they are *teachers*, but because they are *men of solid learning and sound judgment*, in whom the senate and the public have confidence.

But though the above questions are now settled, so far as settlement by legislation goes, that is not all; and a great deal will depend upon how the new Universities Act is carried into effect, who constitute the Senate, and in what proportion the different interests involved are represented in it. One may in the present connection echo the sentiment so beautifully expressed in the following lines:

> "How small of all that human hearts endure,
> The part which laws or kings can cause or cure."

University Regulations to be cautio framed.

I would here venture to express the hope that the regulations under the new Act may be framed with caution so that gradual reformation, and not sudden destruction, of existing educational fabrics may be the result. I yield to none in my desire to raise the standard of education; but my only apprehension is, lest in our enthusiastic effort to raise the height we reduce the base so much as to make the whole fabric come down. Nor must we forget that not only in this now backward country, but in more advanced countries too, it is only a few who are fit for attaining the highest standard, and who study in order to add to the stock of human knowledge, while the great majority of students are able to make but modest progress, and study in order to add to the stock of their own knowledge; and it is no unworthy object of an University, if, while affording facilities to the gifted few to attain the highest eminence. it can help the majority of students to attain a fair amount of knowledge and culture.

It has sometimes been said that this is not the policy of Government which regards spread of high education and the existence of a discontented educated class, as a menace to the peace of the country. I should hesitate much to accept this view. For it is difficult to understand how an enlightened Government under the guidance of a statesman and a scholar of rare intelligence can entertain any such apprehension. If there be any one likely to be troubled by any such fear, to him I would say that considering the circumstances of the country, it is the educated classes and not the ignorant masses, whose deepest interests are concerned with the stability of the Government. It is true the educated classes criticise the acts of Government, and agitate for a few concessions being made to them; but their action is always constitutional and loyal; and if they are occasionally found wanting in proper respect in their tone, the remedy consists not in suppressing high education (which is no longer possible), but in teaching them better things by precept and example, by kindness and not by severity. The maxim that action and reaction are equal and opposite, is as true in the moral as it is in the material world.

Teaching University.

177. A good deal has been said about the inadequacy of our University system, and the necessity of teaching Universities. With all respect for those learned gentlemen who entertain the opposite view, I must observe that our Universities, though requiring improvement in many respects, are not so bad as they are supposed to be, and that it is neither possible nor necessary to convert them completely into teaching Universities. The Indian Universities, though apparently only examining bodies, do really influence and control teaching most materially by prescribing the courses of study for their different examinations, by requiring regular attendance at college as a condition for admission to those examinations, and by framing for the conduct of examinations rules which indicate what importance should be attached to each subject and in what mode (that is whether theoretically only or practically as well) the subjects are to be taught. Then again the extensive jurisdiction and the limited means of an Indian University make its conversion into a teaching University next to impossible. Nor is such conversion necessary. The affiliated colleges which work under the control of the University may be left in charge of teaching up to the B. A. and B. Sc.

standards, and each University should concentrate its efforts in providing for post-graduate teaching. The improvement that is really needed is the establishment of University Chairs in the principal subjects, to be filled by the best men available, who may, by their precept and example, awaken in their pupils an insatiable desire for exploring the infinitudes of matter and mind.

II. Colleges.

178. In regard to Colleges I have not much to say, as the remarks I have made about Schools will apply more or less to Colleges as well. I will only add this, that so long as a College is located in a commodious building and has adequate teaching staff and teaching appliances, the mere want of residential quarters or play grounds or other similar appurtenances should not stand in the way of its affiliation. These appurtenances are in the nature of luxuries which unendowed private Colleges can ill-afford to have. They are doing useful work in disseminating knowledge even if it does not reach the highest standard; and in a country like India where education has made such limited progress that the educated portion of its population is still a much smaller fraction of the whole than it is in other civilized countries, it will do more harm than good if any measures are hastily taken which are calculated to reduce the number of these Colleges. II. Colleges.

19

There is another point connected with Colleges, touching which a few words here will not be out of place. It is said that no College which is established for the profit of the proprietor should be recognized by any University. This is quite sound as a general principle. For the conflict of interests in which the proprietor in such a case, is involved, will generally result in the interests of the College being sacrificed to those of the proprietor. But there is one exception which may with perfect justice be allowed, and that is, where the proprietor, who is an educational expert and is a member of the teaching staff, takes a reasonable remuneration for his professorial work out of the fees realised, all surplus fees being credited to the institution and spent for its improvement.

The Indian Association for the Cultivation of Science.

179. While speaking of Colleges, I may add a word or two relating to the Indian Association for the Cultivation of Science. Our illustrious countryman, the late Dr. Mahendra Lal Sarkar, devoted the best part of his long life and uncommon energy to the establishment of that institution; and aided by the liberality of a few natives of India and the sympathetic co-operation of a distinguished philanthropic foreigner (the Revd. Father Lafont) he succeeded in giving the Association a commodious lecture hall and a well equipped laboratory; but for want of funds he was unable to establish any paid professorships, or to take up the work of original research. A few self sacrificing gentlemen have however been

carrying on the work of teaching; and students of Colleges not fully equipped with scientific appliances may receive training there up to the B. A. and B. Sc. standards up to which the institution may be affiliated to the Calcutta University.

III. Professors.

180. Under this head I have not much to add to what I have said under the head of Teachers in the preceding Chapter. A professor must possess all the qualifications necessary for a good teacher. He must also have greater power of clear exposition than is sufficient for a teacher; because while a teacher in a school may have the opportunity of teaching the students of a class individually, a professor will have to deal with a large class collectively.

III. Professors.

There is another matter connected with professors of colleges touching which I would beg leave respectfully and not without some hesitation, to offer a few remarks. Among professors of colleges there must be many who are Europeans; and Europeans and Indians differ in so many ways, that sometimes from excusable prejudice, oftener from mutual misunderstanding equally excusable, each may find fault with the other when really there is none. I would beg of the European professor to disabuse his mind of the impression, if any there be, that the Indian student is wanting either in intelligence or in respect for authority; and I would on the other hand ask the Indian student to free his mind of all apprehension

Should not assume the intellectual inferiority of Indian students as a class, but should appreciate the difficulties of their situation.

that the European professor may treat him with unkindness or discourtesy. The Indian student (I speak from personal knowledge and not from partiality for my countrymen, pardonable as it may be) is mild and docile; reverence for his teacher whether secular or religious, is strictly enjoined by his religion, and is deeply ingrained in his nature; he may be somewhat sentimental and may expect to be treated gently, and a little kindness is enough to win his heart. If he occasionally appears to be unmannerly or disrespectful, it is due more to his ignorance of the English code of manners or of the English language than to anything else. I may illustrate my meaning by an instance which occurred in my own knowledge. When we were in the third year class in the Calcutta Presidency College, we had for three days in the week History in the first hour taught by Professor Cowell, and Philosophy in the second hour lectured upon by Professor Jones, both very learned and kind teachers, and held in great respect by us all. Professor Cowell, who was often absent-minded, having forgot to call the register for three days in succession during his hour as he ought to have done, a class fellow of mine, a very brilliant and well-behaved student, brought this to the notice of Mr. Jones, day by day, and he supplied the omission on two days; but on the third day he did not do so, feeling perhaps disinclined to do what his colleague ought to have done; thereupon my friend, to make sure that he had been heard and understood, said to Mr. Jones " Sir, do you mean not to call the register," when he really wanted to ascertain whether he had been heard and whether it was the learned professor's pleasure not to call the register that day. The professor with whom our acquaintance had just begun, taking the words in their ordinary sense, naturally considered the conduct of the student most impertinent, and reported the matter to the Principal, Mr. Sutcliffe. The latter, who knew the student from before, sent for him, inquired into the affair, and soon found out that his fault lay in his ignorance of English and not in any intentional show of disrespect to his teacher. My friend apologised for his fault of expression, and the kind-hearted Mr. Jones accepted the apology as sufficient.

I have earnestly entreated our European professors not to accept as correct the view sometimes entertained, that the Indian student is intellectually inferior to students in Europe.

I may be met by the question how to account for the fact of the graduates of Indian Universities having done so little solid work in the fields of literature and science. My answer is that the fact relied upon is due not to any intellectual inferiority of the Indian student, but to his want of sufficient encouragement and stimulus. The Indian students for the most part come from the poorer middle classes. They are soon called upon to earn their living. They have no Fellowships (except one attached to the Calcutta University and tenable only for five years) to encourage them. Nor have they any stimulating atmosphere of literary or scientific activity about them, such as might inspire them to work even without remuneration. As for the pursuit of knowledge for its own sake, that should no doubt be the ideal, as it was the ideal of the Indian student in the good old days when our personal wants were so few. But the increase of these wants has of itself been a serious obstacle in the way of such disinterested pursuit of knowledge. I may here quote a passage from Latham's work on "The Action of Examinations" which occurs in Chapter VII headed "Prize Emoluments in Education," as having an important bearing on the present topic. "First rate genius, it is true" says the learned author "will neither be forced nor suppressed; no emoluments will bribe it into existence and no neglect will extinguish it; but of such geniuses we only see three or four in an age. There are in the country however many young men of assiduity and intelligence who may have a considerable share of intellectual tastes and who, though not geniuses, may do good literary and scientific work. The destination of these persons in life will be determined by the ordinary considerations which influence men, viz., by the prospect of pecuniary profit social position and congenial work; under the last head we must take into account the pleasure which some find in the pursuit of knowledge 'for its own sake.' This expression is somewhat vague, and its exact meaning will be considered further on." And a little further on he adds, "We conclude then that the highest kind of education or attainment is a sort of crop which does not remunerate the producer so directly as to make it likely that it will be grown unless some special market for it is provided.

"Society at present desires that such a crop should be grown and therefore it provides remuneration in the several forms of Scholarships, Fellowships and Government appointments which at present offer this special market for it. The awarding of these Civil Service appointments by competitive examinations makes Fellowships or some University rewards of the kind a necessity if we do not wish the best intellect of the country to be drawn off to official employment" (page 406). If that is the case in advanced England, can we justly complain that knowledge is not pursued for its own sake in backward India? Nor must we overlook or estimate lightly the difficulty under which the Indian student labours by reason of his having to acquire knowledge through the medium of a difficult foreign language, and which not only taxes his energy but also cramps his thought very considerably.

I have entered into what may seem to be a laboured apology for my countrymen, not for any sentimental reasons, but because I deem it necessary in the interests of education. For if a European professor enters on his work with a preconceived notion that his Indian pupils are an intellectually inferior class of men, not only is he likely to treat them with unmerited contempt, but he will have very little inducement to put forth all his energy in doing his work.

But while submitting the foregoing remarks for the consideration of our professors, I must warn my young friends the students against thinking that they are as good as could be wished, and that they need be no better. No. That should never be so. If the Indian student cares to vindicate himself and his race, and if he cherishes with respect the lofty traditions of the intellectual greatness of this classic land in olden times, he should ask for no indulgence, but work on manfully amidst all the difficulties of his situation, and prove by actual solid results that he is fully the equal of his proud brethren of the West; and then even if they dislike him they will not be able to despise him. Let agitations for political, social and industrial reform go on side by side, but let the gifted among Indian graduates and under-graduates work silently and steadily in the pursuit of knowledge, not merely for its own sake but for the sake of a yet higher thing, the honour of their race; and if the pursuit is successful, it will reflect greater honour on the country than success in all the agitations put together.

For those brilliant graduates who have a liking for Law, the attractions of the Bar may be difficult to resist. But I would ask them to remember the remark that Babbage once made. On hearing from a common friend that Maule, the Senior Wrangler of his year and afterwards Mr. Justice Maule, was doing very well at the Bar and that he might one day become the Lord Chancellor of England, Babbage exclaimed, "And if he is Lord Chancellor, what is that to what he might have been ?"[1] that is, if he had stuck to his career as a mathematician.

Professors' Association.

181. Much good is expected to result if professors form themselves into an association. In that case each of them will benefit by the united wisdom of all ; the asperities of individual character will be polished off by mutual contact ; and personal equations will be reduced within the narrowest limits.

IV. TEXT-BOOKS.

IV. Text-books.

182. Of text-books I have already said something when dealing with Education in Boyhood in the last Chapter, and with the course in Mental and Moral Science in this Chapter.

In subjects like Mental and Moral Science, and Physics and Chemistry, text-books ought to be prescribed,

(1) because it is extremely difficult to define the limits of the subject by a mere syllabus ;

(2) because it is exceedingly inconvenient for the student to revise the matter dealt with in previous lectures and to prepare himself to follow with readiness succeedings lectures, unless he has a text-book to refer to ;

---

1 See "The Builders of our Law during the Reign of Queen Victoria" by E. Manson, p. 41.

(3) because it conduces to precision of thought and language on the part of the student if he has a text-book to follow; and

(4) because, after all, it is impossible to avoid having a text-book, the lectures taking its place as far as the teacher is concerned, and the notes of the lectures taking its place as regards the pupil.

As for the two main objections against text-books, namely, that they encourage cramming, and they confine the student to the books when he ought to learn the subjects, they arise only when unsuitable text-books and inefficient modes of teaching are adopted. With suitable text-books and judicious teaching, the evils apprehended will disappear.

The use of text-books will often add a little to the labour of the teacher. For if he has studied his subject and arranged his ideas upon it in a way different from that in which it is treated of in the prescribed text-book, he will have to rearrange his plan to make his teaching follow the text-book. But if the text-book is really a good one, the work of adaptation will be easy and will often result in an improvement on the teacher's original plan. Where a teacher is dissatisfied with any portion of the text-book, he may supplement it by oral teaching. When many teachers are dissatisfied with a text-book, they may have it changed by a representation to the authorities, if they are not themselves the authorities.

The selection of a text-book is no doubt a difficult task. There are in the English language standard classical works in different subjects, such as Bacon's Novum Organum, Newton's Principia, Locke's Essay on the Human Understanding, Hamilton's Lectures on Metaphysics, Adam Smith's Wealth of Nations, Mill's Logic, and Faraday's Researches, which advanced students in those subjects ought to read; but they cannot serve as text-books. The chief requirements of a good text-book are,

(1) that it should be short in extent but full in point of matter;

(2) that it should be concise in language but lucid in exposition;

(3) that it should be direct in its statements but not dogmatic where there is room for doubt; and

(4) that it should observe a just proportion in the treatment of principal and subsidiary matters, and avoid entering into unnecessary details.

In scientific subjects like Economics, Mental Philosophy, and Ethics, which have not yet attained the rank of exact sciences, text-books often involve another difficulty. The language is not the simple and precise language of science, but is under the divided sway of logic and rhetoric; and the graces of style struggle for mastery over the stiffness of scientific diction, to the no small embarrassment of the student who has to exert himself to discover truth in her unadorned plainness, and to be on his guard against yielding to the fascination of language.

But difficult as the task of selecting text-books is, it must be performed; and in the wide range of books produced in the English language, it will be possible to find out good books in almost every subject.

V. Libraries.

V. Libraries.

183. Libraries are useful instruments of education; and to enable students to profit by resorting to them, their course of study ought to be so fixed as to leave them some spare time for voluntary reading. But voluntary reading requires to be guided by proper directions; for misguided or desultory reading will not only be unprofitable, but may be positively injurious. For the purposes of a student, books may be divided into four classes,—

(1) text-books which must be owned by the student and must be read thoroughly;

(2) books referred to in the text-books for which the student may resort to a library and of which (to satisfy and stimulate his curiosity) he should have first hand knowledge at least to the extent of reading their title pages, their tables of contents, and the passages quoted or referred to in his text-book;

(3) the great works of the master minds of the world (or their English translations where the language of the original is not known to the student) selected from Sir John Lubbock's List of One Hundred Books or any other list (books such

as the Chandogya and Katha Upanishad and Vedanta Sutras with Sankara's commentary, portions of Plato's Phedo and the Republic, Meditations of Aurelius, Kant's Critique of Pure Reason, the Pentateuch, the Gospel of St. Mathew, the Quoran (portions of), the Ramayana and Mahabharata (portions of), the Iliad (portions of), the Ænied (portions of), the Paradise Lost, first four Books, Sakuntala, Hamlet, Macbeth, Othello, Julius Cæsar, Merchant of Venice, Bacon's Essays, Ivanhoe, Les Miserables, Pickwick Papers, Boswell's Life of Johnson, Gibbon's Roman Empire, Hallam's Constitutional History, Bentham's Theory of Legislation, Mill's Logic, Mill's Political Economy, Drawin's Origin of Species, &c.) which every general scholar ought to read, and which (arranged in progressive order of course) have a prior claim upon his attention ; and

(4) all other books, that is, other than those coming under the three preceding classes, which the student may read with discrimination.

Every student should prepare for himself with such advice and directions as may be available, a list of books of the third class. It is in regard to the choice of books of the fourth class that great care is necessary. The student should read Harrison's 'Choice of Books' as a guide. He should also try to restrain himself from reading books of the fourth class before he has finished reading those of the preceding classes ; and he should scrupulously avoid reading that class of realistic sensational novels which teach no lesson, and have no lasting effect, except the deadening of the natural abhorrence for vice, the creating of a morbid craving for light reading, and the weakening of the power of sustained thinking. Books of this type are so plentifully produced as to lead one to say with Frederic Harrison that the art of printing has been a boon not unmixed with evil. In the rich and cultivated fields of English literature, they may be likened to rank weeds growing to the injury of useful plants. In the newly formed and unprepared literary soil of Bengal, such products may perhaps serve the useful purpose of preparing the ground for better growths, and they may be compared to the thorn and thistle growing on newly formed sandy alluvial land, only to die and enrich the soil by their decomposition. These few stray leaves of ephemeral existence may, I hope, serve a similar purpose, by preparing the ground for the production of some work of lasting value on Education in India.

Except for the purpose of supplying books of the second class mentioned above, a student's library need not be very full of miscellaneous books. It is not to be a repository of every product of human thought.

VI. Examinations.

VI. Examinations.

184. About Examinations I think I have said enough in the last Chapter. To that I will only add this that of the two things which an Examination is

intended to test, namely, knowledge and capacity, so far as the testing of the former is concerned, an Examination should be so conducted as to be helpful to teaching, by following the lines on which teaching has proceeded, instead of taking both the teacher and the taught by surprise. So far as the testing of capacity is concerned, an Examination must proceed upon ground untrodden by teaching, though not in directions widely divergent from those taken by the teacher. And if Competitive Examinations for Public Service are, as has been proposed, abolished, University Examinations following a prolonged course of study and conducted with a view to test capacity, may well be taken as tests of fitness. To use the words of Mr. Latham,

"If we are guided by Examinations connected with a sound educational course of considerable length, the mere fact that a young man has steadily followed it throughout and has not flinched from the drudgery it involves, affords us a moral index which compensates in a degree for the Examination being less suited than a special one might be for bringing out the cleverest men" (Action of Examinations page 420).

CHAPTER IV.

PROFESSIONAL AND TECHNICAL EDUCATION AND EDUCATION ON NATIONAL LINES.

INTRODUCTORY REMARKS.

Aim of this Chapter. Professional Education.

185. In this Chapter I intend to offer a few brief remarks on Professional and Technical Education, and Education on National Lines.

The Professions recognized by Indian Universities, when the first edition of this book was written, were Law, Medicine and Engineering. And I then remarked "To these the noble profession of Teaching may well be added, and our Universities will do well to grant degrees and licenses in Teaching, with a view to encourage the study of the Science and Art of Education" This has since been done under the new regulations of the Calcutta University. The few imperfect and ill-arranged remarks that I have been submitting for the consideration of the reader in these pages relate to this last mentioned important subject.

Of the three recognised Professions, the only one about which I am at all qualified to speak is Law. I shall deal briefly with Legal Education in the first Section of this Chapter; then make a few observations on Technical Education in the next Section; and conclude with a few remarks on Education on National Lines.

SECTION I.—LEGAL EDUCATION.

Law based on simple maxims, but complex in its application, and requires study.

186. Law in the opinion of many ought to be a simple subject, as it is a body of rules intended to enforce justice, the fundamental principles of which are few and simple. And a poet has feelingly complained—

> "The toils of law what dark insidious men
> Have cumbrous added to perplex the truth,
> And lengthen simple justice into trade,
> How glorious were the day that saw these broke,
> And every man within the reach of right."[1]

This complaint is not well founded. As Mathematics, though based on a few simple axioms about equality and inequality, has, by reason of the complex relations of time and space, developed itself into a highly abstruse subject, so Law, though based upon a few fundamental maxims of justice, is, by reason of the complexity of human transactions, become a difficult subject requiring careful study. A portion of the difficulty, namely, that which is extrinsic and arises from our mode of treatment of the subject, may, in the one science as in the other, be removed, but not the whole. It is, as it ought to be, the aim of the legislator to simplify the Law; and judges, legal practitioners, and even Law students, should try to help the legislator in carrying out this aim.

Preliminary qualifications of a Law student.

187. Law being a subject not free from difficulty, the first question in legal education is what should be the preliminary qualifications of a Law student.

---

[1] Thomson's Winter.

A certain amount of general education is absolutely necessary to qualify one to commence the study of Law. Some are of opinion that the passing of the Intermediate Examination in Arts or Science is sufficient. The Calcutta University requires the obtaining of the B. A. or the B. Sc. degree as a necessary qualification. I think the Calcutta University has taken the right view.

In civilized society, so diversified are the affairs of men leading to litigation, and so varied are the questions arising before Courts of Justice, that there is scarcely any department of knowledge that may not be of use to the lawyer. In addition to his possessing the B. A. or the B. Sc. degree, it will be well for an intending Law student to have some knowledge of Inductive Logic, Elementary Psychology, Political Economy, and the Constitutional History of England.

Period of Law study and number of Law examinations.

188. The points that next arise for consideration are, as to what period a course of Law study should extend over, whether it should be a whole-time study, and whether there should be only one examination at the end of the course, or, an intermediate examination as well.

I think a period of two years sufficient for the study of a fairly complete course in Law. Such study need not be whole-time study. And one examination, namely, that for the degree of Bachelor in Law at the end of the course, is all that is necessary. Those who intend reading for Honours in Law with a view to obtain the Doctor's degree, will have to study much longer; but they may do so while practising their profession.

To prolong the period of Law study beyond two years after the passing of the B. A. or B. Sc. Examination will, I think, be an unnecessary hardship on the student. To insist on his attending the Law class for the whole of his time, will stand in the way of his reading for the M. A. degree, and that is not desirable; for, in my opinion, the Law student who obtains the M. A. degree, is likely to be a better lawyer than one who does not, advanced general scholarship being always helpful to the study of Law. And to institute an intermediate examination would be a needless addition to the pressure of examinations, which is not very wholesome in its effect on the mind. I say this with all respect for the Calcutta University Regulations which have taken a different view.

Attendance at lectures.

189. To the question whether attendance at a regular course of lectures in an affiliated college should be required as a condition for admission to the B. L. Examination, I would unhesitatingly return an affirmative answer. Law is a subject for the proper study of which the beginner certainly requires the help of a trained teacher. It is sometimes said that attendance at Law lectures is often a mere matter of form, and students derive very little benefit from it. If that is so, the remedy lies in improving the lectures, and not in dispensing

with them. When the lectures are attractive, as they should be, and the student finds it profitable to attend to them, I know from personal knowledge that they are attended to.

Central Law College with monopoly of legal teaching not desirable.

190. I am not in favour of having a Central Law College having the monopoly of Law teaching, as that would amount to an undue interference with private colleges, and as, considering the large number of the students who attend the Law classes, it will be practically impossible to provide adequate accommodation and efficient teaching in a single college however well managed.

The subjects for the B. L. Examination—how they are to be studied.

191. The next question for consideration is, what should be the subjects for the B. L. Examination, and how should they be studied.

The B. L. Examination Course should include,—

I. Jurisprudence,

II. Hindu Law,

III. Mahomedan Law,

IV. The Law relating to Persons,

V. The Law of Property,

VI. The Law of Contracts and Torts,

VII. The Law of Limitation, the Law of Evidence and Civil Procedure, and

VIII. The Law relating to Crimes and Criminal Procedure.

I. JURISPRUDENCE.

192. Jurisprudence or the Science of Law must be read by every lawyer who wishes to have a liberal education in Law. The subject has been dealt with differently by different authors, some deducing its principles mainly from facts furnished by History, while others explain them chiefly on *à priori* rational grounds. Many standard works have been written on the subject, which every Law student should read; but most of them are either diffuse or cover only certain parts of the subject, and only a few can be recommended as systematic text-books for the student. One peculiarity which characterises most of these works is the importance they attach to the modes in which juridical ideas have been conceived and juridical principles expounded by Roman and German jurists; and this is quite natural, seeing that it is the writings of these jurists that have materially influenced the development of the science of Law. But as those writings in their original are inaccessible to the Indian Law student owing to his ignorance of Latin and German, the better mode of presenting the subject to him will be the philosophical mode, reference to the Roman Law being made where necessary, by way of illustration only.

Juriprudence to be taught to the beginner in the logical and analytical distin

Interesting as it may be to know that an executory contract of sale is historically a later development than a sale completed at once, and that the Roman lawyers were quite familiar with the idea that a man's assets less his debts constituted his property, it is of greater importance to the Law student to know at the outset that in point of logical order, an executory contract of sale always precedes, though it may not always be followed by, an actual sale, and that as a matter of principle, a person's claims against others less his liabilities to others, must constitute his property, whether the Roman Law or any other system of Law recognises this to be true or not. In fact it is not until a complete logical scheme of legal ideas and principles deduced from an analysis of the relations of human beings in civilised society, as modified by the existence of things capable of appropriation, is presented to the mind of the student, that he can be able adequately to understand and appreciate their historical order of development, or their recognition or non-recognition by any particular system of law. I would therefore suggest that the *logical* and *analytical* mode of treatment of the subject be adopted for teaching jurisprudence to the beginner.

Advantage of this mode.

193. One great advantage of this mode of studying the subject is that it enables the student to have before his mind a tolerably complete and connected scheme of its different parts, though it be in outline or skeleton only, which he may fill up as he proceeds, and which will help him in remembering and arranging its details, and in comparing different systems of Law.

154. In the study of the subject in this mode, its different topics may be arranged under the following heads:— The different topics of Jurisprudence.

1. Analysis of the idea of Law and definition of the term Law.

The sense in which the term is used in the expression International Law.

2. Sources of Law.

(a) Direct Legislation.

(b) Indirect Legislation by adoption by the Legislature of systems or portions of systems of Law not framed by it. Hindu Law and Mahomedan Law in British India are instances of this description.

(c) Indirect Legislation by permission to Judges to decide cases not otherwise provided for, according to justice, equity and good conscience, as in India, or according to Common Law and Equity, as in England.

3. Classification of Rights, with an introductory analysis of the relations between man and man and man and things which give rise to rights.

Rights may be classified in different ways according to different principles of clasification.

Thus Rights are Private or Public, Primary or Secondary (*i. e.*, arising from wrong), of the Person or of Property, *in Rem* or *in Personam*.

Then there are various sub-divisions of these different classes.

4. The Creation, Transfer, and Extinction of Rights.

5. Wrongs—their division into Crimes and Civil Injuries or Torts, the former by reason of their greater heinousness being followed by punishment of the wrong-doer at the instance of the State, and the latter being followed by restitution or compensation to the wronged party who is left to seek his remedy against the wrong doer.

6. The Law of Civil and Criminal Procedure including the Law of Evidence.

The above is only a rough outline of the topics of Jurisprudence, which the student may re-arrange and fill up. He should have a tex-book such as Holland's or Markby's Jurisprudence for his guide; and while following his text-book, he should think for himself and make his own abstract of its substance.

Reasons why particular systems of Law differ.

195. Before entering on the study of any particular system of Law, the student should have some idea of the reasons why particular systems differ from one another. To state shortly, these reasons are to be found in the varying circumstances of different countries, that is, in the differences in their physical environments, and in the sentiments and habits of the races inhabiting them. Thus a country bordering on the sea and having good ports will have

its Maritime-Law more developed than that of an inland country. A country with large rivers cutting away their banks and throwing up large alluvial deposits, has its Law of Alluvial Accretions more elaborately worked out than a country without such rivers. An agricultural country has a more complicated system of Land Tenures and a comparatively simple chapter of Patent and Trade-mark Laws than a manufacturing country.

196. There are two other points of general importance connected with Law, upon which the Law student ought to have clear views at an early stage of his progress. **Lawyer respects authority**

One of these is respect for the opinions of the learned, which marks this department of human affairs more than any other. And there are two good reason's for this respect for authority. In the first place, uniformity in the Law is a matter of great importance, because its absence would disappoint expectations and unsettle society. And to secure uniformity, what one Judge or Jurist has said, others should follow unless there be special reasons for taking a different course. This, no doubt, is a ground of expendiency. But in the second place, there is also a ground of justice for respecting the opinions of others. For, though upon doubtful questions, one's own reason must be the ultimate arbiter, before taking its award, it is necessary to consult the reasons of others; and where there is a consensus of opinion in favour of a certain view, that is more likely to be right than the view entertained by one who stands alone Let us examine the matter a little more closely. Why is it that reasonable men, without any bias one way or the other, and honestly endeavouring to ascertain the right view, differ in opinion? The reason appears to be this, that though we may agree as to our qualitative view of the considerations bearing on any opinion, that is, as to which of them are for, and which against it, it is in estimating their quantitative values and ascertaining how far one consideration should neutralise an opposite one, that different minds, by reason of their diverse training and modes of thought, differ. And a consensus of many opinions must carry with it a proportionate guarantee of correctness.

His conservatism.

Allied to the lawyer's respect for authority is his conservatism. The advocate asks the judge to follow precedent. The judge must follow precedent if it can not be distinguished from the case before him. And even the legislator hesitates to introduce any startling innovation, fearing lest it should unsettle men's minds, and saying to himself it is better to

> "——bear the ills we have
> Than fly to others we know not of."

It is only the speculative jurist, who does not run any such risk, that can safely expose existing errors and recommend change in order to prepare public opinion for its acceptance.

II. Hindu Law.

197. Hindu Law has a double interest for the Indian Law student. It is, in the first place, a living system regulating the affairs of the Hindus in certain classes of cases. And in the second place, it illustrates the gradual growth of an archaic system embodied in the simple texts of the early sages into a more advanced system of Law in the writings of later commentators, who under the guise of interpretation, have introduced substantial changes in the Law, to meet the growing wants and progressive ideas of modern society. The elaborate discussion in the Mitakshara to establish the widow's right of succession, and the still more elaborate and ingenious arguments of the Dayabhaga to extend that right, and to remove the fetters upon the right of a person to alienate his share in joint-property, are instances well worthy of study. If for the legal practitioner it is enough to know the rules of Hindu Law, for the student of Law as a science, the reasons for those rules and their mode of evolution must be matters of greater importance. Hindu Law.

Since the accession of the British Rule, and the authoritative promulgation of the principle that certain classes of cases should be governed by the Hindu Law, that is, the Hindu Law as we find it, the further growth of that Law from within has been arrested, the task of interpreting that Law and of modifying it under the guise of interpretation having been taken away from commentators, and having vested in the judges. These latter, however, have not been altogether inactive. They have, in interpreting the Law, gradually and imperceptibly introduced changes generally for the better. The slow and somewhat fluctuating development of the Mitakshara Law relating to the liability of joint-property in the hands of an heir for ancestral debts, is an instance in point. There are, however, two instances in which the changes introduced have been rather violent and not quite beneficial, and which the student should note as anomalous. These are, (1) the decision in the *Tagore* case[1] based upon a casual remark in the Dayabhaga, that the donee must be a sentient being, which has had the effect of curtailing the testamentary power of a Hindu very much; and (2) the decision in *Moniram Kolita* v. *Kerry Kolitani*[2] to the effect that a Hindu widow does not, for subsequent unchastity forfeit the estate inherited by her from her husband. As these are both decisions of the Privy Council, and are binding on all Indian Courts, and as that tribunal does not review or reconsider its judgments, there is no chance of the Law being altered except by the Legislature. In the first mentioned case, the Law might be altered by an amendment of the Hindu Wills Act; but there is little likelihood of any change in the Law in the second case.

---

[1] 18 Weekly Reporter, 359.

[2] Indian Law Reports, 5 Calcutta Series, p. 776.

The student should not only master the rules of Hindu Law and the reasons for the rules, but he should also direct his attention to the points not covered by those rules, which may arise in the altered conditions of Hindu society. These will furnish excellent problems for exercise which he should endeavour to solve. He should keep a note of the problems and their solutions ; and he will find some of them arising in actual practice.

III. MAHOMEDAN LAW.

198. The student will find the Mahomedan Law equally interesting study. Here also, he should not only learn the rules but should also try to understand the reasons of those rules. Mahomedan Law.

The Mahomedan Law of inheritance is considered by some students to be a little puzzling, but if he reads the Sirajiya with attention, he will find no real difficulty. That Law recognises a plurality of heirs; they are divided into certain classes, some of which exclude others; and among members of a class again, some exclude others. The shares of the different heirs are clearly specified, and the whole Law is stated with mathematical precision. The rules for the working out of the shares of the different co-heirs are worded perhaps in a slightly complicated form ; but our Law-students, who are all acquainted with the doctrine of fractions, will have no difficulty in following them, when they once understand their object, which is to find in any given case, the least number of parts into which the state must be divided so that each co-heir may have an integral number of those parts.

One marked feature of the Mahomedan Law, which the student may notice, and which it has in common with other ancient and mediæval systems, is the importance attached to forms and formalities, of which notable instances are to be found in the Law of Divorce, the Law of Pre-emption and the Law of Endowments. The student should understand the reason for this. Where important legal consequences follow from certain acts of parties, it is necessary to have clear indication of those acts having been really and deliberately done. And it is for the purpose of having this clear indication, that settled forms and formalities are insisted upon.

(IV), (V), (VI), THE LAWS RELATING TO PERSONS, PROPERTY, CONTRACTS AND TORTS.

The Laws relating to Persons, Property, Contracts and Torts.

199. The Law under these three heads, excepting that relating to Torts, is to be found mainly in Codes enacted by the Indian Legislature. As these Codes have been drawn up by English lawyers and are often based on Engliah Law, some knowledge of the corresponding branches of that Law is necessary for a clear understanding of their language and their subject-matter. As text-books on English Law are prescribed side by side with Indian Codes on these subjects, the student should do well to read

the former before commencing the study of the latter.

In reading the Indian Codes, the student should bear in mind the saying of a great lawyer that no Code can be so clear and complete as to dispense with the work of a lawyer, which is to help the judge in construing it and applying it to cases that actually arise.

In reading the Acts relating to these subjects, the student should separate matters of principle from matters of detail, and rules of Substantive Law from those of Adjective Law or procedure; and he should also make a note of the cases not provided for by the Acts, and his proposed modes of dealing with them.

As the Law of Land Tenures in Bengal is somewhat complicated, the annexed tabular view of them may be of use to the student.

(VII), (VIII) CODES OF CIVIL AND CRIMINAL PROCEDURE, LAW OF EVIDENCE, LAW OF LIMITATION, LAW OF CRIMES.

The Laws of Procedure, Evidence, Limitation and Crimes.

200. In reading the Code of Civil Procedure, the student will be best able to appreciate and follow its provisions, if he has before his mind a hypothetical Civil Suit, and carries it through all its successive stages of progress, inquiring at each step how either party should proceed, and referring to the Code to see what provision, if any, is made on the point.

And a similar method may be followed in studying the Code of Criminal Procedure.

In studying the Indian Evidence Act, the student should in the first place understand the necessity of having special rules on the subject, and he should next note that it differs from the English Law of Evidence not only in many matters of detail, but also in its general scheme; and he should have a clear idea of that scheme before entering into the details of its provisions.

In ascertaining any fact in the ordinary affairs of life or in a scientific investigation, as we are not generally pressed for time, we admit evidence upon every connected fact which can throw any possible light upon the point for determination.

But as the time of a Court of Justice is limited, as the production of evidence entails trouble and expense, and as side-lights indiscriminately admitted often produce misleading glare without elucidating the matter to be determined, common sense has dictated the exclusion of evidence upon remotely connected facts, and of secondary or second-hand evidence upon the principle facts where primary or first-hand evidence is procurable. The Law of Evidence aims at excluding evidence that is superfluous or misleading. The scheme of our Evidence Act, the student will observe, is, in the first place, to exclude evidence of all facts except the facts in issue and certain connected facts which are declared to be relevant facts;

in the second place, to exclude secondary evidence except in certain cases; and then in the third place, to exclude oral evidence of certain matters which have been reduced to writing. And the Act then lays down rules regulating the incidence of the burden of proof and the examination of witnesses.

The plan of the Indian Limitation Act is very simple. It gives rules for computation, deduction, and extension of time; it enacts that in certain cases, Limitation not only bars the remedy but also extinguishes the right; it then provides for the acquisition of right to Easements; and it concludes with a Schedule giving the periods of Limitation and their starting points for specified classes of suits, appeals, and applications.

The student need not attempt to remember the details of the Schedule, but he should have a general idea of the periods of Limitation for different classes of suits.

The Indian Penal Code has been considered to be one of the best Codes ever enacted. Its definitions are for the most part clear and exact, and its provisions generally just. It deserves attentive study. The student should carefully go through the general provisions in the earlier chapters; he should next read and understand and try to remember the exact words of the definitions of particular offences, noting the precise points of difference between cognate crimes; and he should have a general idea of the nature of the punishments prescribed for different classes of offences, without endeavouring to carry in his head a detailed account of those punishments.

It may not be quite out of place here to note a few of the points which should occupy the attention of the student of the Indian Penal Code, it being borne in mind, that they are mentioned only by way of example and not by way of enumeration.

SECTION 84. This section lays down the rule of non-liability for crime on the ground of unsoundness of mind, and limits the exemption to the cases in which the mental unsoundness takes the form of obscuration of the cognitive faculty or power of knowing, so as to make the offender incapable of knowing that his act is wrong or contrary to Law: but it does not extend non-liability to cases in which the imbecile has only his control over his will impaired. Many are of opinion that the exemption ought to extend to the latter class of cases as well. That no doubt ought to be so if the act of the offender is an involuntary act, as when a man in moving his limbs in a fit of convulsion, hurts another. But where the act is voluntary, to exempt it from criminal responsibility simply because the agent is by unsoundness of mind deprived of full control over his will, and is excited by irritation and yields to impulse much sooner than a sane man, would be to deprive this class of insane persons of the wholesome effect of fear of punishment in helping them to control their temper and to resist impulse to crime. This is the probable reason why the framers of the Indian Penal Code have limited the exemption to cases of derangement of the cognitive power in which fear of punishment cannot arise. Upon this point the attention of the student may be called to the case of the *Queen-Empress* v. *Kadir Nasya.*[1]

SECTIONS 299 AND 300. *Definitions of Culpable Homicide and Murder.*

These sections puzzle not only students but also practitioners and even judges now and then. The language of the two sections is unambiguous and precise, only it is somewhat involved. The student will find that the mode adopted is to define the lesser offence, Culpable Homicide, first, and then to add, that the lesser offence amounts to the greater in certain cases unless they come under some one or other of the specified exceptions. In other words, Culpable Homicide is not murder, if the case does not come under one of four definite descriptions, or if, coming under them, it is covered by one of the five exceptions ; but it is murder if it is of one of those four descriptions and is not covered by any of the exceptions.

The annexed tabular view of the provisions of sections 299 and 300 may help the student in understanding them.

SECTION 378.—*Theft.* The definition is a very comprehensive one, the essential elements of the offence

---

[1] I. L. R., 23 C., 604.

being, a dishonest removal of movable property from the possession of another without his consent, with intent to take it for a time or permanently; and this definition will include acts which in ordinary language will not be called theft, however wrongful they may be. Thus, the definition will include the case of a creditor taking without the debtor's consent the goods of his debtor of value not exceeding the debt,[1] though in ordinary language such taking will not be considered to be theft; and one would hesitate to stigmatize the creditor in such a case as a thief, however reprehensible his conduct may be. This has given rise to expressions such as *technical theft*. It is not desirable that the language of the Law should be in such conflict with ordinary notions. The Code makes some provision for meeting these cases of technical theft by leaving a wide discretion in the Court in the matter of punishment, which ranges from rigorous imprisonment to a mere fine. But even this does not quite remove the hardship and anomaly. For the Code of Criminal Procedure makes theft a non-bailable offence; so that unless the accused can successfully invoke special interference of the Court, he will, when charged with theft, have to remain in custody until conviction, though after conviction he may be let off with a fine only. This anomaly ought to be removed by the Legislature, either by making theft bailable, or, what is better, by amending the

[1] *Queen-Empress* v. *Sricharan*, I. L. R., 22 C., 1017. But see also *Nabi Buksh* v. *Queen-Empress*, I. L. R., 25 C., 416.

definition of theft so as to exclude the cases of technical theft, and by including them under a new offence which may be called wrongful taking of property.

While speaking of anomalies in the Law, I may call the student's attention to another instance of an anomaly in our Criminal Law which is furnished by section 367 (5) of the Code of Criminal Procedure. That section requires the Court to state its reason for not passing capital sentence in a case which is punishable with death or some other punishment. Considering the irrevocable and extreme nature of the sentence of death, when it and some other punishment are prescribed in the alternative for any offence, the right view to take will be to hold that the former is intended to be reserved for the worst types of the offence, as otherwise there will be no gradation in the scale of punishments; and in that view, one would have expected that section 367 (5) of the Criminal Procedure Code should run in the opposite way, requiring the Court to give its reason for passing the extreme sentence for any offence punishable with some other punishment as well. Perhaps the reason why the section runs in the way in which we find it, is, that the human mind is naturally disinclined to pass capital sentence, and to prevent this disinclination from influencing the judge, the Legislature requires him to give his reason for abstaining from passing sentence of death where the law allows it. Be that as it may, the provision does appear somewhat anomalous, and may either be left out, or modified in the manner in which one would, as I have said above, naturally expect it to run.

Accessories to Legal Education.

201. Besides studying text-books and attending lectures, the Law student should (as he is required by the Rules of the Calcutta High Court if he wishes to be enrolled as a Vakil of that Court on his obtaining his Law Degree) attend a High Court, observe how cases are argued and disposed of, and read, directly from the Law Reports, the reports of the important cases referred to in his text-books.

The student should make for himself condensed abstracts of his text-books, of the cases he reads, and of unsettled legal questions that occur to him, in the different branches of Law.

The Law student should have access to a Law Library. As it is not easy for every college to have a separate Law Library, the Law Professors of the different colleges in every large city may form an association with a small Law Library attached to it, to which their pupils may resort.

Over and above their text-books and Law Reports, Law students should also read books like Campbell's Lives of the Chief Justices, Campbell's Lives of the Lord Chancellors, Serjeant Ballantine's Experiences, Serjeant Robinson's Reminiscences, and Manson's Builders of our Law in the Reign of Queen Victoria, which give accounts of the lives of great lawyers, to remind them that they can make their lives sublime. The story narrated by Lord Campbell[1] of Sir Mathew Hale's refusal to try the case of a plaintiff who had sent him some venison the night before, notwithstanding the remark of the plaintiff that out of a needless apprehension of defeating justice his Lordship was delaying justice, shows with what scrupulous care great English judges have striven to preserve the integrity of the Court safe against all possible suspicion of bias. And the severe retort of the Attorney-General (Sir F. Thesiger) in answer to Chief Baron Pollock's observation that some discretion should be allowed to cross-examining counsel (Mr. Martin, the Chief Baron's son-in-law and favourite),—"My learned friend is allowed discretion in this case and in this Court generally which would not be extended to myself or other counsel in this or in any other Court"[2]—shows how jealous the English Bar is in maintaining the high reputation of the Judicial Bench, and how unsparing it is in criticising the slightest failing in the greatest Judges.

The student of Law cannot better employ his leisure than in studying the noble traditions of Westminster Hall which have made British justice honoured all over the world.

Though studying Law in order to enter the legal profession for the sake of its emoluments, the student

[1] Lives of the Chief Justices, Vol, II, p. 205.

[2] Manson's Builders of our Law in the Reign of Queen Victoria, p. 79.

should be deeply impressed with a due sense of the dignity of the profession which will entrust him with the defence of the life and property of his client. In defending his client's case, which may not always be a just one, he should never stoop to anything mean or sordid. He should, at the outset, let his client know his own view of the case; he should advise him to settle it with his adversary if it is not a hopeful one; and if he has to defend it, he should only ask for his client such relief or protection as the Law gives him. He should remember that that alone is true powerful advocacy which, without overlooking the weak points on its own side, is able to defend them so far as they can be defended, and, without ignoring the strong points on the opposite side, is able to attack them so far as they can be attacked. He should learn not to be content with arguing cases in a mere mechanical way, as for instance by merely urging that the witnesses are discrepant and so they are not to be believed, or that the story is improbable and so it must be false, or that a certain construction of the Law leads to strange results and so it cannot be right. Such routine arguments have very little real force in them, and they arrest but little attention. He should enter a little deeper into matters, and see that what he says has substance in it, and is not a mere form of words. If it is discrepancy in evidence that he wishes to comment upon, he should show that the discrepancy is not such as may result from inaccurate observation and may be consistent with truth, but is incapable of any explanation other than the falsehood of the evidence. If he wants to discredit a story by reason of its improbability, he should dwell upon the degree and nature of the improbability, and show that it is incompatible with truth according to the ordinary course of human transactions. If a proposed construction of any legal provision is to be rejected as incorrect by reason of the strange consequences it would lead to, these should be contrasted with the results of our adopting a contrary construction, and a clear balance shown in favour of the latter.

In forensic arguments as well as in discussions in other departments of life, where conflicting considerations arise on both sides, the real difficulty lies, not in enumerating them in their proper places, but in evaluating them correctly, and in determining on which side the balance of considerations really is.

In the material world, the conflicting matters that require consideration in determining a question, have had their modes of measurement settled. But in the moral world, excepting a few matters like the time of sensation, and the time and energy of volition, which have been sought to be reduced to measurement,[1] the conflicting factors that determine the result in connection with any question, are still incapable of measurement; and different minds, from differences in their constitution and in their training, value them differently, and arrive at different opinions,

---

[1] See Dr. Scripture's New Psychology, Chapters VI, VII, and XV.

to the no small embarrassment of human affairs. The best course for an honest disputant in such cases is, to apply all his powers of analysis to the determination, so far as possible, of the relative if not the absolute values of the conflicting considerations, so as to be able to determine on which side the balance lies. It is by the application of what may be called the differential as distinguished from the absolute method, that any conclusion can be arrived at in such cases.

Another point worthy of the attention of the young lawyer is to bear in mind that in stating his case, it is always convenient to begin from the nearer end and proceed backwards, instead of taking the opposite and in one sense the natural course. For by beginning from the nearer end, you let your hearers know how the case stands, and you avoid going into irrelevant matters; whereas if you begin from the further end, your hearers not knowing how the case finally stands, may not be able to anticipate your object, and you may be going into many things which will, in the end, be found to be wholly unnecessary for consideration.

General directions upon matters like these must necessarily be vague.

The student should watch opportunities of listening to the arguments of the best advocates in particular cases; and he should remember that legal education is not completed merely by the study of Law books.

SECTION II.—TECHNICAL EDUCATION.

202. The necessity of Technical Education for the people of this country is now admitted by all. In the first place it is now clearly understood that if every one were to receive liberal education, the supply of men who received such education will soon exceed the demand, and leave many without employment; so that some of our young men ought to take to Technical Education. In the second place, the fact of our not receiving any Technical Education has reduced us to this unhappy plight, that all our necessaries of life have to be manufactured abroad and imported from other countries. And in the third place, while the raw materials are often produced in this country and carried at considerable cost to other countries to be manufactured into useful articles which are brought back at further cost, if the manufactured articles had been prepared here, we might have had them cheaper by reason of the double cost of carriage being saved. So that for the threefold reason, namely, first, to have work for all, secondly, to manufacture our own necessaries of life, and thirdly, to obtain them cheaper, our young men ought to receive Technical Education in large numbers. Technical Education.

To make them really profit by Technical Education, they should at the outset receive elementary scientific education. They should then be sent to other countries to receive Technical Education by being taught under the best teachers and by observing the working of the most complete machinery. In sending them abroad, care should be taken to have the necessary funds ready beforehand to meet all their expenses. And last, but not least of all, Indian capital must be invested in manufacture, to find employment for them on their return. In what shape such capital will come it is not easy to say. Large investments by millionaires among the landed aristocracy cannot well be expected. They who are accustomed to the security of investment in land are not likely to take the risk of investing largely in manufactures. The capital will therefore have to be raised by joint stock companies. These are matters which should be carefully considered by the Association recently formed for the Advancement of Scientific and Industrial Education.

Commercial Education.

203. Side by side with Industrial Education, Commercial Education claims our attention. Manufacture and Commerce are allied matters, and each will help the progress of the other. Schools and colleges should be established for giving Commercial Education; and the Universities might institute degrees in Commerce. The principal subjects of study will, I presume, be Commercial Arithmetic, Geography, and Political Economy. Educational authorities should in consultation with experts frame a detailed scheme for Commercial Education.

SECTION III. EDUCATION ON NATIONAL LINES.

204. Much has been recently said, and much misconception still exists, regarding National Education

in this country. A few words explaining the true aim and scope of Education on National Lines will not therefore be out of place here.

Education on National Lines.

Love of one's own country and one's own nation is certainly laudable; but education should not be limited by considerations of nationality. It should proceed upon a cosmopolitan basis; and every scheme of national education in this country should provide for the incorporation of the best assimilable ideals of Western life and thought with our own. This is a great truth. But it is not the whole truth. For though this assimilation of foreign ideals is desirable in the later stages of mental growth, in the earlier stages, such assimilation is not possible, and any attempt to force it on, will retard instead of accelerating the healthy development of the mind. Every student, when commencing his school education, brings with him in addition to his outfit of language, his stock of thoughts and sentiments, the gift of his nation, which the teacher instead of ignoring and hastily displacing, should try to utilize and gradually improve. Want of due regard for this elementary principle is, I think, one of the main reasons why the existing system of English education in this country has sometimes failed to produce satisfactory results. The National Education movement recently set on foot has very properly deemed it not only desirable but necessary, that education should be given on national lines, that is, that it should be imparted through the medium of the student's vernacular in the earlier stages at least, and that special importance should be attached to things and thoughts about which he is, or is likely to be, most concerned, to a knowledge of the country, its literature, its history, and its philosophy, and to the study of such branches of the arts and sciences as are best calculated to help the development of the material resources of the country and satisfy its pressing wants. This is, as it should be, the real aim and scope of national education; and there is no reason why such a scheme of education should not receive the support of every one.

INDEX

SUBJECT— PAGE

Tabular view of Land Tenures.

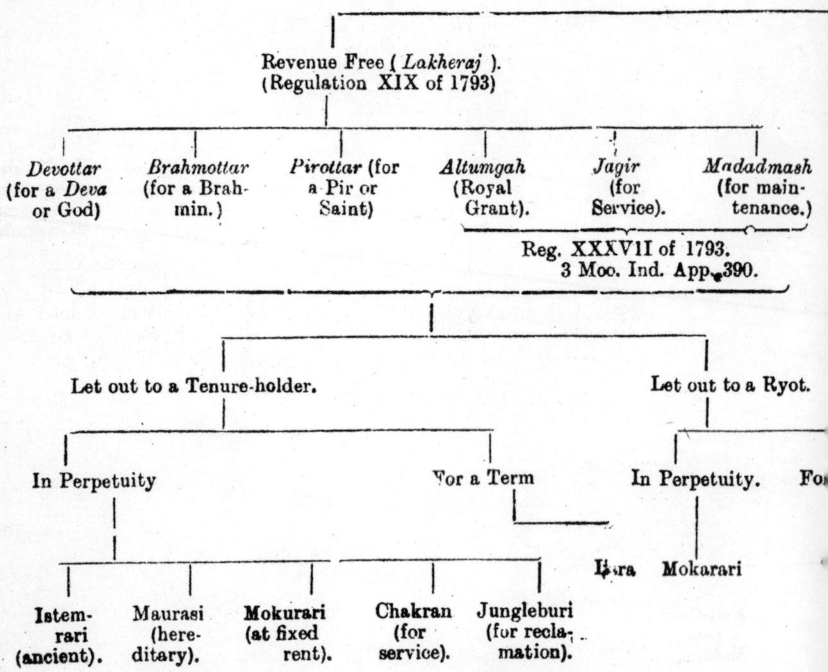

To face page 319.

).

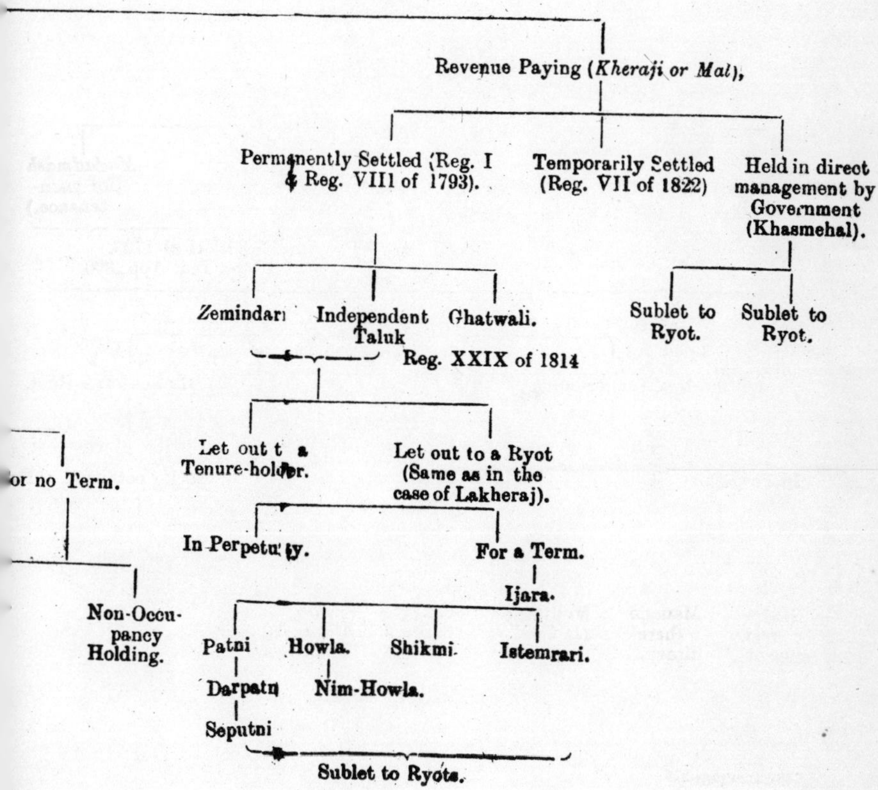
Revenue Paying (*Kheraji or Mal*),
Permanently Settled (Reg. I & Reg. VIII of 1793).
Temporarily Settled (Reg. VII of 1822)
Held in direct management by Government (Khasmehal).
Zemindari
Independent Taluk
Ghatwali.
Reg. XXIX of 1814
Sublet to Ryot.
Sublet to Ryot.
Let out to a Tenure-holder.
Let out to a Ryot (Same as in the case of Lakheraj).
or no Term.
In Perpetuity.
For a Term.
Ijara.
Non-Occupancy Holding.
Patni
Howla.
Shikmi.
Istemrari.
Darpatni
Nim-Howla.
Seputni
Sublet to Ryots.